Pacific Languages

Pacific Languages

AN INTRODUCTION

John Lynch

University of Hawai'i Press
Honolulu

98 99 00 01 02 03 5 4 3 2 1

Library of Congress Cataloging-in-Publication Data

Lynch, John
    Pacific languages : an introduction / [John Lynch].
        p.   cm.
    Includes bibliographical references and index.
    ISBN 0–8248–1898–9 (alk. paper)
    1. Pacific Area—Languages.   I. Title.
P381.P3L96   1998
499—dc21   97–24552
                        CIP

University of Hawai'i Press books are printed on
acid-free paper and meet the guidelines for permanence
and durability of the Council on Library Resources

Designed by Josie Herr

To

Andonia,
Brendan,
and
Steven

Contents

Part 3: The Social and Cultural Context

Illustrations

Tables

Figures

Maps

Preface

This book was born out of frustration. I have lost count of the number of times people have asked me to recommend to them a "good general book on the languages of the Pacific." There are any number of good specialist or technical books on the Austronesian languages as a whole, or on the Papuan languages, or on Australian languages, or on certain subgroups or individual languages—but virtually all of these are aimed at readers who have studied a considerable amount of linguistics.

There are, however, many nonlinguists who want or need to know something about the languages of this region. Language is an important topic of conversation, an important political and social phenomenon, in many if not all Pacific countries and territories. Pacific peoples want to know more about their languages—what other languages they are related to, where they came from, how they compare with, say, English and French, what the other languages in the region are like. People working in Pacific countries need some general information on the languages of the country or the region to assist them in their work and in their appreciation of the cultures and societies of the Pacific. Teachers, sociologists, community workers, government officers, high school and university students—all are affected by language, and most would like to know more.

Hence this book. It has been a long time in the making, but I hope that it will serve a useful purpose. I have tried to steer a middle course between being too simplistic and being too technical. Obviously, to provide detailed coverage in any book of the sound systems and grammars of fourteen hundred languages, their interrelationships and connections with languages outside the region, their history and current status, and the relationships between language, culture, and social organization is quite impossible.

What I have tried to do is to give the general reader a feel for what these languages are like (with a minimum of references) and at the same time offer linguists something to get their teeth into (with references to sources they can follow up).

The book has three major sections. Part 1 describes the geographical distribution of Pacific languages and attempts to summarize what is known of their history. Part 2 is an overview of the phonological and grammatical structure of these languages. This discussion is far from exhaustive. Many areas (e.g., complex sentences) and many thorny problems (e.g., the Polynesian "passive") are omitted or glossed over. But there is enough information to give a general picture of what Pacific languages are like, in what ways they are similar, and how they differ both from each other and from metropolitan languages like English or French. Part 3 looks at the relationship between Pacific societies and cultures and their languages from a number of different points of view. In the Pacific as elsewhere, language is very much a social and cultural phenomenon.

The careful reader will notice a bias toward Oceanic languages in part 2. This results partly from my own professional background and partly from the fact that, while there are good general surveys of Papuan and Australian languages (Foley 1986 and Dixon 1980), there is nothing comparable for Oceanic languages.

The orthography I use in citing language data is generally the standard orthography of the language. For languages lacking such an orthography, I have used a standard set of phonetic symbols (see appendix 2). This has often meant modifying the orthography of the original sources. Similarly, I have consistently used the same name for the same language, even when some sources use different names.

Phrase and sentence examples are presented as shown below.

Fijian

E	*ā*	*rai-<u>ci</u>*	*irau*	*na*	*yalewa*	*na*	*cauravou.*
he	PAST	see- (TRANS)	them:two	the	woman	the	youth

'The young man saw the two women.'

- The first line, in italics, is the phrase or sentence in that language, with hyphens marking morpheme breaks within a word; underlining is used to focus on the particular aspect of grammar being discussed (in this example, the transitive suffix *-ci*).

- The second line is a word-by-word and morpheme-by-morpheme translation. Where a single morpheme expresses more than one item of meaning, these are separated by a colon (thus *irau* 'the two of them' is glossed as 'them:two'). Grammatical categories are given in capitals; a few of these are abbreviated (thus TRANS = transitive), and a list of all such abbreviations appears below. I have tried not to be too technical with these grammatical terms, and have used, for example, "the" or "with" rather than abbreviations like ART (for article) and COM (for comitative), even if these are sometimes too general. Readers interested in more technical aspects of the grammars of any languages cited should consult the sources (appendix 1).

- The last line, in single quotation marks, is the free English translation.

I have tried to be consistent in my use of grammatical terms throughout the book, even where this means using a different term from that in the original source. So, for example, I consistently use "continuous," even though some writers may have used terms like "progressive" or "durative," and I use "completive" where others use "perfective." I have used **small capitals** when a technical term is introduced for the first time in the text. There is a glossary of such terms in appendix 4.

I have generally not directly quoted sources of language data in the text, since this would unnecessarily clutter the text with references. However, a list of data sources for all languages from which data are cited can be found in appendix 1, and the languages' locations are indicated on maps 3 through 7. I have also provided suggestions for further reading at the end of the book.

Acknowledgments

This book originally appeared in 1993 as an in-house text for the University of the South Pacific course "Structure of Pacific Languages." I am grateful to students for their feedback about this earlier version, and to Donn Bayard, Barbara Hauʻofa, Andrew Horn, Ross McKerras, Macha Paris, Mere Pulea, Jeff Siegel, Matthew Spriggs, Jan Tent, Randy Thaman, Howard Van Trease, Vilimaina Vakaciwa, and the Department of Geography of the University of the South Pacific, who either commented on parts of the earlier version or provided useful information.

I take particular pleasure in expressing my gratitude to Niko Besnier, Terry Crowley, Ken Rehg, Malcolm Ross, and Nick Thieberger, without whose assistance this book would not be what it is. I reserve, of course, all blame for errors and misinterpretations.

I am also deeply indebted to a number of Pacific people who have opened the doors of their languages to me. I am especially grateful to John Davani, Tom Hiua, John Naupa, Julie Piau, Tuʻa Taumoepeau-Tupou, Philip Tepahae, and Apenisa Tusulu, to the people of Uje and Anelcauhat (Aneityum) and west Tanna in Vanuatu, and to my *tambu*s in Kond and Anigl in Papua New Guinea.

My sons Brendan and Steven have lived with this book over the past few years, and the backs of discarded drafts have been of great use in helping to develop their artistic talents. My wife Andonia has been a source of constant encouragement, and I am eternally grateful for her love and support. I dedicate this book to them.

Terms Used

The following abbreviations are used in the text:

°	(a) marks a phrase or sentence as ungrammatical; (b) marks a phoneme or word as having been reconstructed for some proto-language
Ø	zero
1	first person
2	second person
3	third person
C:S	construct suffix
DIFF:SUBJ	different subject
EXC	exclusive
INC	inclusive
NOM	nominalizer
O	object
PL	plural
POSS	possessive
S	subject
SG	singular
SAME:SUBJ	same subject
TRANS	transitive
V	verb

CHAPTER

1

Linguistics:
Some Basic Concepts

1.1. The Structure of Language

Linguistics is the systematic study of language, and **descriptive linguistics** is the branch of linguistics that deals with the analysis and description of languages. Each language is a system with various units and rules for the combination of these units into larger units. These rules are not always formulated in grammar books, but they are there nevertheless—in the brains of speakers of the language.

One simple way of seeing the operation of these rules is through the mistakes children make when they are learning a language. When a four-year-old says *The mans goed away*, the sentence is clearly incorrect English. It does, however, follow a pattern. First, the child has deduced that, to make a noun plural in English, you add *s* to it. She has already produced large numbers of plural nouns, like *dogs, cats, cups, bananas*, and so on, following this rule. Second, she has also deduced that, to put a verb into the past tense, you add *ed* to it. Again, she has already produced many English verbs in the past tense this way—*laughed, cried, kicked, washed*, etc.

In producing the sentence *The mans goed away*, the child is not imitating what adults say, since no adult speaker of English would say that sentence. Instead, she is applying two of the many rules she has formulated on the basis of observing how English is spoken.

1. NOUN + *s* = PLURAL
2. VERB + *ed* = PAST TENSE

The only problem is that the noun *man* happens to be an exception to rule (1), and the verb *go* an exception to rule (2). Looking at this ungrammatical utterance gives us insight into how the child's brain is functioning in terms of rules that combine units into larger units.

What are these units I have been talking about? If you asked a non-linguist that question, the answer would probably be sounds, words, and sentences. Unfortunately, the situation is more complex than that.

1.1.1. The Sounds of Language

At the "lowest" level of language we have **sounds**, which linguists enclose in square brackets [ ] to distinguish them from letters. Individual sounds, like [t], [e], and [n] are meaningless in themselves. Only combinations of sounds provide meaningful utterances: [t] + [e] + [n] = *ten*, [n] + [e] + [t] = *net*.

No language uses all the speech sounds human beings can make, and the sound systems of different languages are organized in different ways. The study of sounds is known as **phonetics**, and the study of the way in which sounds are organized into a system in a language is called **phonology** (or sometimes **phonemics**). (A chart of all phonetic symbols used in this book appears in appendix 2.)

Let us take as an example the sounds [p] (represented by the letters *p* or *pp*) and [f] (represented by *f* or *ff*). These are quite different sounds, but is the difference between them important? In some languages, for example English, it is, as the pairs of words below show.

pull	*full*
pig	*fig*
supper	*suffer*
cup	*cuff*

The only difference in sound between the words in each pair is the difference between the sounds [p] and [f], but each word has a very different meaning. In English, the sounds [p] and [f] belong to different **phonemes**; that is, they are different *significant units of sound* in the language. And linguists write phonemes in slant lines / / to distinguish them from both sounds and letters. Thus English has the phonemes /p/ and /f/.

Compare the same two sounds in the Tok Pisin language of Papua New Guinea:

paia	*faia*	both mean 'fire'
pasim	*fasim*	both mean 'tie'
mipela	*mifela*	both mean 'we'
lap	*laf*	both mean 'laugh'

In this language, the difference between [p] and [f] is not significant. You can use either sound without changing the meaning of a word. In Tok Pisin, [p] and [f] belong to the same phoneme, usually written /p/. The same sounds in different languages may therefore have quite different functions in the systems in which they occur, and quite different relationships with each other.

Note that we are dealing with sounds and phonemes here, not with the letters that are used to write them. In the English words we looked at above, the phoneme /f/ is represented by the letter *f* in *full* as well as by the combination *ff* in *suffer*. The same phoneme /f/ is also represented by *ph* in *phone*, by *gh* in *enough*, and so on. Our principal concern is with the sound systems of Pacific languages, though we will also look at their **orthographies**, or writing systems.

1.1.2. The Composition of Words

Phonemes combine to form larger units. Consider the following English examples:

act
acted
react
reacted

Each of these consists of a number of phonemes, and each is also a word, since it has meaning by itself and, in the written language, appears with a space before and after. The second and third words, however, can also be divided into two meaningful parts, *act* 'carry out' + *ed* 'past tense' and *re* 'back' + *act*. The fourth word consists of three meaningful parts: *re* + *act* + *ed*.

These smallest meaningful units are called **morphemes**. Some single morphemes are words (*act, dog, house, desire*, for example). Other words (*acted, react, reacted, dogs, housewife, desirable*, for example), consist of multiple morphemes. The study of morphemes and of the way morphemes combine to form words, is known as **morphology**, a term also used to refer to the patterns by which morphemes combine to form words in a particular language.

The examples given above show one other feature of morphemes. While *act* can stand on its own as a word (as a **free morpheme**), *re* and *ed* cannot. Morphemes like *re* and *ed* are known as **affixes**, and they must be attached to another morpheme. There are a number of different kinds of affixes, the most common being **prefixes**, which, like *re*, come before the root in a word, and **suffixes**, which, like *ed*, come after the root. The convention in linguistics is to write prefixes with a following hyphen (*re-*) and suffixes with a preceding hyphen (*-ed*), the hyphen indicating where the join takes place.

Another kind of affix occurs in some Pacific languages, namely, the **infix**, which is placed *within* the root. In Roviana (Solomon Islands), for example, verbs are converted to nouns by inserting the infix *-in-* (note the hyphens both before and after the infix) before the first vowel of the root:

habu	'to fish'	*hinabu*	'a catch of fish'
kera	'to sing'	*kinera*	'a song'
moho	'to be sick'	*minoho*	'sickness, disease'
toa	'to be alive'	*tinoa*	'life'
zama	'to talk'	*zinama*	'language'

When morphemes combine to form words, the sounds at the boundaries of these morphemes often change. For example, I said above that the four-year-old had learned to form plurals by adding the suffix *-s*, but this is not strictly true. The regular plural morpheme has two spellings and three or four pronunciations in English. The pronunciation of the letter *s* in plurals like *cats, cups, socks* is indeed the phoneme /s/, but the letter *s* of plurals like *dogs, bugs, homes* is pronounced as the phoneme /z/, not as /s/; and the same letter in plurals like *inches, buses, dishes* is pronounced /ɪz/ or /əz/, depending on the dialect. I also said that the child had learned to form the past tense by adding *-ed* to verbs. Again, this is not strictly true. The pronunciation of *-ed* is /ɪd/ or /əd/ in words like *banded* and *slotted*, /d/ in *killed* and *conned*, and /t/ in *laughed* and *kissed*.

In these examples, the sound at the end of the noun or verb determines the pronunciation of the plural or past-tense suffix. The study of sound changes that take place when morphemes combine to form words is known as **morphophonemics**.

1.1.3. Above the Word Level

Words combine to form **phrases**. A phrase is a group of words that functions as a unit in a sentence. Look at the following English sentence (where / marks the boundary between phrases):

The young boys / were killing / the cats / on the beach.

Each of these phrases is a unit. When each is moved to some other position in the sentence, it must be moved as a whole entity. For example, the passive equivalent of the sentence above is

The cats / were being killed / by the young boys / on the beach.

and not something like

°The young the cats were being killed by boys on the beach.

(The asterisk marks the sentence as ungrammatical.) That is, it is not just the noun *boys* that moves in this change from active to passive, but the whole noun phrase *the young boys*.

There are different types of phrases. In this book, I refer to **noun phrases**, which are phrases that function like nouns and can be replaced by a single noun or a pronoun—*the young boys* and *the cats* in our sentence above are both noun phrases (and could be replaced, for example, by *they* and *them*). I also refer to **prepositional phrases**, which are noun phrases introduced by a preposition: *on the beach* and *by the young boys* in the examples above are prepositional phrases, introduced by the **prepositions** *on* and *by*. I use the term **verb complex** to refer to phrases that function like verbs: *were killing* and *were being killed* in the sentences above are both verb complexes.[1]

Phrases combine to form clauses. A **clause** is a group of phrases containing a **subject** (the topic being talked about) and a **predicate** (what is being said about the topic). A **sentence** is a group of one or more clauses that can stand alone. If we return to our example of the cat-killing boys, none of the following is a sentence, since each requires other phrases to make it complete.[2]

°*The young boys*
°*Were killing the cats*
°*The young boys on the beach*

English and many other languages usually require each predicate to contain a verb complex, so that a sentence must have at least one verb. Many languages of the Pacific, however, do not require this, since in these languages there is no verb equivalent to English *be* (with its various forms *is, are*, etc.). So, for example, English demands the verb *be* in equational sentences like *That man is a doctor*, but many Pacific languages have no verb in equivalent sentences. In the Lenakel language of Vanuatu, for example, the same sentence would be *Wus aan tokta*, literally 'man that doctor,' with no verb.

1.2. Common Grammatical Categories and Functions

1.2.1. Subject and Object

The terms **subject** and **object** traditionally refer to the performer and receiver of the action of the verb, respectively. In the sentence *The boy is petting the pig*, the performer of the action, *the boy*, is called the subject, and the receiver, *the pig*, is the object. In many languages the verb changes with a change of subject. In the sentence *The boys are petting the pig*, the plurality of the subject, *the boys*, causes the verb to change from singular (*is petting*) to plural (*are petting*).

This fact is important, because the subject is not always the performer of the action. Look at these sentences:

The boy likes the pig.
The boy was bitten by the pig.

In these sentences, *the boy* is still the subject, because we can see the same kinds of changes in the verb when *the boy* becomes plural:

The boys like the pig.
The boys were bitten by the pig.

In the second case, however, *the boy* is not performing the action. The pig is performing the action on the boy.

In other languages, the subject and the object behave in ways different from the way in which English subjects and objects behave, and we cannot give a universal definition of these concepts. But the subject often performs the action, and the object usually receives it.

1.2.2. Transitivity and Voice

A sentence that contains no object is **intransitive**, while one that does contain an object is **transitive**. Examples:

Intransitive:	*Mele is eating.*
	The dogs are sleeping.
Transitive:	*Mele is eating a banana.*
	The dogs chased the children away.

An **active** sentence—a sentence in the **active voice**—is one in which the subject performs the action or where the object has the action performed on it. A **passive** sentence is one in which the action is performed on the subject. For example:

Active:	*Mele ate the banana.*
	The men cut down the tree.
Passive:	*The banana was eaten by Mele.*
	The tree was cut down.

1.2.3. Adjectives and Verbs

Many Pacific languages do not distinguish between adjectives and verbs in the same way English does. The distinction in English is related to the existence of the verb *be*. In English, an **adjective**—like *good*, for example—can either precede the noun it describes or follow the verb *be* (or similar verbs like *seem* or *appear*), as in *A good chief looks after his people* and *Our chief is/seems good.*

In many Pacific languages, however, adjectives belong to a class of **stative** verbs, verbs that indicate a state rather than an action. In Fijian, for example, a verb is marked as stative by one of a number of markers (e.g., *e* 'third person singular subject'). In the first sentence below, the verb is *kana* 'eat,' and the word *levu* 'big' follows the noun it modifies, *vuaka* 'pig':

> *E kana na vuaka levu oqō.*
> 'This big pig is eating.' it eats the pig big this

In the next sentence, the word *levu* 'big' behaves like a verb, that is, just as *kana* 'eat' does in the sentence above.

> *E levu na vuaka oqō.*
> 'This pig is big.' it big the pig this

A stative sentence is an intransitive sentence expressing a state rather than an action. Thus while *Mele is eating* expresses an action, *Mele is fat* or *Mele is a teacher* express a state.

1.2.4. Person, Number, and Gender

In English, we are used to distinguishing first, second, and third person pronouns as well as subject, object, and possessive forms. Both nouns and pronouns occur in singular and plural, and in some cases they have masculine, feminine, or neuter gender. The English subject, object, and possessive pronouns illustrate this:

	Singular	**Plural**
First person	*I, me, my*	*we, us, our*
Second person	*you, your*	*you, your*
Third person		
Masculine	*he, him, his*	*they, them, their*
Feminine	*she, her*	*they, them, their*
Neuter	*it, its*	*they, them, their*

Pacific languages differ in a number of ways from the English model.

1. Most Pacific languages do not show gender in pronouns. Rarotongan (Cook Islands) *ia*, or Fijian *o koya*, or Anejom̃ (Vanuatu) *aen* all mean 'he,' 'she,' and 'it.'

2. A large number of Pacific languages distinguish *two* types of first person pronouns. **Inclusive** first person pronouns refer to the speaker and the addressee(s). **Exclusive** first person pronouns refer to the speaker and some other person(s), but *not* the addressee(s). In

Bislama, the national language of Vanuatu, for example, *yumi* is the first person inclusive pronoun ('I + you'), while *mifala* is the first person exclusive pronoun ('I + he/she/it/them [not you]').

3. Many Pacific languages distinguish more than two numbers, the most common (apart from singular and plural) being the **dual** number, which refers to two and only two; the **trial** number, referring to three and only three; and the **paucal** number, used for a few (three to six or so), or to a small group that is part of a much larger one.

   The function of the plural changes depending on how many numbers a language recognizes. In a language with a singular, a dual, a trial or a paucal, and a plural, the role of the plural is much smaller than it is in a language with only a singular and a plural. In Fijian, for example, we have *o koya* 'he/she/it' (singular), *o irau* 'they two' (dual), *o iratou* 'they (a few)' (paucal), and *o ira* 'they (many)' (plural).

4. Many Pacific languages have separate object and possessive forms of the pronoun, as English does. But in addition, and unlike English, many also distinguish between an **independent** pronoun and a subject pronoun. The independent pronoun can be used as an answer to a question, and *may* be used as a subject, but when it is it is usually emphatic. In Lenakel, for example, *in* is the third person singular independent pronoun, and *r-* is the corresponding subject pronoun. The sentences *In r-am-apul* and *R-am-apul* both mean 'He/she is asleep.' But while the second one is a neutral statement, the first emphasizes that it is he or she, not someone else, who is asleep.

1.2.5. Possessives and Classifiers

In languages like English, there is usually only one kind of possessive construction. No matter what the possessed noun refers to, or what the possessor's relationship is to that noun, the same construction is used: *my hand, my father, my house, my dog* are all possessed in the same way, by means of the possessive, *my*.

Now look at translations of those four phrases in Motu (spoken around Port Moresby in Papua New Guinea), in which the suffix *-gu* translates 'my.' The nouns are *ima, tama, ruma,* and *sisia*:

ima-gu	'my hand'
tama-gu	'my father'
e-gu ruma	'my house'
e-gu sisia	'my dog'

Here we can see that there are two different constructions: The words for 'hand' and 'father' attach *-gu* directly to the noun. I call this type a **direct**

possessive construction. The words for 'house' and 'dog' do not attach *-gu* directly to the noun, but attach it instead to the morpheme *e-*, and this word (*e-gu*) precedes the noun. This I call an **indirect possessive construction**.

In one way or another, most Pacific languages distinguish two types of possessive constructions to which different linguists have given different labels, and which have different semantics. These two types could be classified as follows:

- Close, or subordinate, or **inalienable possession** is often manifested by direct constructions. This involves the possession of something over which the possessor has no control, and which cannot (normally) be acquired or disposed of. It may be an integral part of the possessor (like a hand), or a relative (we cannot control who our father is).
- Remote, or dominant, or **alienable possession** is frequently manifested by indirect constructions. This involves the possession of something over which the possessor has control. It can be acquired and disposed of, given away or sold, like a house or a dog.

Some languages are more complex than this, using a system of **classifiers**, often in both possession and counting, to show what type of thing the noun is, just as in English we normally do not say *ten cattle* or *four breads*, but *ten head of cattle* or *four loaves of bread*, using *head* and *loaf* as kinds of classifiers. Look at the following examples from Ponapean (spoken in Pohnpei, Micronesia):

kene-i mahi
edible:thing-my breadfruit
'my breadfruit'

nime-i uhpw
drinking:thing-my coconut
'my drinking coconut'

sehu pah-sop
sugarcane four-stalk
'four stalks of sugarcane'

Ponapean has more than twenty possessive classifiers (like *kene-* and *nime-* above), and approximately thirty numeral classifiers (like *-sop* above).

1.3. Reconstructing Linguistic History

1.3.1. Genetic Relationship

All languages change. The process of change is gradual, but it is also constant. There are various kinds of evidence for this. For example, earlier written records show a version of the language different from the modern version, though both are often still recognizable as the "same" language. The two examples given below, of the beginning of the Lord's Prayer in the English of about 1400 and in modern English, illustrate this principle.

> *Oure fadir that art in heuenes halowid be thi name, thi kyngdom come to, be thi wille don in erthe es in heuene.*

> *Our Father, who is in heaven, may your name be kept holy. May your kingdom come into being. May your will be followed on earth, just as it is in heaven.*

Even if a language does not have written records going back a long time, the fact that people of different generations speak the same language slightly differently shows that languages change. We can even observe changes taking place in a language when we notice competing forms, like the two different pronunciations of a word like *either* in English (one with an initial vowel sound like that of *niece* and the other with a vowel like that of *nice*), or the past tense of the verb *dive—dived* and *dove—*in many dialects of American English. Perhaps the most obvious example of language change, however, is the continual introduction of new words into all languages (and, less obvious but also quite frequent, the gradual loss of words that, for one reason or another, have become obsolete).

Imagine now that we have a single speech community speaking a language we will call X. This community splits into four separate groups, A, B, C, and D. Because language change is inevitable and continuous, after a few hundred years these four communities would speak different dialects of the same language.[3] But after a thousand years or more, these four dialects would have changed so much that they had become separate languages, as shown in figure 1. The languages would share many similarities in vocabulary and grammar, since language change is relatively slow. But a speaker of language A would have considerable difficulty in holding a conversation with a speaker of B, C, or D.

Languages A, B, C, and D in figure 1 are all **genetically related** to each other, because they all descend from language X, which is their **common ancestor**. Languages A, B, C, and D are often referred to as **daughter languages** of X, and all four languages belong to the same **language family**. Figure 1, which represents their relationship, is their **family tree**.

Where there are historical records of the ancestor language and of the whole period of change, it is easy to establish the relationship between the daughter languages and to see how diversification took place. But in the Pacific, as in many other parts of the world, such records do not go back anywhere near far enough for us to have concrete proof of diversification and relationship. How, then, do linguists establish such languages' relationship?

Related languages share a number of similarities in vocabulary, pronun-

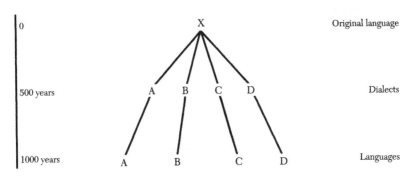

Figure 1. Genetic Relationship

ciation, and grammar. Linguists look for similarities between various languages, and if the similarities are numerous enough, they assume that the languages involved are related despite the absence of documentary proof and derive from a hypothesized common ancestor, which is referred to as a **protolanguage**.

But not all similarities between languages can be attributed to genetic relationship. There are two other possible explanations. One is that the similarities are purely accidental. In Motu, Fijian, and many other Pacific languages, the word for 'eye' is *mata*, while in Modern Greek the word for 'eye' is *mati*. This, however, is a purely accidental resemblance, as there are no other connections between Greek and Motu or Fijian. If two or more languages share only a few similarities, these are probably coincidental. It is virtually impossible, however, that languages could accidentally have hundreds of similarities.

The second explanation for similarities between languages is **copying** or **borrowing**—that a language has adopted a word (or some other linguistic feature) from some other language. For example, in many Pacific languages the word for 'radio' is something like *retio* or *ledio*. This word has been copied from English, but this does not mean that these languages are related either to English or to each other.

Copying is a very common phenomenon in all languages (see chapter 9). When new items of technology, new social practices, or new ideas are introduced into a society from outside, often the words for them, modified to fit local pronunciation, will be brought in at the same time. English is full of words copied from other languages: *Algebra, boomerang, coup, demonstrator, ghetto, junta, taboo, thug,* and *yen* are just a few examples.

Copying is more likely to take place in certain areas of the lexicon than in others. For example, words like *snow, coconut, ice cream, church, team,* and *television* could be easily introduced into a language, since they represent things or concepts that are by no means found in all cultures or environments.

But words like *hand, leg, one, two, black, white, eat, sleep* are much less likely to be taken from another language, since all languages probably have their own words for these concepts, irrespective of the culture of their speakers or the physical environment in which they live. There would be no need for a language to supplement its vocabulary by borrowing them. For similar reasons, certain aspects of grammar (the morphological structure of words, for example) are less likely to be borrowed than others (like word order).

If similarities between two languages are only in areas where we might expect to see copying, they do not constitute evidence of genetic relationship. If, however, the similarities are in areas of vocabulary and grammar where borrowing is much less likely to take place, we can reasonably conclude that these are not due to chance or borrowing, but to **genetic inheritance**. The words and structures were present in some form in an ancestor language and have been retained, usually in a modified form, in the daughter languages. This then leads to the conclusion that the languages sharing these similarities are related, belong to the same language family, and derive from the same protolanguage.

1.3.2. Reconstructing a Protolanguage

In addition to being able to show, with reasonable confidence, that a set of languages are related and derive from the same common ancestor, historical-comparative linguists can reconstruct what many of the sounds, words, and grammatical structures in the protolanguage were probably like.

An important principle in reconstruction, especially in dealing with similarities in vocabulary, is that of the **regularity of sound correspondences**. Look at the following examples from the Aroma, Hula, and Sinagoro languages spoken on the coast east of Port Moresby in Papua New Guinea:

	Aroma	**Hula**	**Sinagoro**
'father'	*ama*	*ama*	*tama*
'milk'	*laa*	*laa*	*lata*
'sew'	*uli*	*uli*	*tuli*
'grandparent'	*upu*	*upu*	*tubu*
'sago'	*lapia*	*lapia*	*labia*
'pigeon'	*pune*	*pune*	*pune*
'skin'	*opi*	*kopi*	*kopi*
'bird'	*manu*	*manu*	*manu*
'mosquito'	*nemo*	*nemo*	*nemo*

There are a number of correspondences between identical phonemes. Aroma *m* corresponds to Hula *m* and Sinagoro *m*. This correspondence is abbreviated as *m:m:m*. We can also see all the vowels (*a:a:a*, *i:i:i*, and so on). But there are also some correspondences between different phonemes: First, although we have the set *p:p:p* (as in *pune : pune : pune* 'pigeon'), we also have another set *p:p:b* (as in *lapia : lapia : labia* 'sago'). Then, we also have the set *∅:∅:t* (where ∅ represents the absence of a sound), as in *uli : uli : tuli* 'sew.' The important thing about both types of correspondence sets is that they are regular. They are not random, but occur again and again in many words. Even in the short list above, you can see a number of examples of each.

In the case of correspondence sets of the type *m:m:m*, the original language almost certainly had *m*, and the daughter languages have not altered it. The protolanguage, then, had a phoneme °*m*, where the asterisk denotes a reconstructed form.

In the case of correspondence sets of the type *p:p:p* and *p:p:b*, however, one or more daughter languages has changed. The logical assumption here is that the set *p:p:p* reflects an original °*p*, while the set *p:p:b* represents an original °*b*, which Aroma and Hula have changed to *p*. The **merger** of phonetically similar phonemes is a very common phenomenon, and this is what seems to have happened: The distinction between the two phonemes *p* and *b* has been lost in these two languages (in the same way as the distinction between the voiced *w* in *witch* and the voiceless *w* in *which* is being lost in most varieties of English). Similarly, the set *∅:∅:t* probably represents an earlier °*t*, which has been lost in Aroma and Hula; again, loss of a phoneme is far more common and natural than the addition of a phoneme.

Using this principle of regularity of correspondence, and also making use of what linguists know generally about language change, it is possible to **reconstruct** elements of a protolanguage—to make an educated guess about what the phonemes, words, and grammar of the ancestor language might have been. Given that Aroma *nemo*, Hula *nemo*, and Sinagoro *nemo* all mean 'mosquito,' for example, and that the correspondences *n:n:n*, *e:e:e*, *m:m:m*, and *o:o:o* are regular, linguists would reconstruct the word °*nemo* 'mosquito' in the language ancestral to these three languages. The full set of protoforms for the words given above would be:

°*tama*	'father'
°*lata*	'milk'
°*tuli*	'sew'
°*tubu*	'grandparent'
°*labia*	'sago'
°*pune*	'pigeon'

°*kopi*   'skin'
°*manu*   'bird'
°*nemo*   'mosquito'

1.3.3. Families and Subgroups

The original split of a community may be followed by later splits. Similarly, the original split of a protolanguage may be followed by subsequent splits in intermediate ancestral languages, sometimes called **interstage languages**. Look at the family tree in figure 2, which represents the following historical sequence of events.

First, the original ancestral language, X, initially split into three daughter languages, P, Q, and R. Some time later, (1) language P suffered sufficient divisions to result in the modern languages A and B; (2) language Q split into Z and the modern language C; (3) language Z itself underwent a further split, into the modern languages D and E; and (4) language R split, giving rise to the modern languages F, G, and H.

All of these languages are related, since they all derive from a common ancestor, X. There are, differing however, degrees of relationship in this family tree. For example, languages A and B are more closely related to each other than either is to any other modern member of the family because they share a period of common development that the other languages do not—the period when language P was separated from the others. Similarly, languages F, G, and H are more closely related to each other than to any other modern member of the family. Languages C, D, and E can also be

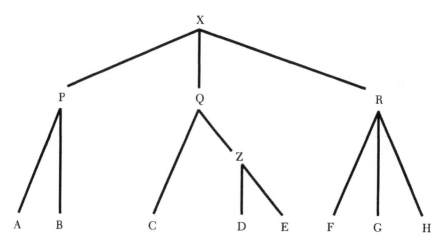

Figure 2. Subgroups of a Family

grouped together, but within the group, D and E are more closely related to each other than either is to language C.

Linguists generally use the term **subgroup** to refer to two or more languages within a family that are more closely related to each other than to the rest of the family. In figure 2, A and B form one subgroup and F, G, and H another. C, D, and E make up a third subgroup within which exists a further, lower-level, subgroup (sometimes called a subsubgroup), D and E.

When the history of a language family is known through written records, the subgrouping of languages within that family can also usually be established by examining those records. But how do we determine subgroups of a language family in an area like the Pacific, where written records of languages either do not exist at all or date only from recent times?

One technique for doing this is known as **lexicostatistics**. This involves the comparison of the basic vocabulary of the languages we are interested in (using a standard one-hundred- or two-hundred-word list), and expressing the degree of relationship between any two languages in the sample as a percentage, which represents the **cognates** (similar vocabulary items presumed to derive from the same original word in the protolanguage) shared by each pair of languages. A higher percentage corresponds to a closer relationship, and members of subgroups should show the highest percentages.

Lexicostatistics has the advantage of allowing quick formulation and quantification of the internal relationships of a language family, but it also has many problems. Some of these are theoretical or methodological and need not concern us here. One obvious problem, however, is that a list of even two hundred words represents only an extremely small part of a whole language, and the figures obtained from comparing such lists may not accurately represent the relationship between two languages. Today, most linguists do not rely heavily on lexicostatistics as a method for subgrouping languages, although they might use it to get a preliminary indication of the possible subgrouping.

The chief method linguists use to establish subgroups is examination of **shared innovations**. If you go back to the Aroma, Hula, and Sinagoro examples in the last section, you will see that two changes, or innovations, have taken place: (1) original °*t* has been lost in both Aroma and Hula (but not in Sinagoro); and (2) the distinction between original °*b* and °*p* has been retained in Sinagoro, but it has been lost in both Aroma and Hula, where these two phonemes merge as the single phoneme *p*.

Aroma and Hula share two innovations that Sinagoro does not, which would suggest that the two languages are more closely related to each other than either is to Sinagoro. The family tree in figure 3 shows how these three descendants of Proto East-Central Papuan are related.

Rather than suggesting that Aroma and Hula both quite independently

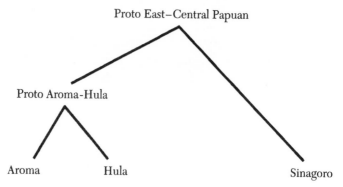

Figure 3. Subgroups of Proto East-Central Papuan

made the changes °t > Ø, °b > p inferred from a comparison of cognates, it seems logical to assume that the changes happened only once, in the inter-stage language, Proto Aroma-Hula. In this way Aroma and Hula came to share two innovations missing in Sinagoro, which suggests that they belong together in a subgroup.

There are various kinds of innovations which, if shared by two or more languages exclusive of others in the family, can be solid evidence for assigning those languages to the same subgroup. Phonological innovations (like the example above) and innovations in morphology are fairly strong evidence; innovations in vocabulary and syntax (sentence structure) are less strong, since changes take place in vocabulary much more easily and rapidly than in phonology or morphology. Quantity is also a factor. Generally speaking, if languages share more innovations (of the stronger kind) the hypothesis that they form a subgroup is more secure.

1.3.4. Reconstructing Linguistic and Cultural History

What use can linguists and others can make of the conclusions reached about the relationships between languages, the subgroups of a language family, and the reconstructed protolanguage?

The branch of linguistics I have been discussing is known as **comparative linguistics** or **historical-comparative linguistics**. It involves comparing languages in order to find out something about their history. This branch of linguistics is one of the disciplines contributing to the study of **prehistory**, the time preceding the existence of written records. (Other such disciplines include archaeology, social anthropology, the study of oral literature and oral traditions, and so on.) So, what can comparative linguistics tell us about prehistory?

First, the fact that languages are related implies that they have a common origin. This often (though not always) implies that the people who speak those languages have a common origin as well, telling us something about the origins of and historical connections between the peoples of a region.

Second, information about subgroupings can give us an idea of the chronology of language divisions (and presumably also divisions in a community), as well as providing indications about the directions in which people migrated. As an example of this, let us consider just the following Pacific languages: Fijian, Tongan, Pukapuka (spoken in the Cook Islands), Tahitian, and Rapanui (Easter Island). A simple family tree for just these five languages would look like the one in figure 4.

The most recent split in this family (which includes hundreds of other languages) is that between Tahitian and Rapanui, with the next most recent that between Pukapuka and the ancestor of Tahitian and Rapanui. Somewhat earlier Tongan and "Proto Pukapuka-Tahitian-Rapanui" divided, and the first split was between Fijian and all the other languages. As you can see by looking at map 1, the splits proceeded from west to east.

On the basis of this subgrouping, most linguists would assume (1) that the original homeland of this group of people was probably somewhere around the Fiji-Tonga area; and (2) that the general direction of migration of these peoples was probably from west to east, as shown in map 1. Note that I have used the terms "assume," "probably," and "somewhere." These conclusions are merely the best educated guesses we can make from the data. We would still want to find supporting evidence from other disciplines—archaeological dates, oral traditions, or the like—before adopting these conclusions firmly.

Third, comparative linguistics can tell us something about the culture of the people who spoke the protolanguage, and about the changes that have taken place in that culture. If a set of words can be reconstructed for a

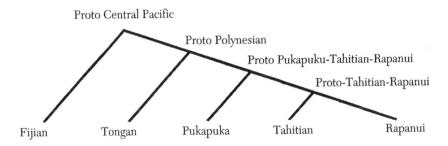

Figure 4. Establishing Migration Patterns

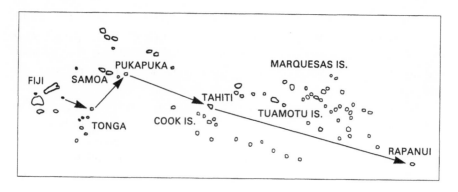

Map 1. Reconstructing Migration Patterns

protolanguage, the items or concepts they refer to were probably also present in the protoculture. For example, if we could reconstruct for a protolanguage words for *taro, yam, coconut*, and *breadfruit*, then we could presume that these items were in the original culture of the people who spoke that language. And if the daughter languages have quite unrelated words for *peanut, rice, coffee*, and *sweet potato*, then we could assume that these items were not in the original culture, but represent later innovations. The identification of copied words can also tell us quite a bit about another aspect of linguistic and social history—cultural contact between groups of people speaking (related or unrelated) languages.

1.3.5. Time Depths

Finally, a word of warning. The principles and techniques of comparative linguistics allow linguists to trace relationships between languages going back perhaps eight or ten thousand years, and to make associated conclusions regarding migrations, cultures, and so on. If, however, the initial breakup of a language family took place longer ago than about ten thousand years, linguists often cannot find sufficient evidence to prove that the languages involved are related. The changes that have taken place in each language over the millennia are usually so great that very few similarities can be distinguished or reconstructed.

The hypothetical family tree in figure 5 helps illustrate this point. The similarities currently existing between the modern languages P through Y would probably lead comparative linguists to divide them into four *unrelated* families:

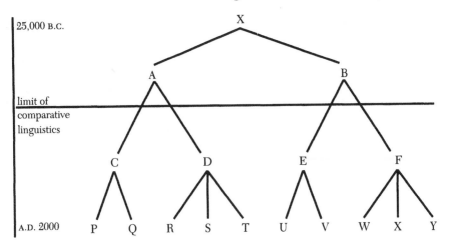

Figure 5. Time Limits on Comparative Linguistics

1. the C family, with members P and Q;
2. the D family, with members R, S, and T;
3. the E family, with members U and V; and
4. the F family, with members W, X, and Y.

The true historical picture is presented in the diagram, which shows how all these languages are related, deriving from a common ancestor X. Because of the length of time involved, however, the changes have been so great that most similarities between, say, languages P and Y have been lost, which is why linguists would treat these languages as belonging to four distinct families.

The study of prehistory relies heavily on comparative linguistics for many different kinds of information. But it is important also to realize that—at least with the techniques currently at our disposal—comparative linguistics has limitations.

PART ONE

Geography and History

2

The Languages
of the Pacific

When different people speak of the Pacific region, they often mean different things. In some senses, people from such Pacific Rim countries as Japan and Korea, Canada and the United States, and Colombia and Peru are as much a part of the region as are those from Papua New Guinea, Fiji, the Marshall Islands, Tonga, and so on. In this book, however, I use the term "the Pacific" to refer to the island countries and territories of the Pacific Basin, including Australia and New Zealand.

This Pacific has traditionally been divided into four regions: Melanesia, Micronesia, Polynesia, and Australia (see map 2). Australia is clearly separate from the remainder of the Pacific culturally, ethnically, and linguistically. The other three regions are just as clearly *not* separate from one another according to all of these criteria. There is considerable ethnic, cultural, and linguistic diversity within each of these regions, and the boundaries usually drawn between them do not necessarily coincide with clear physical, cultural, or linguistic differences. These regions, and the boundaries drawn between them, are largely artifacts of the western propensity, even weakness, for classification, as the continuing and quite futile debate over whether Fijians are Polynesians or Melanesians illustrates.

Having said this, however, I will nevertheless continue to use the terms "Melanesia," "Micronesia," and "Polynesia" to refer to different *geographical* areas within the Pacific basin, without prejudice to the relationships of the languages or the cultures of people of each region.

2.1. How Many Languages?

This book deals mainly with the indigenous languages of the Pacific region. There are many other languages that can be called "Pacific languages," for

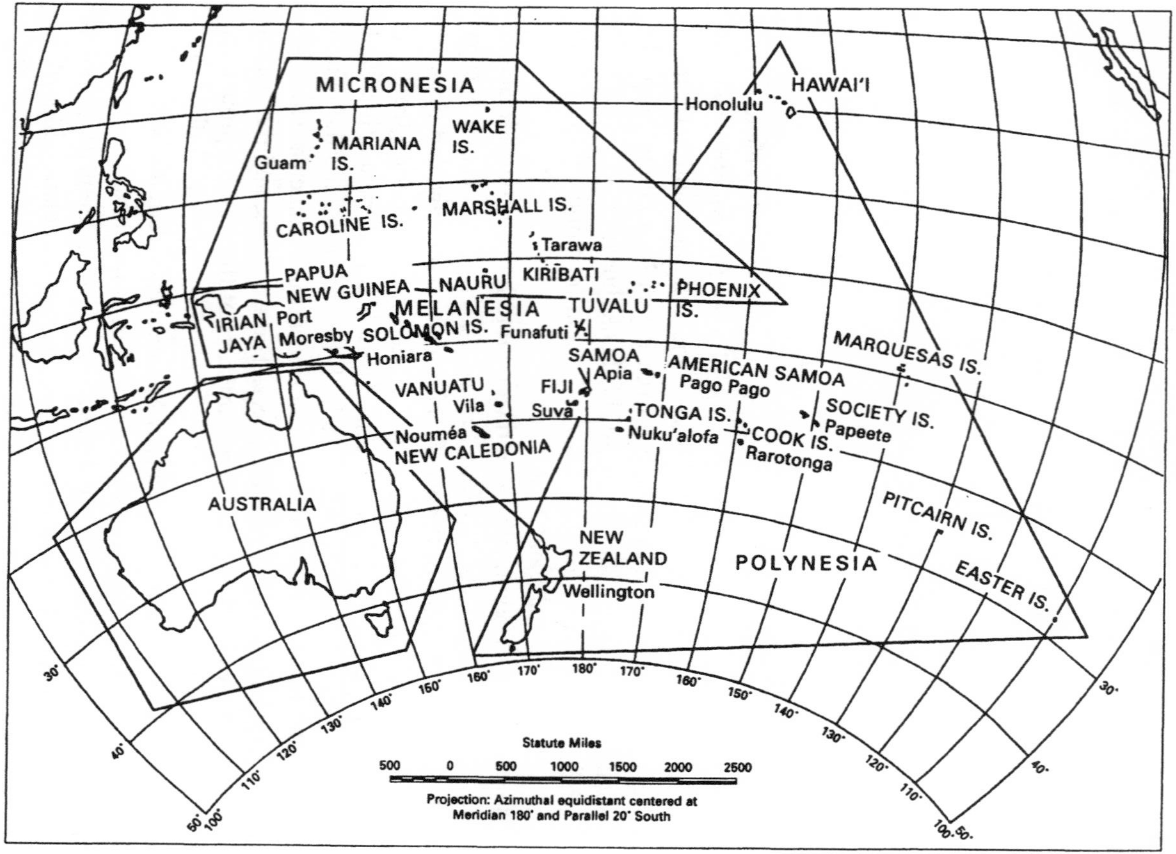

Map 2. The Pacific

example, languages that have developed fairly recently, such as Hawaiian Creole, Fiji Hindi, Hiri Motu (Papua New Guinea), Melanesian Pidgin (known as Tok Pisin in Papua New Guinea, Pijin in Solomon Islands, and Bislama in Vanuatu), Broken and Kriol (Australia), and others. There are also the languages of the metropolitan powers, particularly English and French, which are widely used throughout the region, but also Bahasa Indonesia in Irian Jaya and Spanish in Easter Island. And there are small but substantial numbers of speakers of various Chinese languages, of Vietnamese, and of other "intrusive" languages in Pacific towns. (These languages receive some attention in part 3.)

When it comes to what we might call "true" Pacific languages, we find that this region is probably the most linguistically complex in the world. There are, or were, almost fourteen hundred distinct languages spoken in the Pacific, or about one quarter of the world's languages. And these fourteen hundred languages are spoken by not much more than 0.1 percent of the world's population![1] Further, so far as we can tell, these languages do not all belong to a single language family. There are a number of language families in the Pacific.

Let us look first at the nature of the differences between languages in this region. Many people describe the languages of the Pacific as "dialects," partly because most are spoken by small populations and are unimportant in terms of world politics, and partly because many are unwritten. But linguists use the terms "language" and "dialect" with quite specific meanings.

Speakers of the same language living in geographically separate areas often speak differently, though these differences are usually not great enough to prevent communication between them. For example, many Americans say *sidewalk, diaper,* and *flashlight* where English people would use *footpath, nappy,* and *torch.* And while most English people pronounce words like *half, past,* and *mast* with the same vowel as the first vowel in *father,* most Americans pronounce them with the same vowel as in *hat.* But despite these obvious differences in vocabulary, in pronunciation, and in grammar as well, the Americans and the English can still communicate quite easily. We would therefore say that they are speaking different **dialects** of the same language. But Americans or English people must learn French to understand a French person, as English and French are different languages.

Mutual intelligibility—whether speakers from one group can or cannot carry on a normal conversation with speakers of another—is just one way of looking at the distinction between language and dialect. In many parts of the Pacific, it is difficult to test for mutual intelligibility, because people not only speak the language of their own community, but also acquire an understanding, either active or passive, of the languages of neighboring communities from a very early age. People from two communities can quite often carry on a conversation in two different languages, so testing for mutual intelligibility is fraught with all sorts of problems. In cases like these, linguists have to use their own judgment about how many languages are involved.

Perhaps more important than the issue of mutual intelligibility is the issue of social identity. People believe that their language is the same as—or is different from—another group's language for a variety of social rather than linguistic reasons. Here are two examples of this:

1. On the basis of mutual intelligibility, Hindi and Urdu would be classified as dialects of the same language. Hindi is the national language of India. It is written in the Devanagari script and is closely associated in people's minds with Hinduism. Urdu is the national language of Pakistan. It is written in Arabic script and is closely associated with Islam. For these nonlinguistic reasons, most speakers would say that Hindi and Urdu are two different languages.

2. Many people refer to Fijian as if it were one language. It is associated with a group of people who are ethnically and culturally fairly homogeneous, and there is just one written version, which all literate Fijians read and write. But people in the eastern part of Fiji cannot understand people from the western area when they speak (unless they have learned the western Fijian language).

There is a further problem with differentiating and counting languages that relates to the phenomenon known as a **dialect chain**. A dialect chain is found in a series of communities in which each community has a different dialect. Close neighbors can quite easily understand each other, but people have greater difficulty in understanding or communicating with people from communities farther along the chain. Imagine that the following villages are spread along the coast of a large island:

A   B   C   D   E   F   G   H   I   J

People from, say, village C can easily communicate with their close neighbors (A and B to the west, D and E to the east); they have some difficulty communicating with people from F and G; and they cannot communicate well at all with people from H, I, and J. On the other hand, people from village E can communicate easily with those from C, D, F, and G, have some difficulty with those from B, H, and I, but find people from A and J unintelligible. People from A would be unable to communicate with those from

J, so it would seem from looking just at the two ends of the chain that two different *languages* are involved. But there is nowhere in the middle of the chain where we can draw a language boundary, since everyone can communicate with their immediate neighbors. So are we dealing with one language or two?

In one sense, this is really a problem only when one tries to count the number of languages, to tidy up the situation with a neat classification. Some linguists would say that the villages I have described share one language, made up of a complex dialect chain. Others would say it is two, with, however, no distinct boundary between the western language and the eastern one. Situations like this are found in Fiji, in the Caroline Islands of Micronesia, and in a number of areas in Papua New Guinea. This is one reason that different authorities give different numbers of languages for certain areas of the Pacific.

Despite these complications, when I say that there are about fourteen hundred languages spoken in the Pacific, I do mean languages, not dialects. Some, of course, are quite similar to each other, as French is to Spanish and Italian, or even as Hindi is to Urdu. But there are also differences of the same order of magnitude as those between English and Chinese. And many of these languages are spoken in a number of dialects as well.

There are two other reasons why we cannot be exact about the number of languages in the Pacific. Some languages are moribund—that is, at last report they were spoken by just a small number of old people—and therefore are almost extinct. Many Australian languages fall into this category, but there are some in Melanesia as well. The other reason is that, at least in certain parts of the Pacific, we have insufficient information. The interior of Irian Jaya is an especially good example, though not the only one. In such cases we are forced to make educated guesses.

Table 1 gives the number of languages spoken in each of the main regions of the Pacific and in each of the countries and territories within each region. For the reasons discussed above, the figures given are approximate.

2.2. Linguistic Demography

2.2.1. Polynesia and Micronesia

With a few exceptions, we can say that in Polynesia there is generally one language per island or per island group. Ignoring minor problems ("Are they two languages or two dialects?"), there are twenty-one languages spoken in what is referred to as the Polynesian Triangle (including the extinct Moriori language).[2] Map 3 shows the location of all these languages.

Table 1.   Pacific Languages by Region and Country

Melanesia	1151+
Irian Jaya	205+
Papua New Guinea	750+
Solomon Islands	63
Vanuatu	105
New Caledonia	28
Micronesia	16
Belau	1
Northern Marianas and Guam	2[a]
Marshall Islands	1
Kiribati	1
Nauru	1
Federated States of Micronesia	11
Fiji and Polynesia	22
Fiji, including Rotuma	3
Tonga	2
Niue	1
The Samoas	1
Tuvalu	1
Tokelau	1
Wallis and Futuna	2
Cook Islands	3
Hawai'i	1
French Polynesia	5
Easter Island	1
New Zealand	1
Australia	200[b]
Total	1389+

[a] One of these is a dialect of Carolinian, other dialects of which are spoken in the Federated States of Micronesia.
[b] Many of these have become extinct or are moribund.

Speakers of many of these languages now live outside their home countries. There are significant communities of speakers of, for example, East Uvea (Wallisian) in New Caledonia and Vanuatu, and of Tongan and Samoan in both New Zealand and the United States. About as many

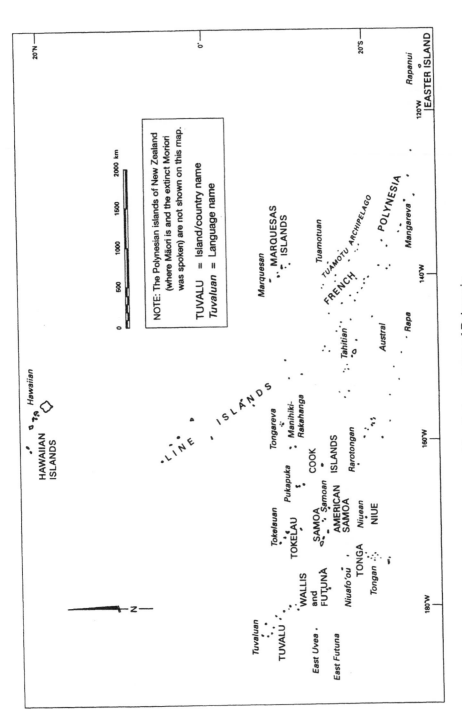

Map 3. Languages of Polynesia

Rarotongan speakers, and many more speakers of Niuean, live in New Zealand as in the Cook Islands and Niue, respectively.

Some Polynesian languages have large numbers of speakers. Samoan probably has about 250,000 speakers, Tongan, Tahitian, and New Zealand Māori each approximately 100,000. Rarotongan, with more than 30,000 speakers, and Wallisian, with 10,000, are also large in Pacific terms. In contrast, some of the languages of French Polynesia other than Tahitian are spoken by fewer than a thousand people.

Micronesia is similar to Polynesia in having—as a rule—only one language per island or island group, although there are difficulties in deciding exactly how many languages there are. Bender and Wang (1985, 54–56) have a good brief discussion of this problem. While many of the speech traditions of Micronesia are clearly identifiable as discrete languages, the Trukic group of speech communities, extending from Chuuk (Truk) Lagoon to Tobi, presents a major problem. Different linguists have divided this complex continuum into three, seven, and eleven distinct languages, which makes the exercise of counting languages difficult and probably futile. I have taken Bender and Wang's figure of three languages for this continuum, and this gives the somewhat arbitrary figure of sixteen languages spoken in Micronesia. Map 4 shows the location of these languages, but also indicates the named varieties of the three Trukic languages that some linguists treat as distinct.

Many speakers of Micronesian languages also live outside their home countries, particularly in Guam and the United States. Fiji, Nauru, and Solomon Islands possess sizable Kiribati-speaking communities. Kiribati and Chamorro, each with more than 50,000 speakers, have the greatest number of speakers in Micronesia. Lagoon Trukese, Ponapean, and Marshallese all have about 20,000 speakers, and most of the other languages (depending on how they are defined) number in the thousands. A number of languages or dialects, however,—including Sonsorolese, Satawalese, Namonuito, Ngatikese, Kapingamarangi, and Nukuoro—have fewer than a thousand speakers.

2.2.2. Melanesia

For the purposes of this discussion, Melanesia is taken as including the independent states of Papua New Guinea, Solomon Islands, Vanuatu, Fiji, the Indonesian province of Irian Jaya, and the French overseas territory of New Caledonia. Melanesia differs from Polynesia and Micronesia; here it is the rule rather than the exception for there to be many languages per island. In this general survey of the linguistic situation in Melanesia, maps 5 through 10 locate all the languages of Melanesia mentioned in this book.

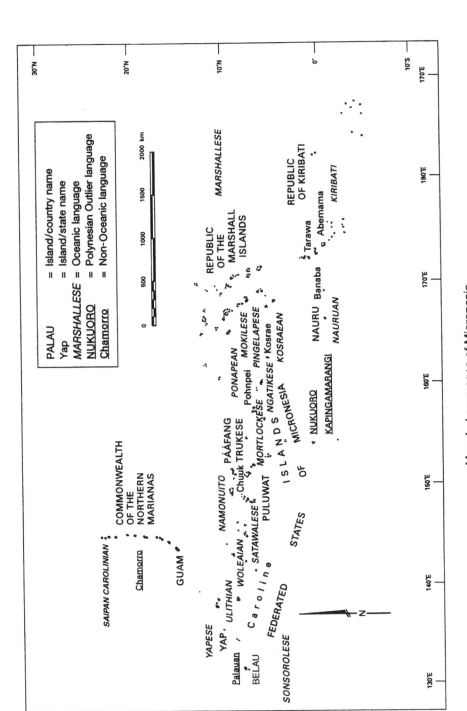

Map 4. Languages of Micronesia

Fiji and Rotuma

Rotuma is home to a distinct language spoken by around 10,000 people, but linguists disagree about how many languages are spoken in the rest of Fiji. Certainly there are many different varieties of "Fijian" spoken by the 300,000 or so ethnic Fijians in Viti Levu, Vanua Levu, and the offshore islands. The situation is further complicated by the fact that the dialect of the

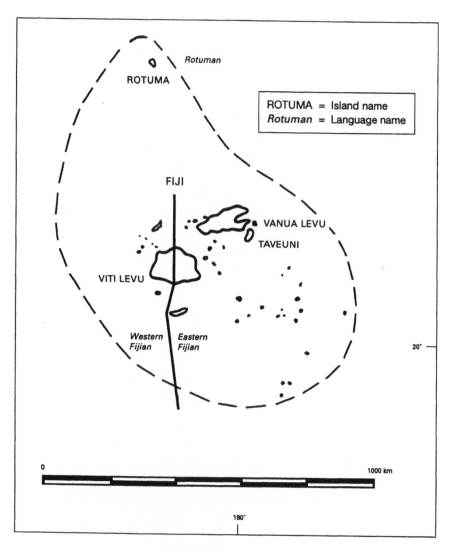

Map 5. Languages of Fiji and Rotuma

island of Bau, southeast of Viti Levu, has been adopted as the standard for the written language, for education, and for certain public occasions, so that many Fijians who speak another dialect also know that one. "Fijian" consists of a chain of perhaps thirty or forty dialects. Most linguists would probably divide this chain into two languages, Western Fijian (spoken in the western half of Viti Levu), and Eastern Fijian (spoken in the rest of the country, excluding Rotuma).

New Caledonia and the Loyalty Islands

There are twenty-eight languages in the French territory of New Caledonia, all spoken by small populations. The two languages with the largest number of speakers are Drehu, with about 7,000 speakers, and Paicî, with just under 5,000; but five of the territory's twenty-eight languages have fewer than two hundred speakers. (Map 6 shows only those languages that I mention in this book.)

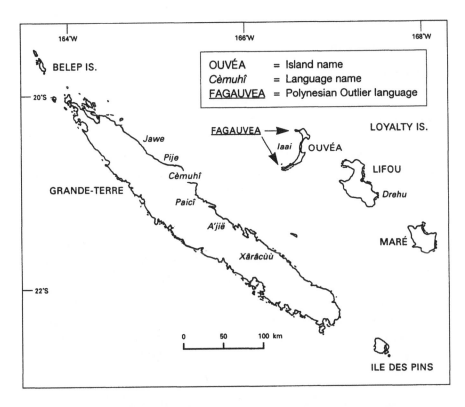

Map 6. New Caledonia (showing languages referred to in the text)

Vanuatu

The Republic of Vanuatu is home to between one hundred and 110 languages (Tryon 1976). As in New Caledonia, all of these are spoken by very small populations. Recent estimates (Tryon and Charpentier 1989) show that Northeast Ambae on Ambae Island, with 4,300 speakers, Lenakel and Whitesands on Tanna, each with 4,000, and Apma on Pentecost, with 3,800 have the largest number of speakers.[3] Forty-one languages, or almost half the languages of the country have two hundred speakers or fewer; five of these forty-one have fewer than fifty speakers. (Map 7 shows only those languages mentioned in the text.)

Solomon Islands

The most recent linguistic survey of Solomon Islands (Tryon and Hackman 1983) lists sixty-three languages as being spoken in that country. Those with the largest populations are the North Malaita dialect chain, with 13,500, and Kwara'ae, with 12,500, both on Malaita. No other language has more than 10,000 speakers. Twelve languages have fewer than two hundred speakers; six of these twelve have fewer than fifty. (Map 8 includes only those languages discussed in the text.)

Papua New Guinea

Papua New Guinea is probably the most linguistically diverse nation in the modern world. A population of around four million people speak well over seven hundred distinct languages. Wurm and Hattori's (1981) linguistic atlas of the region estimates that there are 750 languages spoken in Papua New Guinea. This may be a slightly conservative figure. Other estimates usually count more than these. Some differences lie in the distinctions made between dialect and language. Map 9 shows only a few of these languages.

According to Wurm and Hattori's figures, in the 1970s, nine of the languages of Papua New Guinea were spoken by more than 40,000 people. All of these except Tolai are spoken in the Highlands. These languages are:

Enga	165,000	Huli	60,000
Kuman (Simbu)	140,000	Kewa	48,000
Hagen	100,000	Mendi	45,000
Kamano	85,000	Wahgi	45,000
Tolai	65,000		

At the same time, a staggering 114 languages in Papua New Guinea are listed as being spoken by populations of fewer than two hundred people.

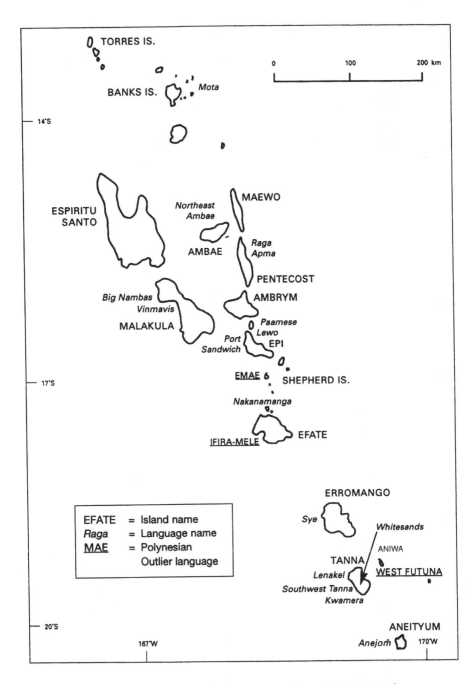

Map 7. Vanuatu (showing languages referred to in the text)

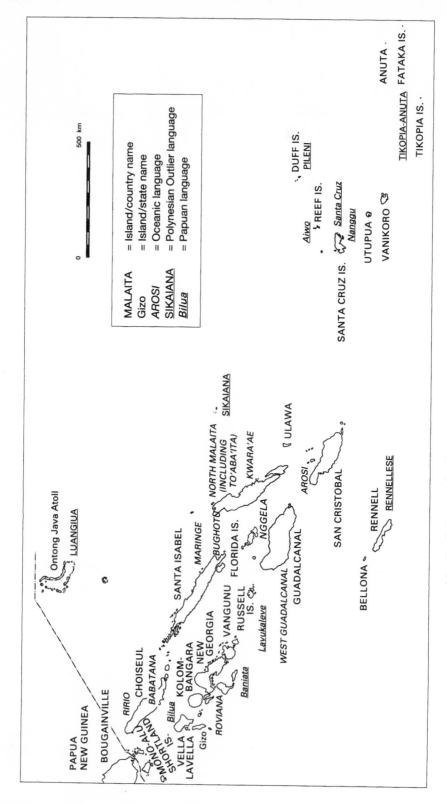

Map 8. Solomon Islands (showing languages referred to in the text)

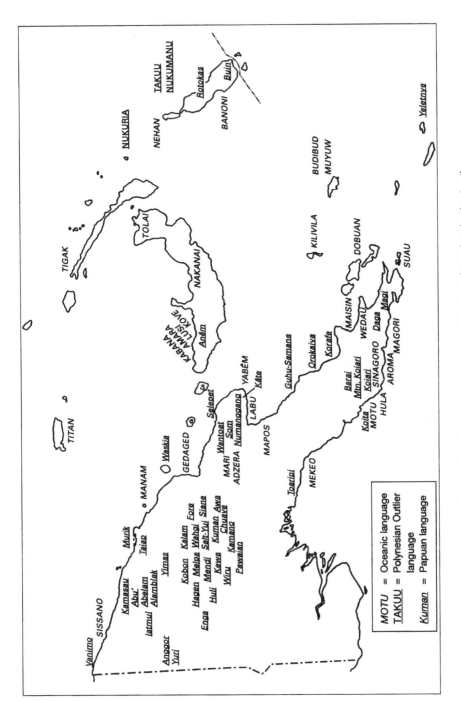

Map 9. Papua New Guinea (showing languages referred to in the text)

Irian Jaya

The situation in Irian Jaya is less clear than anywhere else in the Melanesian region, since much less research has been done on these languages than on those of any other part of the Pacific. Wurm and Hattori (1981) believe that slightly more than two hundred languages are spoken in this Indonesian province, only four of them by 40,000 people or more. These four are:

Western Dani	100,000
Grand Valley Dani	75,000
Ekagi	65,000
Biak-Numfor	40,000

In contrast, Wurm and Hattori list forty languages—20 percent of those in the province—as being spoken by two hundred or fewer people. (Map 10 names only the languages mentioned in this book.)

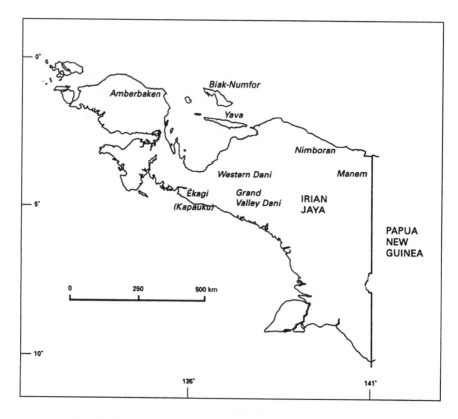

Map 10. Irian Jaya (showing languages referred to in the text)

2.2.3. Australia

Dixon (1980) says that, at the time of first European settlement, there were probably about two hundred different languages spoken in Australia. We will never know the exact figure, since many languages had disappeared before any linguistic work had been carried out on them. Of these two hundred, the Western Desert language had the largest number of speakers, around 6,000. It was spoken over an area of about 1.3 million square kilometers.[4]

The survival of Australian languages (and of the people who speak them) has been severely threatened in the last two centuries. Whole tribes and their languages died out in many areas, while other tribes assimilated to varying degrees to the invading culture, losing their languages in the process. Of the current language situation in Australia, Dixon says:

> Of the 200 languages spoken in Australia before the European invasion 50 are now extinct, the last speakers having died some years ago; in most cases there are still some people who would claim tribal membership but they know only a dozen or so isolated words of what was once a full and flourishing language. Then there are probably around

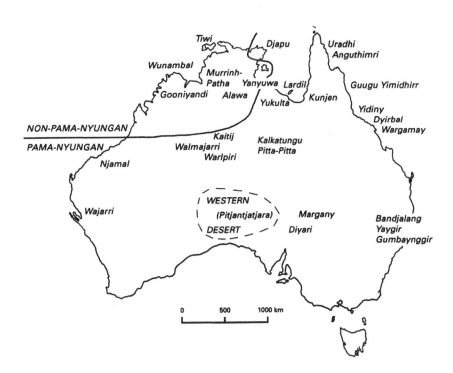

Map 11. Australia (showing languages referred to in the text)

100 languages that are on the path towards extinction. Some are remembered by only a handful of old people, and will cease to be spoken or remembered within a very few years; others may be being
learnt by children in a few families but the total number of speakers is
so small—a few dozen or less—that these languages seem bound grad-
ually to drop out of use over the next few generations. Finally, perhaps
50 languages are in a relatively healthy state—spoken as first language
by a few hundred (or, in one or two cases, by a few thousand) people
and preserving their full range of use in everyday affairs and in cere-
mony and ritual. (Dixon 1980, 18)

While the languages of the rest of the Pacific region are generally quite viable, the Australian languages, which once spread right across the continent, are in rapid decline. The number of speakers of each diminishes with
the shift toward English and the decimation of the population.

2.3. Language Names

Language names in the Pacific can be problematic. Some languages are
known by one, and only one, name. It may be the people's own name for the
language (Nakanamanga in Vanuatu), the name of the people themselves
(Motu in Papua New Guinea), an English version of a local name (Tongan),
or a compound expression referring to some feature of the language
(Pitjantjatjara, the name of a dialect of the Western Desert language of
Australia, which means "having the word *pitjantja* 'come' ").

In some areas, however, people do not have a name for their own language, but refer to it as "the language," "our language," or "correct/good language." The Tolai language of New Britain, for example, has been referred
to in the literature as Tuna, from *a tinata tuna* 'the real language.'
Languages of this kind are often named in the literature after the locality in
which they are spoken. For example, linguists call the languages spoken on
the islands of Paama and Mota in Vanuatu Paamese and Mota.

People sometimes invent names for languages lacking a specific appella-
tion. Discussing the names of some languages of the Torricelli Phylum in
the Sepik area of Papua New Guinea, Laycock (1975b, 774) says, "The languages are named, when not after a village or area, by the translation into
that language of *no* or *there is none*; this practice has been widespread in the
Lumi area for some time, and may antedate European contact, and the
principle has been extended in naming languages outside the Lumi area."
This practice explains why a number of languages in this area have very similar names (Olo, Alu, Galu, Aru, Aruop, and so on).

Even when people do have their own name for a language, some other name is often given, usually a geographical one. On the island of Tanna in Vanuatu, for example, the "real" names of the languages spoken in the Lenakel and Whitesands areas are, respectively, Netvaar and Nɨrak. But these languages are almost universally known as Lenakel and Whitesands not only to outsiders but also to their speakers.

In many cases the same language goes by a number of different names, a name in the local language and a geographical name, or a series of names for different dialects or different localities in the language area, for example. The language spoken (in two dialects) on the islands of Rennell and Bellona in Solomon Islands is known variously as Rennell-Bellona, Rennellese, Bellonese, Moiki, Munggava, and Munggiki. The Nakanamanga language of central Vanuatu is perhaps better known to linguists as Nguna or Ngunese, which is the dialect that has received the most attention.[5]

Again, there are cases where names may refer only to different dialects. West Guadalcanal (Solomon Islands), for example, has a number of named dialects, some of which appear in the linguistic literature as if they were separate languages (Gari or Ghari, Kerebuto, Nggae, Sughu, and Vaturanga). Early mission grammars or dictionaries often named the language after the location of the mission, while the name in current use is different (Lamalanga [name assigned by missionaries] for Raga, spoken in Pentecost Island in Vanuatu). Hyphenated language names (e.g., Mono-Alu in Solomon Islands) can indicate that there are (at least) two named dialects but no overall local name for the language. Spelling variations also occur. The name of the Baniata language of Rendova in Solomon Islands has also been spelled Bañata and Mbaniata, while another Solomons language, spoken in New Georgia, has been variously spelled Bareke, Bariki, Mbareke, and Mbariki.

In this book I try to use the most generally accepted name for any language with consistency, even if (1) the language has other names, and (2) these other names are used in my sources.

2.4. A Brief History of Pacific Language Research

The first information on Pacific languages came from European navigators, who published lists of words and occasional sentences in various languages (and sometimes commented on the similarities between some of them). Missionaries followed, translating religious materials into various Pacific languages, but also producing grammars, dictionaries, and the like. Some colonial government officials also made contributions.

Professional linguists were rather late on the scene. In general, their interests have been threefold.

1. Comparative-historical: attempting to establish relationships between languages within the Pacific, and between Pacific languages and languages outside the region, thus contributing to the study of Pacific prehistory.
2. Descriptive: analysis of the grammars of Pacific languages, compilation of dictionaries, and so on.
3. Theoretical: testing or formulating general claims about the nature of language and of language change on the basis of data from Pacific languages.

2.4.1. Fiji and Polynesia

Our knowledge of the Fijian and Polynesian languages is more complete than our knowledge of most other Pacific languages for a number of reasons. There is usually only one language per country (or island). The languages are not especially difficult phonologically and are quite closely related, so that a knowledge of one makes a good stepping-stone to learning another. And in general, the Polynesian languages and Fijian have been studied for far longer than have those of the rest of the region.

Missionary endeavors and the work of some colonial officials provided a firm foundation for the description of many of these languages, with a good number of grammatical studies and dictionaries being written in the nineteenth and early twentieth centuries. The first grammar and the first dictionary of Fijian, for example, were published in 1850 (Hazlewood 1850a, 1850b), and there were also early studies of the languages of Tonga, Samoa, and various parts of eastern Polynesia, including New Zealand. In many of the countries of Polynesia, governments have also taken a keen interest in the preservation of traditional culture and language, encouraging the use of Polynesian languages in schools and churches, on radio and television, in books and newspapers, and elsewhere in the public domain. So there are good grammars and/or dictionaries for most of the languages of Fiji and Polynesia, and there are numerous publications in and on these languages of both an academic and a general nature.

2.4.2. Micronesia

Given Micronesia's checkered colonial history, it is not surprising that little was known about most of its languages until after the Second World War. Some of the early information on Micronesian languages was written in German or Japanese.

Bender (1984, viii–x) gives a brief summary of the history of Micronesian linguistics since 1945. Initial studies focused on applied linguistics to assist the American government in education and other areas. But these studies often had a more academic side as well. The decision in 1966 to send Peace Corps volunteers to Micronesia meant that language courses had to be written, providing a fresh impetus for linguistic research. These language lessons often developed into full-scale grammars and dictionaries, mainly under the auspices of the University of Hawai'i, which continues to be the major center for the study of Micronesian languages.

As a result of the last fifty years' research good grammars or dictionaries exist for most Micronesian languages. Orthographies have been developed for virtually all the languages, and many are or have been used as classroom languages in Micronesian educational systems.

2.4.3. Melanesia

In Melanesia, some languages have been well known to linguists for a long time, but a very large number remain almost completely unstudied. Apart from a few wordlists published by early explorers, it was once again the missionaries who undertook the first serious study of any of the Melanesian languages. For many of these languages missionary grammars and dictionaries (in French, German, or Dutch as well as English) remain the only publications of a linguistic nature. By the turn of the twentieth century, there were publications on a handful of these languages, including the comparative studies of von der Gabelentz (1861–1873), Codrington (1885), and Ray (1926), which presented grammatical sketches of a number of languages. But even into the 1920s, very little indeed had been published about the languages of Melanesia.

During the twentieth century, missionary linguistic work has continued in anglophone Melanesia. Scholars from various universities have also published grammatical and lexical studies of a number of Melanesian languages, while the Summer Institute of Linguistics has engaged in a massive amount of research into languages of the New Guinea area especially. Until recently, the pioneering work of Leenhardt (1946) remained the major source of information for the languages of francophone Melanesia, though recent work by a number of French and other linguists has dramatically increased our knowledge of the languages of New Caledonia and the Loyalty Islands.

2.4.4. Australia

Apart from a few missionaries and colonial officials, very few of the early white settlers paid much attention to Australian languages. Given their attitudes toward Aboriginal people and Aboriginal society, which ranged from classifying them as primitive, attempting to assimilate them, and treating them with "benign neglect" to downright extermination and genocide, one would not have expected much linguistic work to be done on these languages in the first century of contact.

In the earlier part of the twentieth century, some linguistic study accompanied anthropological studies. In his survey of the languages of Australia Dixon notes that, in the fifty years between 1910 and 1960, there was only *one* linguist, Arthur Capell, active in the field. In more recent years, linguists from a number of universities in Australia and elsewhere, as well as those working with the Summer Institute of Linguistics, have produced a considerable body of descriptive and comparative work. Much of this falls into the category of salvage linguistics, recording a language before it becomes extinct. Many salvage attempts are just sketches, containing gaps in lexicon and grammar that can never be filled.

3

The History of the Austronesian Languages

Comparative-historical linguists have divided the fourteen hundred or so languages of the Pacific into three broad groups. About 450 are classified as belonging to the *Austronesian* family, a very large family of languages with another six or seven hundred members spoken outside the Pacific Basin. Seven hundred or so languages spoken on the island of New Guinea, or on islands not far from it, belong to a number of apparently unrelated families. All are grouped under the cover term *Papuan*. The two hundred *Australian* languages belong to a third broad genetic grouping. We know much more about both the present and the past of the Austronesian languages of the Pacific than we do about the Papuan or Australian languages. For this reason I discuss the history of the Austronesian languages first.

3.1. The Austronesian Family

The **Austronesian** language family is one of the two largest language families in the world in number of member languages. (The other is the Benue-Congo family in Africa.) The family as a whole has somewhere between a thousand and twelve hundred languages, spoken by almost three hundred million people.[1] Map 12 shows the distribution of Austronesian languages. Outside the Pacific Basin, Austronesian languages are spoken in Taiwan, in Malaysia and a few small pockets on the Asian mainland, in Madagascar, and in almost all of island Southeast Asia. All the languages of the Philippines and almost all the languages of Indonesia (excluding most of Irian Jaya) are Austronesian.

About 450 Austronesian languages are spoken within the Pacific region. These include all the languages of Polynesia, Micronesia, Fiji, New Caledonia, and Vanuatu, as well as almost all the languages of Solomon Islands. Only about one quarter of the languages of the New Guinea area

Map 12. Austronesian Languages

belong to this family, however. Speakers of these languages generally occupy New Guinea's offshore islands and some coastal areas, but very few inhabit inland areas.

While linguists are still not in full agreement as to the major subgroups of Austronesian, figure 6 shows one widely accepted view of the higher-order branches of this family. Nearly all of the Austronesian languages discussed in this book belong to the Oceanic subgroup. The family tree suggests an Asian origin for speakers of Austronesian, and the archaeological evidence tends to corroborate this.

3.2. The Oceanic Languages

Two languages spoken in Micronesia, Palauan and Chamorro, belong to one of the Western Malayo-Polynesian subgroups of Austronesian, and the Austronesian languages of the western part of Irian Jaya belong to the South Halmahera–West New Guinea subgroup. All of the other Austronesian languages in the Pacific belong to the **Oceanic** subgroup. This subgroup was originally established by the German linguist Dempwolff (1934–1938). He referred to it as *Urmelanesisch* 'Proto Melanesian.' All Oceanic languages share a number of phonological, grammatical, and lexical innovations that are absent from the other Austronesian languages.

3.2.1. Internal Relationships of the Oceanic Languages

Scholars have been debating the internal relationships of Oceanic for some time. They agree that the initial branching of Oceanic was in the western part of the Pacific, but the poor state of our knowledge of Melanesian languages has made it difficult to determine just what that initial branching looked like. Fijian and the Polynesian languages have been thoroughly studied for more than a century, and their interrelationships are fairly clear. They form, however, only one small subsubgroup of Oceanic, and studying them has not helped a great deal in determining the overall structure of the Oceanic subgroup.

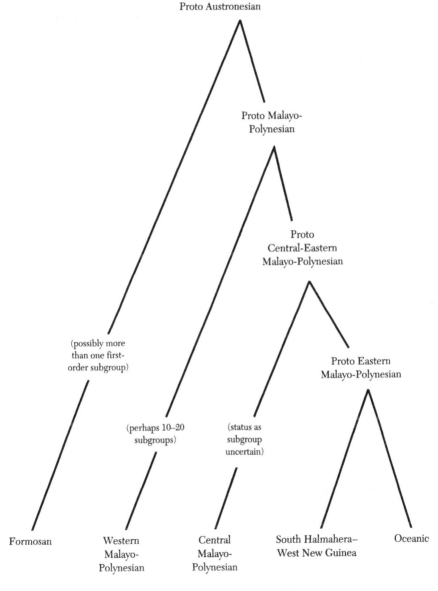

Figure 6.   An Austonesian Family Tree

Only in fairly recent years has a coherent picture of the Oceanic sub-group begun to emerge. Currently the groups within this subgroup include:

1. **Yapese**, spoken on the island of Yap in Micronesia (Ross 1995). This *may* prove to form part of the Admiralty Islands group.
2. The **Admiralty Islands** group, namely, the languages of Manus and neighboring islands to the north of the New Guinea mainland.
3. The **Saint Matthias Islands** group, two languages spoken on small islands immediately to the north of New Ireland in Papua New Guinea. This also may prove to be part of the Admiralty Islands group.
4. The **Western Oceanic** group, a very large grouping consisting of:
   a. The **North New Guinea** subgroup, comprising all the Oceanic languages of western and southern New Britain plus those spoken along the northern coast of Papua New Guinea from just south of the Markham Valley westward to the Irian Jaya border.
   b. The **Papuan Tip** subgroup, all the Oceanic languages of the Papuan mainland and the neighboring islands.
   c. The **Meso-Melanesian** subgroup, made up of the Oceanic languages of northern and eastern New Britain, New Ireland, Bougainville (and their offshore islands), and the Oceanic languages of the western half of the Solomon Islands (excluding a handful of Polynesian Outlier languages—see 3.2.2 below).
   d. The **Sarmi-Jayapura** subgroup, made up of the Oceanic languages of the northeast coast of Irian Jaya (Ross 1996). (These are included here because they may turn out to be part of the North New Guinea subgroup.)
5. The **Southeast Solomons** group includes the Oceanic languages of Guadalcanal, Malaita, and Makira, plus Bughotu on Isabel. This group may possibly also include the languages of Utupua and Vanikoro in the Temotu Province of Solomon Islands, though it is more likely that these form one or even two separate subgroups.
6. The **Southern Oceanic** group (Lynch 1997), consisting of:
   a. The **North-Central Vanuatu** subgroup, in which are the non-Polynesian languages of north and central Vanuatu from the Torres Islands in the north to Efate in the central south.
   b. The **Southern Melanesian** subgroup, with the non-Polynesian languages of Southern Vanuatu (Erromango, Tanna, and Aneityum), New Caledonia, and the Loyalty Islands.
7. The **Micronesian** group, all non-Polynesian Oceanic languages in geographical Micronesia, excluding Yapese; note that the status of Nauruan within this group is still problematic.

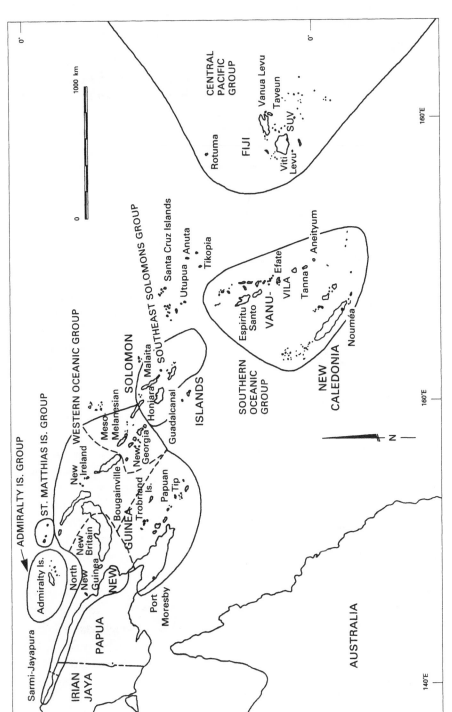

Map 13. Oceanic Subgroups in Melanesia

8. The **Central Pacific** group, consisting of Rotuman, the languages of Fiji, and all Polynesian languages, including the Polynesian Outliers discussed below.[2]

Attempts have been made to try to link two or more of these groupings together into a higher-order group, but they have so far been unsuccessful. Groups 5–8 above have recently been linked into a putative Central-Eastern Oceanic subgroup (Lynch, Ross, and Crowley 1998) whose validity is still being investigated. Because of this, trying to present a family tree of Oceanic would serve no real purpose at this stage of our research.

3.2.2. Oceanic Subgroups and Geographical Regions

Given the subgrouping of Oceanic just outlined, it should be obvious that the boundaries dividing the three traditional geographical-cultural regions of the Pacific—Melanesia, Micronesia, and Polynesia—do not correspond to the linguistic facts. About twenty languages are spoken in the geographical area known as Polynesia. Outside Polynesia are fourteen other languages that are very clearly genetically "Polynesian." These are referred to as **Polynesian Outliers**, and most scholars assume that they are the result of migrations into Melanesia and Micronesia from western Polynesia after its settlement by the ancestors of the modern Polynesians. Table 2 gives a list, with locations, of the fourteen Polynesian Outliers. (See also maps 4, 6–9). Figure 7 shows the interrelationships of the Polynesian languages and their immediate relatives in the Central Pacific group. The primary split in Polynesian occurred between the Tongic subgroup (consisting of just Tongan and Niuean) and the Nuclear Polynesian subgroup (consisting of all other Polynesian languages including the Outliers). The closest Outliers' relatives within Polynesian appear to be Samoan, Tokelauan, Tuvaluan, East Uvea, East Futuna, Niuafo'ou, and Pukapuka. Although all the languages of Polynesia are Polynesian in the genetic sense, not all Polynesian languages are spoken in Polynesia.

In Micronesia the situation is somewhat different. The "Micronesian" subgroup consists of most, but not all, of the languages of geographical Micronesia. Not only are two Polynesian Outliers, Nukuoro and Kapingamarangi, spoken in Micronesia, but Yapese appears to be a single member of a subgroup separate from all other Oceanic languages. To complicate matters further, the nature of the relationship of Nauruan to the other Micronesian languages is unclear, and Palauan and Chamorro are not even Oceanic languages at all, but have as their closest relatives languages in Indonesia and the Philippines.

Nowhere, however, is the mismatch between so-called cultural areas and linguistic classification more glaring than in Melanesia. Hundreds of

Table 2.   Polynesian Outliers

Country or territory	Location	Language
Federated States of Micronesia	Nukuoro Island	Nukuoro
	Kapingamarangi Island	Kapingamarangi
Papua New Guinea	Nukuria Island	Nukuria
	Mortlock Island	Takuu
	Tasman Island	Nukumanu
Solomon Islands	Ontong Java	Luangiua
	Stewart Island	Sikaiana
	Rennell Island, Bellona Island	Rennellese
	Duff Island	Pileni
	Tikopia Island, Anuta Island	Tikopia-Anuta
Vanuatu	Emae Island	Emae
	Port Vila harbor	Ifira-Mele
	Futuna Island, Aniwa Island	West Futuna
New Caledonia	Ouvéa, Loyalty Islands	Fagauvea (West Uvea)

Papuan languages are spoken in Melanesia, as are a number of Oceanic languages, including a dozen or so Polynesian Outliers (see table 3).

But more important is the fact that, although we can speak of a Polynesian subgroup, and even of a Micronesian subgroup, that have *some* correlation with geography, there is no such thing as a Melanesian subgroup of Oceanic. Of the eight major subgroups of Oceanic, six are located wholly or partly in Melanesia.

3.3. The Settlement of Oceania

Linguists construct hypotheses about the interrelationships of languages to attempt to find out about the past. These theories about past languages and language splits generally lead to theories about the origins and migrations of peoples. In many cases, one can compare linguistic and archaeological hypotheses in an effort to put both on a firmer footing.

3.3.1. Origins of Oceanic Speakers

The Oceanic subgroup's position on the Austronesian family tree (figure 6) indicates that the speakers of Proto Oceanic migrated from Southeast Asia

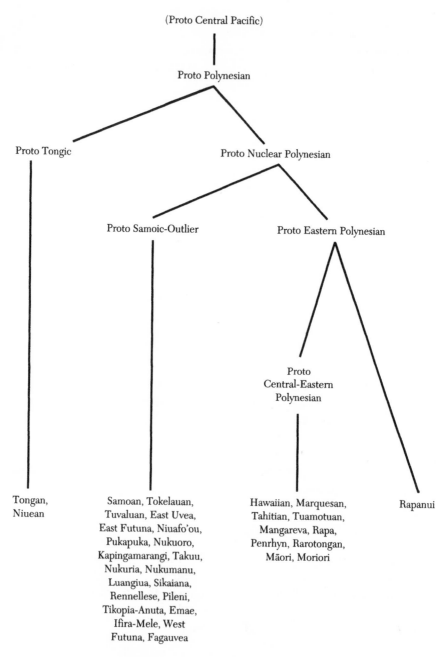

Figure 7. The Polynesian Subgroup

Table 3. Languages of Melanesia

	Austronesian	Papuan	Total
New Caledonia	28	—	28
Vanuatu	105	—	105
Solomon Islands	56	7	63
Papua New Guinea	210	540	750
Irian Jaya	45	160	205
Totals	444	707	1151

to the Pacific region. This thesis is almost universally accepted. Some evidence suggests that the closest external relatives of the Austronesian languages may be (1) the Thai-Kadai group of languages, spoken mainly in Thailand and Laos, and (2) the languages of the neighboring Austroasiatic group, spoken mainly in Cambodia and Vietnam. Both of these groups also have members in southern China and in parts of Malaysia. Archaeologists suspect that dramatic improvements in agricultural practices, accompanied by significant population growth, led to expansions of human populations on the Southeast Asian mainland around 5,000 B.C. (Bellwood 1995).

The Austronesians were one of these populations. The linguistic family tree presented in figure 6 is compatible with the archaeological evidence pointing to an Austronesian homeland on the Asian mainland. The first noticeable expansion was into Taiwan, and then, after some centuries, from Taiwan to the Philippines. Later some Austronesian speakers migrated to Malaysia, Indonesia, and Madagascar.

The closest relatives of Oceanic are its immediate western neighbors in the Cenderawasih Bay area and the Halmahera Islands in western Irian Jaya. The immediate ancestors of the Proto Oceanic speakers migrated from eastern Indonesia through western Irian Jaya into the Bismarck Archipelago (Manus, New Britain, and New Ireland), and settled there—possibly around the Willaumez Peninsula in New Britain—for some time. Map 14 gives some idea of the various migrations.

3.3.2. The Dispersal of Oceanic Speakers

Oceanic speakers were not the first to arrive in the New Guinea area; speakers of Papuan languages had been there for a long time. The New Britain area, for example, has been settled for more than thirty thousand years, and parts of the mainland of New Guinea for much longer even than that. Contact between the original Papuan-speaking settlers and the invading

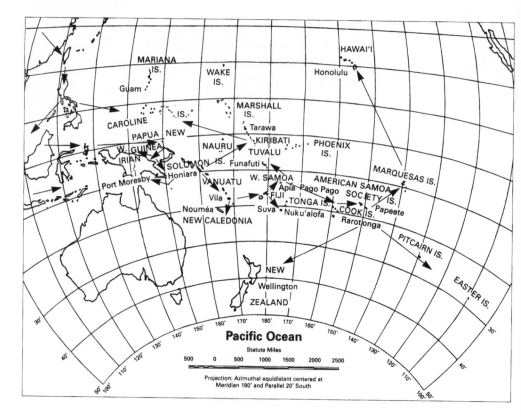

Map 14.   Austronesian Migrations

Austronesians must have been varied in nature. In some situations the two groups probably engaged in open warfare. In others, the relationship would have been uneasy but not particularly hostile. Yet others no doubt involved total integration and intermarriage.

Some speakers of Proto Oceanic and its early descendants limited their settlements, moving slowly to settle the Admiralties and New Britain. Others went farther: Yap may have been settled from the Admiralties, for example, as were New Ireland and the western Solomons. Oceanic speakers also crossed the Vitiaz Strait to reach the New Guinea mainland, with one group progressively settling the north coast from east to west, and another moving into the Milne Bay area and the south coast.

Some Oceanic speakers seem to have been more adventurous still. If indeed they originated in the New Britain area, they have left no trace there, but seem to have moved first southeast into the Solomons, then south into northern and central Vanuatu and north into Micronesia, probably the Kiribati–Marshall Islands area, from which location they settled the rest of Micronesia. There were also movements further south, into southern

Vanuatu, the Loyalty Islands, and New Caledonia, and further east to Fiji, from where Polynesia was settled. Map 14 outlines these movements.

We should be careful, however, not to think of all of these migrations as major colonizing expeditions. Spriggs (1995), for example, suggests that there were probably initial long-distance scouting parties, followed by more than one movement of people along fairly well defined routes. Back-migrations of some people also took place. The migrations may have been deliberate, as such factors as population pressure, food shortages, or political turmoil forced people to seek somewhere else to live. They may also have been accidental, at least initially, as fishermen were blown off course and ended up on new islands. Many settlements succeeded, but a great number no doubt failed because of disease, attacks by speakers of Papuan languages, and all kinds of other reasons.

Such factors complicate the neat splitting of communities suggested by family trees. On the one hand, a language community may not have actually split, but rather slowly diversified as contact between its subgroups became less and less intense. On the other hand, different related languages could have influenced each other, blurring any innovations that might have been developing in one or another of them. Speed of settlement is another complicating factor. In the islands east of the Bismarcks no one seems to have stayed in one place long enough for telltale linguistic innovations to appear. Under these circumstances, definitive higher-order subgroups of Oceanic are hard to establish.

If the settlement of the Pacific proceeded in the direction and at the speed discussed above, it begins to make sense that Micronesians and Polynesians, although originating in Melanesia, nevertheless physically resemble their Southeast Asian ancestors more than they do Melanesians. Some Oceanic speakers moved through Melanesia quickly enough to retain Asian genetic features, and these people "became" Polynesians and Micronesians. Others remained in Melanesia, where centuries of intermarriage with the physically different Papuan speakers have led to quite different genetic developments (Pawley and Ross 1995, 60).

3.3.3. Dating Dispersals: The "Lapita People"

Trying to establish a chronological framework for these migrations purely on linguistic grounds is presently—and will probably remain—impossible. A family tree provides **relative datings** of language divisions, telling us that one such split occurred before or after another, but it does not offer any **absolute dating**.

In the 1950s and 1960s, linguists made an attempt to derive actual dates from lexicostatistical data.[3] (The term for this is **glottochronology**.)

Concrete dates for the breakup of Proto Indo-European and its various subgroups were, for example, proposed. Glottochronology, however, was strongly criticized by many scholars, not only because of some of the dates it generated, but also because of inherent weaknesses in its methodology and underlying assumptions. The practice has been almost universally abandoned.

But although there is no linguistic technique for determining absolute dates for divisions in protolanguages or for migrations, linguists can try to match their relative dating sequences with archaeological evidence, which is on surer ground when it comes to absolute dating. In the Oceanic region, this cooperative enterprise has led to some interesting results.

Archaeologists use the term **Lapita** to refer to a distinctive style of pottery. (The name comes from a place in New Caledonia, one of the first sites excavated with this pottery.) The term **Lapita culture** refers to the cultural complex associated with this pottery style, including the introduction of pigs, dogs, and chickens; distinctive stone adzes and shell ornaments; the development of larger villages; and the intensification of agriculture (Spriggs 1995; 116–118).

Lapita culture first appears in the archaeological record of the Bismarck Archipelago about 1600 B.C. It seems to have reached as far as Vanuatu and New Caledonia by about 1200 B.C., and Fiji and western Polynesia by about 1000 B.C. In Vanuatu and islands farther south and east, Lapita people were the first settlers: There is no evidence of any pre-Lapita people (Papuans or others) in eastern Melanesia and Polynesia, and this absence of competition for land would have made settlement much easier than it was farther north and west.

This notion of a very rapid movement of people through island Melanesia correlates very well with the linguistic subgrouping that I discussed in the last section: That is, the fact that the Oceanic group seemed to have a number of first-order subgroups (a "flat" tree), rather than two or three subgroups that themselves have only two or three subsubgroups, suggests fairly quick movement over a wide area. Much slower settlement patterns would have allowed more time for distinctive innovations and would present a more layered family tree, with the eastern languages much lower down the tree than the western ones.

Archaeologists tell us that the original Polynesians settled in the Samoa-Tonga area about 1000 B.C., remaining in that area for five hundred or even a thousand years. At around the turn of the era, some moved into eastern Polynesia, while others migrated to the western Pacific to establish the Outliers. By about A.D. 1000, all the major eastern Polynesian island groups had been settled (Bellwood 1978; 318).

In Micronesia, there is evidence that the Mariana Islands may have been settled from Southeast Asia about 1000 B.C. The rest of Micronesia, however, appears to have been settled for only about two thousand years—probably by Lapita people from somewhere in Melanesia, though neither linguistics nor archaeology is able to tell us precisely where.

Significantly less archaeological work has been done in the western and northern parts of the Pacific than in the eastern part, so that linguists working on the Polynesian languages, who are dealing with a relatively short period, have reliable archaeological information with which to correlate their findings. But those working in Melanesia and Micronesia have to deal with a longer period of time, much less archaeological information against which to test their hypotheses, and, in some areas at least, occupation by pre-Oceanic peoples.

3.3.4. Rapid Diversification in Melanesia

Many linguists have commented on and tried to explain the much greater diversity exhibited by the Austronesian languages of Melanesia than by any other part of the Austronesian family. This is partly a function of time. Austronesian languages have had more time to change in Melanesia than in Polynesia or Micronesia, and so appear less similar to each other. But there is more to the problem—and to Austronesian language history—than the time factor. After all, Austronesians have not been in Melanesia for countless eons longer than they have been in Polynesia and Micronesia.

Some of the Austronesian languages of Melanesia seem to have changed more rapidly than others. This is due in part to contact between Austronesian and Papuan languages. Fairly clear evidence shows that some languages of the Oceanic subgroup have changed radically as a result of contact with Papuan languages. Among the most radical are languages like Magori and Maisin in Papua New Guinea, where linguists have had difficulty in deciding whether or not they are Austronesian at all! So the history of the Austronesian languages of Melanesia—especially western Melanesia—is complicated by the fact that they not only neighbor Papuan languages but have in many cases been in intimate contact with them.

But certainly all of the major differences between Melanesian languages cannot be explained by Papuan contact. Many of the more aberrant Oceanic languages in Melanesia, like those of New Caledonia, are far away from the nearest Papuan language. Rapid change can be an internal matter as well as an external one, and many of the differences between languages in this region have come about without external influence. The small scale of many Melanesian societies can allow changes to spread more quickly than they might in larger societies, although smallness does not *cause* rapid change.

The notion of the **emblematic function** (Grace 1981) of language in Melanesia is an important one to mention here. Linguistic differences can be important as badges of membership in a particular social group, and people often focus on these differences as markers of in-group or out-group status (in the same way that young people in many societies use slang expressions to mark their in-group status). In Melanesia especially, differences between neighboring languages may have been exaggerated—even manufactured—in order to preserve this emblematic function. Such a process leads to more rapid diversification than normally expected.

3.4. Reconstructing Culture

Much of the effort of comparative-historical linguists has gone into the reconstruction of the vocabulary of Proto Oceanic. An examination of this reconstructed vocabulary gives us insights into the culture of the speakers of the language in a number of ways:

1. An examination of words that can be reconstructed for Proto Oceanic can help us make inferences about the culture of the speakers of that language.
2. Identification of widespread cultural items for which terms can *not* be reconstructed for Proto Oceanic suggests that such items were more recent introductions.
3. An examination of reconstructed Proto Austronesian words not reflected in Proto Oceanic can indicate which original Austronesian cultural items were lost or abandoned by Oceanic speakers as they moved eastward into the Pacific.

As an example of the last point, we can reconstruct Proto Austronesian words referring to different kinds of rice and millet, and to rice and millet cultivation, but no such reconstructions can be made for Proto Oceanic. Presumably these crops were abandoned by Oceanic speakers in their migration from Southeast Asia to the Pacific.

Terms we can reconstruct for Proto Oceanic embrace a wide cultural range.[4] A few of the subject areas are:

- *Canoes and fishing.* Terms for two types of outrigger canoes (large and small), outrigger float and boom, matting sail, paddle, bailer, launching rollers, rudder, and anchor, as well as terms for various parts of the canoe and for steering and sailing. There are also many reconstructed terms for a number of aspects of fishing technology, and of course names of many different kinds of fish, shellfish, and crustaceans.

- *Pottery.* Various kinds of pots, clay and techniques of clay pot manufacture, decorations, and accessories like lids, as well as terms for different kinds of cooking (roasting, boiling, steaming, stone or earth oven, etc.).

- *Food crops.* Several kinds of yam, taro, banana, pandanus, breadfruit, sago, and sugar cane, as well as terms associated with horticultural practices.

- *Fruits and nuts.* A wide range of terms relating to the coconut has been reconstructed, including those for different stages of growth and parts of the fruit or tree. The words for a number of fruit and nut trees, for betel nut, and for plants like ginger and turmeric have also been reconstructed.

- *Animals and birds.* Proto Oceanic terms in this area include words for wild and domesticated pig, dog, fowl, rat, bandicoot, cassowary, cuscus (possum), and numerous bird names.

- *Social structure.* A fairly complete set of kinship terms has been reconstructed, as have terms relating to chieftainship and the societal hierarchy.

These and other reconstructed words paint the following picture of early Oceanic culture. The original speakers of Proto Oceanic were clearly a maritime people. They used outrigger canoes, fished with hooks and nets, and generally exploited the resources of the maritime environment. They grew a number of crops, including yam, taro, banana, and sugar cane, and gathered fruits and nuts. They had domesticated fowls, pigs, and dogs (and suffered the rat!), used the spear and the bow and arrow for hunting or warfare, made clay pots, and built houses with shelves and platforms (as well as probably building more temporary shelters in gardens or on the beach). They had a fairly hierarchical society, with chiefs and probably other social ranks as well. They believed in gods or spirits and probably practiced sorcery.

But some words cannot be reconstructed for Proto Oceanic despite the fact that the items they name are found in most parts of the Pacific today. The sweet potato, for example, is grown and eaten across the Pacific, yet there is no Proto Oceanic reconstruction for it. Apparently the sweet potato was introduced after the dispersal of Oceanic speakers. Archaeological evidence confirms this. Other items that also fall into this category include the pawpaw and the cassava (manioc). Our linguistic evidence, particularly when paired with the archaeological testimony, gives us a partial understanding of Pacific prehistory, although much remains to be done.

4

The History of the Papuan and Australian Languages

Almost a thousand languages spoken in the Pacific region do not belong to the Austronesian family. Of these, more than seven hundred are spoken in or near New Guinea and are known by the general term "Papuan"; the remaining two hundred or so are, or were, spoken in Australia. We know much less about the history of these languages than about the history of the Austronesian languages.

The majority of Papuan languages are located in the interior of the island of New Guinea. This area experienced no European contact until shortly before (and even in some cases some time after) World War II. So while many of the languages east of New Guinea had been written for a hundred years or more, and had been studied in some detail, most Papuan languages were unknown to the outside world until very recently.

Missionary linguists (especially those working with the Summer Institute of Linguistics) were largely responsible for dramatically increasing our knowledge of Papuan languages in the decades after 1945, and the picture is considerably clearer than it was in, say, the 1960s. Nevertheless, there are still very many Papuan languages about which almost nothing is known, and the work of comparative linguistics has barely begun. Where Australia is concerned, the death of many languages before they had been properly recorded leaves us with gaps of a different kind. Much of the evidence needed to make historical inferences has disappeared, and formulating and testing historical hypotheses is hampered at every turn.

As if these problems were not enough, we are faced with a much longer period of human habitation in both Australia and New Guinea than in most of the rest of the Austronesian-speaking world. The longer a group of languages have had to diversify, the fewer will be their apparent similarities. In dealing with the history of both Papuan and Australian languages, I can make only general and tentative statements.

4.1. Interrelationships of Papuan Languages

4.1.1. Papuan Language Families

The term **Papuan** refers to those languages of the Pacific region, excluding Australia, that are not members of the Austronesian language family. It does *not* refer to a single family of languages: "Papuan languages are not all genetically related. They do not all trace their origins back to a single ancestral language. On the basis of present knowledge, they belong to *at least sixty different language families*, all with their own common ancestral language" (Foley 1986, 3; emphasis mine). Some linguists prefer the label "Non-Austronesian" for these languages, since it does not imply the genetic unity that a positive label like "Papuan" does. "Non-Austronesian," however, like any negative label, has its own problems—Russian, Chinese, English, and Swahili, after all, are also non-Austronesian languages—so I use the term "Papuan" in this book.

While Foley does not explicitly define the criteria he uses in deciding membership or nonmembership of a family, it is clear from his conclusions that relatively close relationship is involved. As far as these sixty or so families are concerned, their "wider relations [are] not yet conclusively demonstrated. Undoubtedly, with more careful and complete comparative work, this picture will become simpler; a number of families will probably combine into larger families, as Romance, Germanic and Slavic combine into the Indo-European family" (Foley 1986, 3).

In this initial discussion of Papuan language families, I follow Foley's conservative view; later I discuss proposed combinations of these families. The list of Papuan families in table 4 proceeds generally on a west-to-east basis, with the number for each family corresponding to that on map 15. The locations given in table 4 refer to geographical regions in Irian Jaya and to province names in Papua New Guinea.

The situation is, however, even more complicated than table 4 indicates. Not every Papuan language belongs in a (smaller or larger) family. A number of Papuan languages are currently classified as isolates. The term **isolate** refers to a one-member family, a language that, on the basis of current evidence, appears to have no relatives.

4.1.2. Possible Wider Groupings of Papuan Families

Naturally enough, the existence of so many language families in such a relatively small geographical area has caused many linguists to look for wider re-

Table 4. Papuan Language Families

Family	Location[a]	Number of languages
West of the New Guinea mainland		
1 Timor-Alor-Pantar	Timor area	18
2 Northern Halmahera	Halmahera Islands	11
Mainland Irian Jaya only[b]		
3 West Bird's Head	Bird's Head	6
4 Central Bird's Head	Bird's Head	4
5 Borai-Hattam	Bird's Head	2
6 South Bird's Head	Bird's Head	10
7 East Bird's Head	Bird's Head	3
8 Mairasi–Tanah Merah	western	4
9 West Bomberai	western	3
10 East Cenderwasih Bay	western	4
11 Tor–Lake Plain	northern	20
12 Nimboran	northeast	3
13 Kaure	northeast	3
14 Pauwasi	northeast	4
15 Sentani	northeast	4
16 Dani-Kwerba	central	11
17 Wissel Lakes	central	4
18 Mek (Goliath)	eastern	9
19 Kayagar	southeast	3
20 Yelmek-Maklew	southeast	2
21 Kolopom	Frederick Hendrik Island	3
Both sides of the Irian Jaya–Papua New Guinea border[c]		
22 Sko	north coast	8
23 Border	northern	12
24 Kwomtari	northern	5
25 Senagi	northern	2
26 Central-South New Guinea	central	54
27 Marind	southern	6
28 Trans-Fly	south coast	25
Mainland Papua New Guinea only[d]		
29 Torricelli	East & West Sepik, Madang	48
30 Upper Sepik	East Sepik	16

Table 4. *Continued*

	Family	Location[a]	Number of languages
31	Ram	West Sepik	3
32	Tama	East and West Sepik	5
33	Yellow River	West Sepik	3
34	Middle Sepik	East Sepik	12
35	Sepik Hills	East Sepik	15
36	Leonhard Schulze	East Sepik and Western	6
37	Nor-Pondo	East Sepik	6
38	Yuat	East Sepik	6
39	Mongol-Langam	East Sepik	3
40	Waibuk	Enga, Madang	4
41	Arafundi	East Sepik	2
42	Keram (Grass)	East Sepik, Madang	5
43	Ruboni	East Sepik, Madang	8
44	Goam	Madang	11
45	Annaberg	Madang	3
46	Arai	East Sepik	6
47	Amto-Musian	West Sepik	2
48	Mugil-Isumrud-Pihom	Madang	28
49	Josephstaal-Wanang	Madang	12
50	Brahman	Madang	4
51	Mabuso	Madang	29
52	Rai Coast	Madang	29
53	East New Guinea Highlands	all Highlands provinces	42
54	Finisterre-Huon	Morobe	65
55	Gogodala-Suki	Western	3
56	Kutubuan	Southern Highlands	5
57	Turama-Kikorian	Gulf	4
58	Teberan-Pawaian	Simbu, Gulf	3
59	Inland Gulf	Gulf	5
60	Eleman	Gulf	7
61	Angan	Gulf	12
62	Binanderean	Oro	16
63	Central-Southeast New Guinea	Central, Milne Bay	36

Continued

Table 4. *Continued*

Family	Location[a]	Number of languages
East of the New Guinea mainland		
64 New Britain	East New Britain, New Ireland	8
65 South Bougainville	Bougainville	4
66 North Bougainville	Bougainville	4
67 Yele-Solomons	Milne Bay, Solomon Islands	5
68 Reefs–Santa Cruz	Solomon Islands	4

[a] Geographical designations in Irian Jaya; province names in Papua New Guinea.
[b] There are a number of isolates in addition to the languages listed here.
[c] The isolate Yuri belongs in this group.
[d] Several isolates occur in this group.

lationships between them. If the neighboring Austronesian languages can apparently be classified into a single large family, then can we not at least reduce the number of Papuan language families? Scholars at the Australian National University, particularly S. A. Wurm, have attempted to establish larger groupings of Papuan languages on the basis of what seem to be shared features. Lack of adequate information about many languages has hampered this work. While some of the proposals rest on solid data, others are much more impressionistic. Map 16 shows the locations of proposed wider groupings.

Wurm borrowed terms from the biological sciences to refer to some of these wider groupings of languages. A **stock** is a group of language families that appear to be reasonably closely related to each other, while a **phylum** is a group of distantly related families or stocks. In table 4, I have often treated as families groups that other linguists refer to as stocks. The degree of relationship between Papuan languages of the same stock roughly parallels that between geographically dispersed members of the Austronesian family, but the concept of a phylum is quite different, as it implies only a very distant relationship. The techniques and procedures of comparative linguistics have not yet been able to prove the existence of such attenuated relationships.

One proposed phylum is the **West Papuan phylum**, consisting of the Northern Halmahera, West Bird's Head, Central Bird's Head, and Borai-Hattam families (families 2 through 5 in table 4) along with the Amberbaken isolate, for a total of twenty-four languages, all in the extreme

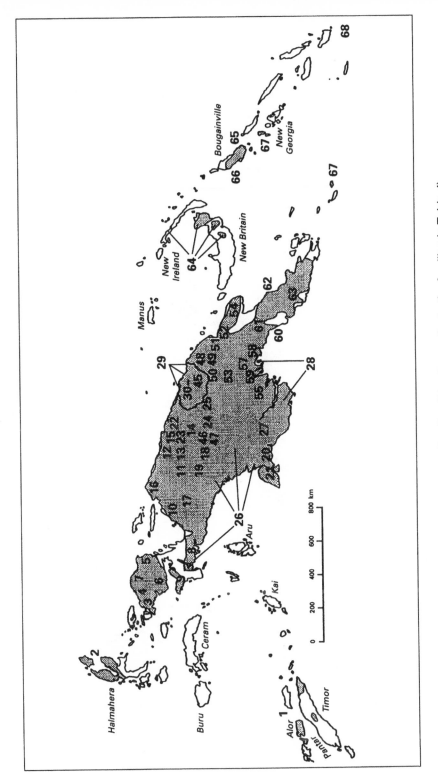

Map 15. Papuan Language Families (Numbers refer to the families in Table 4)

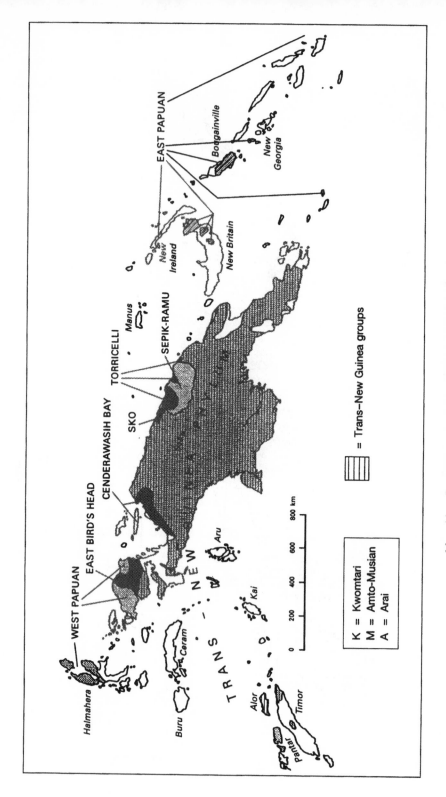

Map 16. Possible Wider Groupings of Papuan Families

K = Kwomtari
M = Amto-Musian
A = Arai

||||| = Trans–New Guinea groups

west of Irian Jaya. These languages have in common a certain amount of lexical similarity and some grammatical features (e.g., the marking of subject and object by verbal prefixes rather than suffixes [Wurm 1982, 208]).

Another suggested wider grouping is the **Sepik-Ramu phylum**, consisting of more than one hundred languages belonging to sixteen different families (numbered 30 through 45 in table 4) and spoken mainly in the East Sepik, West Sepik, and Madang provinces of Papua New Guinea. (A few nearby isolates would also be members of this phylum.) These languages share a number of distinct phonological features, such as a very small number of vowel phonemes, and also have some common grammatical features (Wurm 1982, 210).

The Torricelli family (29 in table 4) is treated by Wurm as the **Torricelli phylum**, composed of perhaps five or six families. Foley (1986, 241–242), however, treats this as a single family, largely because these languages share a number of grammatical features not found elsewhere among Papuan languages. (Subject prefixes and complex noun-class systems are two examples.)

Wurm has also grouped the Papuan languages spoken east of the New Guinea mainland into the **East Papuan phylum**. This consists of twenty-five languages belonging to the New Britain, South Bougainville, North Bougainville, Yele-Solomons, and Reefs–Santa Cruz families (64 through 68 in table 4). There appears to be some lexical and grammatical evidence for the existence of this group, though it is not very strong, and the situation is complicated by the heavy Austronesian-language influence on some of the members of the phylum.

The largest and possibly most controversial genetic grouping Wurm proposes is the **Trans–New Guinea phylum**. This hypothesis, in its most extreme form, proposes that almost all the rest of the Papuan languages—with the exceptions of a few small families and some isolates—belong to a single genetic group of about five hundred languages stretching from Timor in the west to Milne Bay in the east. It would include all of the languages of the southern and central part of the mainland, as well as some spoken in the north (1, 6, 8, 9, 11–21, 23, 25–27, and 48–63 in table 4). There are certain phonological and grammatical features shared by at least some members of this group, but the existence of the phylum as a whole—at least at this stage of our research—seems tenuous, to say the least. Some support for the hypothesis can be found in Pawley (1995).

A number of the families listed in table 4 cannot at present be assigned to any phylum even under the most liberal application of the comparative method. These lone families are the East Bird's Head, Cenderawasih Bay (plus the isolate Yava), Sko, Kwomtari, Arai, and Amto-Musian families (see map 16).

4.2. Interrelationships of Australian Languages

4.2.1. Mainland Australia

Some linguists have divided the languages of mainland Australia into two pseudogenetic groups. The **Pama-Nyungan** group of languages occupies about three-quarters of the mainland. Its name comes from the words meaning 'man' at the northeastern and southwestern extremes of the group (Dixon 1980, 221). These languages are very similar typologically in both phonology and grammar. The remaining languages—referred to by the negative term **Non–Pama-Nyungan**—occupy the northwest of the mainland (see map 11 in chapter 2). They are phonologically fairly similar to the Pama-Nyungan languages, but grammatically quite different.

In the 1960s a lexicostatistical classification of the Australian languages divided the languages into twenty-six "phylic families" (those sharing 15 percent basic vocabulary or less). Of these groups, one was Pama-Nyungan, and each of the remaining twenty-five—Non–Pama-Nyungan—groups was held to be a "phylic family" on a par with Pama-Nyungan (Dixon 1980, 263).

Dixon himself is highly distrustful of this classification. A majority of linguists now agrees that all the mainland languages belong to a single, **Australian**, family. The differences between Pama-Nyungan and Non–Pama-Nyungan languages are developmental rather than original: "It seems clear . . . that nearly all the languages of Australia form one genetic family, going back to a single ancestral language, proto Australian" (Dixon 1980, 228). Because of the thousands of years of contact between Australian languages, however, shared innovations supporting subgrouping hypotheses are extremely hard to find: "Present knowledge of the relationships between Australian languages is not sufficient to justify any sort of fully articulated 'family tree' model. . . . It could perhaps be that the continual levelling due to diffusion of features of every sort has obscured those genetic splits that did take place in the development of Australian languages, so that it will not be possible to reconstruct them" (Dixon 1980, 264–265).

4.2.2. Tasmania

Genocide in Tasmania has led to the loss of all Tasmanian languages. An Aboriginal population of possibly five thousand people at the time of first European contact, speaking somewhere between eight and twelve languages, was exterminated in less than eighty years. The last full-blooded Tasmanian died in 1888, although there are still about four thousand people of partial Tasmanian Aboriginal descent living in Tasmania and elsewhere. So little was recorded of these languages that it is almost impossible to say anything about them (Crowley 1993). As regards their history, Dixon (1980, 233) says, "All we can conclude is this—there is NO evidence that the Tasmanian languages were NOT of the regular Australian type. They have been separated off for so long, and the available materials are so poor, that the likelihood of a genetic connection cannot be confirmed. The genetic affiliation of Tasmanian is, and must remain, unproven."

4.3. Possible External Links

Suggestions about the wider relationships of Papuan and Australian languages have not been lacking, but given the long periods of time involved, most of these can remain no more than suggestions. Greenberg's (1971) Indo-Pacific Hypothesis attempts to link Papuan languages with those of Tasmania (but not mainland Australia) and of the Andaman Islands in the Indian Ocean. Greenberg speculated that Australian languages are related to the Dravidian languages of South India. Scholars and amateurs have also looked for relationships between Papuan or Australian languages and those of Africa and Asia. None of these hypotheses seems to be based on any evidence more solid than typological similarities or a few possibly accidental lexical similarities.

Foley (1986, 271–275), however, has recently presented a small but tantalizing amount of evidence for the existence of a genetic link between Australian languages and the languages of the Eastern Highlands of Papua New Guinea. A small number of basic vocabulary items look as if they might be cognate. But he says that this evidence "in no way constitutes **proof** of a genetic relationship between Australian and Eastern Highlands languages. . . . Much more detailed and careful research needs to be done before a convincing proof is provided, and, given the time depth, that may never be possible. Rather, the above data represent a first attempt at marshalling some evidence for a genetic link between Australian and Papuan languages" (Foley 1986, 275).

Up until around eight thousand years ago, New Guinea and Australia were one continent. Only then did sea levels start rising after the last Ice Age to form what is now the Torres Strait. It is distinctly possible that Australia was settled from the New Guinea area, so the idea of a genetic link between the two areas cannot be ruled out.

4.4. Implications for Prehistory

4.4.1. Origins

The New Guinea mainland was probably occupied at least fifty thousand years ago, presumably by the ancestors of the speakers of (some) Papuan languages; Australia was also settled at about the same time. Since comparative linguistics cannot reach back more than about eight or ten thousand years, most of that fifty-thousand-year period is lost to linguistics.

It is possible that all the Papuan families are related, descending from a single "Proto Papuan" ancestor that we cannot even dimly imagine. A single language, spoken somewhere in the New Guinea area around 50,000 B.C., could have given rise, over time, to all of the modern Papuan languages, and this language may have been the ancestral language from which all Australian languages ultimately derive.

We also have no evidence to indicate the origins of the first speakers of Papuan or Australian languages. Linguistic connections with Asia or Africa are nothing more than highly speculative, nor would we expect otherwise. If the time elapsed is too great to show interrelationships among all Papuan languages, it is certainly too great to show genetic relationships between these languages and those to the north, south, or west.

But perhaps this very lack of evidence for external relatives means that the Papuan languages do, or did, form a genetic unity, and that the same could be said about the Australian languages. If the diversity existing among modern Papuan and Australian families is due to different origins and different migrations of people at various times from various locations, one might expect to find some genetic connections between individual Papuan or Australian families and Asian or African language families. The fact that we do not, while not strong enough to be called evidence, does suggest that the Papuan languages may have formed a single linguistic grouping in the very distant past, and that the same may be true of Australian, Tasmanian included.

In only a few instances has there been anything in the way of comprehensive reconstruction of the phonology, grammar, and vocabulary of any of the larger Papuan families, and the situation in Australia is pretty similar. Little can be said about relations with other families, origins and migration routes, and earlier stages of Papuan or Australian culture, and the little that has been said on these topics must be treated as highly speculative.

4.4.2. Diversification

One question that must be asked in any study of the Papuan and Australian situations is, if both New Guinea and Australia have been settled for about the same length of time, why do we find such incredible genetic diversity among Papuan languages, whereas Australian languages all seem to belong to just a single family?

Physical geography, and its effect on wide-ranging human movement, is one contributing factor: "Most of New Guinea is difficult country indeed, steep, forest-covered mountains with precipitous drops, swirling rivers, dense, nearly impenetrable rainforests and endless tracts of swampland. The terrain thus poses some genuine barriers to human social interaction and would certainly favour, rather than inhibit, linguistic diversity" (Foley 1986, 9). Geographical barriers like these were often bolstered by social barriers. Hostile relations were the rule between neighboring communities, and the tendency of language to take on emblematic functions and to be considered as a mark of group identity throughout Melanesia is one sign of communities' desires to set themselves apart. People often created linguistic differences, or exaggerated differences that already existed, in order to preserve their group membership.

Kulick (1992, 2–3), for example, quotes the following observation made by Ken McElhanon, who worked among Selepet speakers in Papua New Guinea: "The people living in the Selepet-speaking village of Indu had gathered together for a meeting. During this meeting, a decision was reached to 'be different' from other Selepet speakers. It was agreed that the villagers of Indu would immediately stop using their usual word for 'no,' *bia*, which was shared by all their fellow speakers of Selepet. Instead, they would begin saying *buŋɛ*, which they did and have continued doing since that time." There are many other similar examples. In Buin (spoken in Bougainville), speakers of the Usai dialect have reversed all gender agreements: masculine markers in other dialects become feminine in Usai, and feminine markers become masculine (Laycock 1982a). Similar phenomena can be observed in Oceanic languages. Speakers of Ririo (Choiseul, Solomon Islands) seem to have deliberately transposed the last consonant and vowel of words to make them sound more different from their counterparts in the neighboring closely related language of Babatana (Laycock 1982b, 274–276):

Babatana	Ririo	
soso*le*	susu*el*	'naked'
vu*mi*	vu*im*	'beard'
pi*ru*	pi*ur*	'wild'
bo*se*	bu*es*	'man'

The Australian continent is in some ways less difficult geographically than New Guinea, and physical barriers to long-distance communication are generally much less extreme. Though Australians belonged to distinct tribal and linguistic groups, there was much more social interaction between these groups, typically accompanied by transfer of vocabulary items from one group to another. Rather that accentuating differences, Australians seem to have made an active effort to keep different languages from becoming *too* different. Dixon (1980, 239) refers to "a gradual but constant shifting of tribal groups," through which people came into contact with different languages. He also mentions mergers of different tribal groups whose numbers had been reduced by famine or disease. Such factors conspired to keep Australian languages more similar to each other than one might expect, especially in comparison to Papuan languages.

Both Papuan and Australian languages have been in the Pacific region for a very long time indeed. We know nothing of where they came from and little of how their speakers moved around the region. We do not know how far east or west of the New Guinea mainland Papuan speakers might have originally settled or much about their connections with Australian languages. All we can reasonably deduce is that, by the time speakers of Austronesian languages arrived in this area about four to five thousand years ago or so, speakers of Papuan and Australian languages were very much entrenched.

PART TWO

Structure

Sound Systems

The sound systems of languages in different parts of the Pacific vary enormously, sometimes even when the languages themselves are closely related. Major similarities and differences exist between languages of the three broad genetic groups—Austronesian, Papuan, and Australian. Below I discuss the vowel systems, consonant systems, stress and tone, and the way in which words are structured in each group, touching briefly as well on the development of orthographies.[1]

5.1. Oceanic Languages[2]

5.1.1. Vowel Systems

The great majority of Oceanic languages have five vowel phonemes, which is also the commonest system found among the world's languages generally. A vowel's position in the diagram corresponds to how it is described, e.g., *i* is a high front vowel.

$$
\begin{array}{ccc}
\text{i} & & \text{u} \\
\text{e} & & \text{o} \\
& \text{a} &
\end{array}
$$

This system is universal in the languages of Polynesia and widespread in Melanesia, though among Micronesian languages only Kiribati has five phonemic vowels. This same system has also been reconstructed for Proto Oceanic. In many languages there is also a phonemic (significant) difference between **short vowels** and **long vowels**, a long vowel being one that takes almost twice as much time to articulate as a short vowel. The examples below show, in various languages, that vowel length alone is sufficient to distinguish two otherwise identical words. A long vowel is marked with a following colon: /a:/ is long, and /a/ is short.

Samoan

| /malo/ | 'loincloth' | /malo:/ | 'hard' |
| /lulu/ | 'barn owl' | /lu:lu:/ | 'shake' |

Nukuoro

| /nui/ | 'coconut' | /nu:i/ | 'green' |
| /ahe/ | 'go back' | /ahe:/ | 'when?' |

Paamese

| /men/ | 'it's ripe' | /me:n/ | 'his tongue' |
| /vati/ | 'he stopped' | /va:ti/ | 'he'll bite it' |

A handful of languages have fewer than five vowels. One Micronesian language, Marshallese, has been analyzed as having only four vowel phonemes. These are written *i, ẹ, e,* and *a,* but they have wide variations in pronunciation. The vowel *e,* for example, is variously pronounced [ɛ], [ə] and [o], depending on the neighboring consonants. Some languages in the Morobe Province of Papua New Guinea also have fewer than five vowels: Mari, for example, has just /i a u/, Adzera /i a o u/.

Quite a few languages have more than five phonemic vowels. Rotuman, for example, has ten. Almost all of the languages of Micronesia have more than five vowels: Kosraean has twelve, Lagoon Trukese and Saipan Carolinian each have nine, Yapese and Ulithian eight, Mokilese seven, and Nauruan, Chamorro, and Palauan six. Some dialects of Ponapean have seven vowel phonemes, others six. (See appendix 3 for the vowel inventories of Kosraean and Mokilese.) Vowel length is also significant in Micronesian languages, as the example shows.

Mokilese

| /paj/ | 'nest' | /pa:j/ | 'hollow of canoe' |
| /ros/ | 'darkness' | /ro:s/ | 'flower' |

In Melanesia, most languages with more than five vowels have just one or two extra ones. In Tanna and Malakula (Vanuatu), as well as in New Ireland (Papua New Guinea), languages with six vowels generally add /ə/ (the sound of *a* in English words like *ago* or *sofa*). Some languages in Melanesia have developed seven-vowel systems, the basic five vowels plus either front rounded vowels (like the vowels in French *rue* and *heureux*), or a contrast between two different *e*-sounds and two different *o*-sounds (/e/ and /ɛ/, /o/ and /ɔ/).

The most complex Oceanic vowel systems, however, are almost certainly those of New Caledonia (see appendix 3). Iaai in the Loyalty Islands, for example, has eleven short vowels, all of which can also occur long; while Xârâcùù, on the mainland, has ten oral and seven nasal vowel phonemes, each of which can occur short or long, yielding thirty-four vowel contrasts!

How do such complex vowel systems evolve out of an original five-vowel system? The changes that took place in different Oceanic languages are very different. Here I give just two kinds of examples. First, phonemes often have more than one pronunciation, depending on their phonetic environment. Imagine that the phoneme /a/ was pronounced [æ] (the sound represented by *a* in English *cat*) when the vowel in the next syllable was /i/, but as [a] (like in *father*) elsewhere. We would have pairs of words like:

| /mati/ | 'sick' | [mæti] |
| /mata/ | 'eye' | [mata] |

The pronunciation of phonemic /a/—[æ] or [a]—is totally predictable. Now imagine that this language drops out all vowels at the end of words, as has happened in many Oceanic languages. The following changes occur:

| [mæti] | > | [mæt] | 'sick' |
| [mata] | > | [mat] | 'eye' |

Now the contrast between [æ] and [a] creates a minimal pair, and /æ/ has been added to the language's phonemic (as opposed to phonetic) inventory.

Rotuman illustrates a second kind of process. Most Rotuman words have "long" and "short" forms that are used in different grammatical contexts.[3] In some cases, the short form simply drops the final vowel of the long form. (Note that the symbol ŋ represents the *ng* sound in English *sing*, while ʔ represents the glottal stop.)

Rotuman

Long form	Short form	
haŋa	haŋ	'feed'
heleʔu	heleʔ	'arrive'

Metathesis, however—two phonemes exchanging places—is more common. With some vowel combinations, metathesis has no further phonological repercussions:

Rotuman

Long form	Short form	
hosa	hoas	'flower'
tiko	tiok	'flesh'
pepa	peap	'paper'

But with other combinations, the two vowels that came into contact have fused to produce a third, different vowel. (The vowel ö is a bit like the vowel in French *heureux*, while ü is the vowel in French *rue*.)

Rotuman

Long form		**Short form**	
mose	(> moes >)	mös	'sleep'
futi	(> fuit >)	füt	'pull'

Because of this Rotuman, which originally probably had five vowels, now has ten.

5.1.2. Consonant Systems

Polynesian Languages

In general terms, the Polynesian languages have the simplest consonant systems of all the Oceanic languages. Tongan has the largest inventory of consonant phonemes of all of the Polynesian Triangle languages, with twelve. A number of Polynesian languages, for example, Hawaiian, have only eight consonants:

Tongan					**Hawaiian**			
p	t	k	ʔ		p		k	ʔ
v					w			
f	s		h					h
m	n	ŋ			m	n		
	l					l		

The consonant systems of the Polynesian Outlier languages are generally slightly more complex (Krupa 1982). In some cases this is a result of contact with neighboring non-Polynesian languages. First, unlike any Polynesian Triangle language, quite a few Outliers, among them West Futuna, Ifira-Mele, Emae, and Takuu, make a distinction between /l/ and /r/. Second, in addition to the normal Polynesian **stop** consonants /p t k ʔ/, some Outliers show a contrast with the **aspirated** stops /pʰ tʰ kʰ/ (e.g., Takuu and Kapingamarangi), with the **voiced** stops /b d g/ (Fagauvea), or with the **prenasalized** stops /ᵐb ⁿd/ (e.g., Emae and Pileni). Third, there is contrast between the ordinary nasals /m n ŋ/ and one or more of the voiceless nasals /m̥ n̥ / in Kapingamarangi, Fagauvea, and Pileni.

Micronesia

The consonant systems of the languages of Micronesia are quite different from those of the Fijian and Polynesian languages. Lagoon Trukese is fairly typical of the majority of these languages. It has the following fourteen consonants (/tʃ/ represents a sound something like *ch* in English *church*, but with the tongue turned back).

Lagoon Trukese

pʷ	p	t	tʃ	k
mʷ	m	n		ŋ
	f	s		
		r		
w			y	

All consonants except /w/ and /y/ have both short and long forms.

Lagoon Trukese

/sɨk/	'appear'	/s:ɨk/	'bleed'
/kamʷe/	'clam'	/kamʷ:et/	'sweetheart'
/tʃi:mʷ/	'head'	/tʃ:in/	'speedy'
/takir/	'laugh'	/tak:itʃ/	'torch-fishing'

Most other Micronesian languages have similar consonant systems (including the distinction between short and long consonants), although Kiribati has no phonemic **fricatives**. A number have, in addition to the trilled /r̃/, either a flapped /r/ or an /l/. Some, like Kosraean, Nauruan, and Yapese (see appendix 3), have more complex systems of consonants.

Melanesia

There is a considerable variety of consonant systems in Melanesia, and although neighboring languages often have similar systems, one cannot make broad generalizations on a geographical basis. It is fair to say, however, that the consonant systems of New Caledonia are considerably more complex than those of the rest of this region.

Some of the simpler consonant systems in this region are found in the New Guinea area. Below, for example, are the consonants of the Tigak language of New Ireland:

Tigak

p	t	k
b		g
	s	
v		
m	n	ŋ
	r	
	l	

Probably half of the Melanesian languages would fall into a category of medium complexity as far as any classification of consonant systems is concerned. This complexity usually involves one or more of the following: (1) contrast between oral and prenasalized stops; (2) contrast between simple and aspirated stops; (3) contrast between voiced and voiceless fricatives; and (4) contrast between simple and labialized or velarized consonants. Standard Fijian and the Toʻabaʻita dialect of North Malaita (Solomon Islands) illustrate such phonological systems.

Fijian				Toʻabaʻita				
p	t	k			t	k	kʷ	ʔ
ᵐb	ⁿd	ᵑg		ᵐb		ⁿd	ᵑg	ᵑgʷ
f	s			f	θ	s		
v	ð							
m	n	ŋ		m		n	ŋ	
	l					l		
	r							
w	y			w				

An unusual phonological feature of some of the languages of north Malakula and east Santo in Vanuatu are the **apico-labial** consonants /p̃ ṽ m̃/, which are produced with the tip of the tongue touching the upper lip.

The most complex consonant systems in Melanesia are those of the languages of New Caledonia (see appendix 3 for two examples). The Drehu language of the Loyalty Islands has twenty-eight consonant phonemes, including a contrast between the alveolar stops /t d/ and the **retroflex** stops /ṭ ḍ/ (similar to that found in many Indian languages)—a fairly rare contrast in Oceanic languages. Both Drehu and Pije, a language of the northern mainland that has thirty-five consonant phonemes, contrast voiced and voiceless nasal, lateral, and semivowel phonemes.

5.1.3. Prosodic Features

The system of consonants and vowels in a language is often referred to as the **segmental phonology** of the language, since linguists break up (segment) a stream of speech into discrete units. Other features of speech that do not belong to individual segments—consonants or vowels—but to syllables or words are known as **suprasegmental** or **prosodic** features. Stress and tone are two of the most important of these.

Stress

The term **stress** refers to the relatively greater prominence given to one syllable in a word through extra effort, extra loudness, a change in pitch, or some combination of these factors. The underlined syllables in the English words *temptation*, *absolute*, *absolutely*, and *resist* receive greater stress than the other syllables in those words.

In the majority of Oceanic languages, the position of stress in a word is predictable. Let us take Samoan as an example. The basic pattern in Samoan is one of **penultimate stress**. Stress (marked here by an acute accent over the vowel of the syllable) falls on the next-to-last syllable of the word.

Samoan

/túli/	'dismiss'		/táma/	'child'
/tulíŋa/	'dismissal'		/tamáʔi/	'young of animals'

When a suffix is added to a word in Samoan, the stress shifts to the right so that it still falls on the penultimate syllable: /túli/ becomes /tulíŋa/.

When a Samoan word ends in a diphthong (like /ae ai au/, for example) or in a long vowel, stress falls on this final diphthong or long vowel:

Samoan

/atamái/	'clever'		/faifeʔáu/	'pastor'
/tamá:/	'father'		/paʔú:/	'fall'

Most Oceanic languages seem to have a predictable pattern of penultimate stress, but in some languages, while stress is predictable, the patterns are different. One such language is Māori. There are three rules involved in the assignment of stress in Māori: (a) The first long vowel in a word is stressed, as in the examples in (a) below; (b) if there are no long vowels, the first vowel cluster is stressed, as in (b); and (c) if there are no long vowels or vowel clusters, as in (c), then the first vowel is stressed.

Māori

(a)	/maná:ki/	'support'	/pá:tu:tahi/	'a village'
(b)	/tamáiti/	'child'	/táutau/	'barking'
(c)	/támariki/	'children'	/hóro/	'fast'

Languages with unpredictable stress patterns are relatively uncommon in the Pacific, although they do exist. In many languages of this type, however, there seems to be one common stress pattern, other patterns being very much in the minority. The Big Nambas language of Malakula in Vanuatu is an example of this type of language. In it the majority of words are stressed on the penultimate syllable:

Big Nambas

/áɣau/	'go away!'		/patiráni/	'put it up'
/ipáli/	'he'll burn it'		/iputakmáni/	'he'll spoil it'

But sometimes stress falls on the final syllable. Compare the two pairs below, identical except for stress:

Big Nambas

/áɣau/	'go away!'	/aɣáu/	'chief's wife'
/ipáli/	'he'll burn it'	/ipalí/	'he'll tie it'

Further, as is not the case in Samoan, the stress remains in its original position even when suffixes are added:

Big Nambas

/ɣápat/	'chief'	/ɣápatak/	'my chief'
/prápar/	'sow (pig)'	/práparan/	'his sow'

Tone

Phonemic **tone** refers to contrasting pitch occurring at the word level. The same string of consonants and vowels can mean different things if the pitch of the voice is high or low, rising or falling. While common in Asian and African languages—and in Papuan languages as well—tone is fairly rare in the rest of the Pacific. Among Oceanic languages, just a few in New Caledonia (like Cèmuhî) and a few more in the Morobe Province of Papua New Guinea (like Yabêm), have phonemic tone.

Cèmuhî has three tones: high (marked here with an acute accent), mid (marked with a macron), and low (marked with a grave accent), as exemplified in the following words:

Cèmuhî

/tí:/	'destroy'
/tī:/	'gather'
/tì:/	'write'

Yabêm has two tones, high and low:

Yabêm

/áwá/	'valuables'	/àwà/	'his/her mouth'
/wá/	'mango'	/wà/	'crocodile'
/sá?/	'to hammer'	/sà?/	'put on top of'
/ólí/	'body'	/òlì/	'wages'

Because tone is a rare phenomenon in Oceanic, we assume that the few languages that have it have developed it some time after they split off from most of their other relatives. But how do languages develop tone systems? Let us look briefly at what seems to have happened in Yabêm and closely related languages (Bradshaw 1979, Ross 1993).

At one time there was probably a rule in Yabêm that a syllable containing a voiceless stop or fricative (like *p t k s*) would have high tone, but one with a voiced stop or fricative (*b d g j*) would have low tone.[4] For example, /kápúŋ/ 'I plant' and /kátáŋ/ 'I make a sound,' but /gàbù/ 'I insult' and

/gàdù?/ 'I bow.' Some consonants that conditioned high or low tone have since changed their voicing (or even disappeared), but they have left their tone "trace" behind. For example, earlier °*s* remained /s/ in Yabêm and, because it is, and was, voiceless, it is associated with high tone.

Yabêm

| °*sipo* | > | /sép/ | 'go down' |
| °*saqit* | > | /sí/ | 'sew' |

On the other hand, earlier °*j* was voiced, and it conditioned low tone on the following syllable, but later became voiceless /s/:

Yabêm

°*jóŋi*	>	/sòŋ/	'stop up, plug'
°*joRi*	>	/sò/	'tie'
°*lejan*	>	lésɛ́ŋ	'nit'

5.1.4. Word Structure

Some Oceanic languages allow only **open syllables**, meaning that each syllable may begin with a consonant but may not end with one. These languages do not permit **consonant clusters**—two or more consonants coming together without an intervening vowel. Using C for consonant, V for vowel, and ( ) to indicate that whatever is enclosed is optional, the general structure of words in languages of this type is built on the pattern (C)V(C)V . . . , where vowels (and, in some languages, consonants) may be short or long.

Languages that allow only open syllables occur in some parts of Papua New Guinea and Vanuatu, the southeastern Solomons, most of Fiji, and Polynesia. Examples:

Mekeo

/akaikia/	'great'
/oisofai/	'off you go!'
/ekapaisau/	'he made me'

Arosi

/taroha/	'news'
/amamu/	'your father'
/ha?aheuheu/	'change form'

Fijian

/veitau/	'friends'
/vakasalataka/	'advise'
/ᵐbataᵐbata:/	'cold'

Hawaiian

/pauloa/	'everything'
/hoaha:nau/	'cousin'
/ku:konukonu/	'excessive'

Probably the majority of Austronesian languages, however, allow both open and closed syllables (syllables ending in a consonant). In some cases, only a few consonants (most frequently nasals) can close a syllable. In such cases there are few consonant clusters, and they mainly occur across morpheme boundaries. Here are some Banoni examples (note that /ts/ represents a single phoneme in Banoni, not a consonant cluster):

Banoni

/matam/	'your eye'
/βatamumam/	'make us eat'
/teŋtapatsi/	'broken off and scattered'

In other cases, however, consonant clusters are frequent and can occur in syllable-initial position as well as across syllable boundaries:

Adzera

/tatariʔ/	'fowl'
/romgam/	'yourself'
/tafa-ŋga-^{n}ʔ/	'our ancestors'

Maringe

/fnakno/	'famous'
/kñaokñar$_o$o/	'be stringy'
/snaplu/	'slip out'

Big Nambas

/prapar/	'sow (female pig)'
/vənmaran/	'old woman'
/kətəɣsrasr/	'you've swept'

Most Oceanic languages have a large amount of **reduplication**, a process wherein all or part of a word is repeated. Look at the following examples from Hawaiian:

Hawaiian

/ʔaki/	'to take a nip and let go'
/ʔakiʔaki/	'to nibble (as a fish)'
/ʔaʔaki/	'to nip repeatedly'

The basic verb is /ʔaki/. The verb /ʔakiʔaki/ shows **complete reduplication**, with the whole verb root being repeated, while the verb /ʔaʔaki/ is an example of **partial reduplication**, in which only part of the verb (in this case, the first syllable) is repeated. Reduplication commonly has a number of functions in the languages in which it is productive. Take a look at these examples.

1. Repetition or continuous action.

   Māori

/paki/	'pat'	/pakipaki/	'clap'
/kimo/	'wink'	/kimokimo/	'blink, wink repeatedly'

2. Intensity.

   Tahitian

/hiʔo/	'look at'	/hiʔohiʔo/	'stare at'
/parau/	'converse'	/parauparau/	'talk a lot'

3. Similarity or diminution. The reduplicated word refers to something similar to, but often smaller or more moderate than, its unreduplicated counterpart.

   Tongan

/viku/	'wet all over'	/vikuviku/	'damp'
/havili/	'strong wind'	/havilivili/	'gentle wind, breeze'

4. Change in part of speech, e.g., making a noun into an adjective.

   Kosraean

/pʌk/	'sand'	/pʌkpʌk/	'sandy'
/pʷeŋ/	'news'	/pʷeŋpʷeŋ/	'famous'

5. Change from transitive to intransitive. (In the transitive verbs below, the suffix /-i/ marks the third person singular object.)

   Tigak

Transitive		Intransitive	
/nol-i/	'think about'	/nonol/	'be thinking'
/vis-i/	'hit him'	/visvis/	'fight'
/kalum-i/	'see it'	/kalkalum/	'look, appear'

6. Indication of plurality, usually of the subject of a verb, but sometimes of some other aspect of the action. (In the examples below, the reduplicated form is used if the subject of the verb is plural.)

Samoan

Singular	Plural	
/ʔai/	/ʔaʔai/	'eat'
/tu:/	/tutu:/	'stand'
/ŋalue/	/ŋalulue/	'work'

Nearly all the examples so far have been from Polynesian and Micronesian languages. Here is a set of examples from a Melanesian language, the Nguna Island dialect of Nakanamanga (Vanuatu). The function of each example of reduplication is given in the right-hand column.

Nakanamanga (Nguna dialect)

/kati/	'bite'	/katikati/	'nibble'	diminution
/ta:ki/	'throw'	/tata:ki/	'continually throw'	repetition
/namalo/	'piece'	/namalomalo/	'pieces'	plurality
/vano/	'go'	/vanovano/	'travel around'	randomness
/ta:re/	'white'	/ta:reare/	'very white'	intensification

When reduplication is partial, it may be prefixed, suffixed, or infixed, occurring before, after, or in the middle of the root. A rare example of infixed reduplication, given above, is Samoan /ŋalue/ 'work (singular),' /ŋalulue/ 'work (plural).' Below are four examples from Manam. The first two show partial prefixed reduplication and the last two partial suffixed reduplication:

Manam

/salaga/	'be long'	/sasalaga/	'long (plural)'
/eno/	'sleep'	/eneno/	'always sleep'
/sapara/	'branch'	/saparapara/	'having branches'
/ʔulan/	'desire'	/ʔulanlaŋ/	'desirable'

The last Manam example shows that there are often morphophonemic changes involved with reduplication, so that the reduplicated part of the word is not always phonologically identical to the unreduplicated part. In Tongan, vowels undergo changes in many reduplicated words. Some of these changes involve differences in length, others differences in vowel quality:

Tongan

/poʔuli/	'be dark'	/po:po:ʔuli/	'be somewhat dark'
/mafi/	'powerful'	/ma:fimafi/	'almighty'
/teliŋa/	'ear'	/taliŋeliŋa/	'fungus'
/muʔa/	'front'	/muʔomuʔa/	'go in front'

In Ponapean, when certain categories of consonants come together across a morpheme boundary as a result of reduplication, the first is replaced by a nasal, as in (a) below. In other cases, a vowel is introduced to break up the consonant cluster, as in (b).

Ponapean

(a)	/pap/	'swim'	/pampap/
	/kak/	'able'	/kaŋkak/
	/sas/	'stagger'	/saṇsas/
	/ṭiṭ/	'build a wall'	/ṭiṇṭiṭ/
(b)	/tsep/	'begin'	/tsepitsep/
	/katso:re/	'subtract'	/katsikatso:re/
	/kaṭek/	'be kind'	/kaṭakaṭek/
	/masukuṇ/	'be blind'	/masamasukuṇ/

5.2. Papuan Languages

5.2.1. Vowel Systems

The majority of Papuan languages have the standard five-vowel system found among the Austronesian languages as well:

i	u
e	o
	a

Although this is the most common system, some Papuan languages, including many of those in the Sepik area of Papua New Guinea, have fewer than five phonemic vowels, while others have more. Compare Iatmul's three vowels to Vanimo's eight:

Iatmul   **Vanimo**

Iatmul		Vanimo		
ɨ		i		u
ə		e	ə	o
		ɛ		ɔ
a			a	

Foley (1986, 54) says that no Papuan language with more than eight phonemic vowels has been attested.

A number of Papuan languages, for example, Pawaian, contrast oral and nasalized vowels. (The examples below are all low tone.)

Pawaian

/sù/	'ginger'	/yè/	'ancestor'
/sũ̀/	'road'	/yẽ̀/	'type of nut'

Distinctions of vowel length do occur in Papuan languages, though this feature is much rarer than it is in Oceanic languages.

5.1.2. Consonant Systems

Consonant inventories in many Papuan languages are relatively small (a sample of Papuan consonant inventories is given in appendix 3). No language in the world has a smaller consonant inventory than Rotokas (spoken on Bougainville), which has only six consonant phonemes.[5]

Rotokas

p	t	k
v	r	g

There are, however, Papuan languages with more complex consonant systems. A number of languages distinguish prenasalized and simple stops, while some languages (like Kâte, for example) have **coarticulated** labial-velar stops. In addition to the labial stops /p/ and /b/, made by closing the lips, and the velar stops /k/ and /g/, made by putting the tongue up in the back of the mouth, there are the coarticulated stops /^{k}p/ and /$^{\mathfrak{g}}$b/, produced by simultaneously closing the lips and raising the tongue at the back of the mouth.

Languages of the Highlands of Papua New Guinea are well known for, among other things, their range of **laterals** (or *l*-like sounds). Kobon, for example, has three laterals: an alveolar lateral /l/, rather like English *l*; a retroflex lateral /ḷ/, with the tip of the tongue turned back to the roof of the mouth; and a palatal lateral /λ/, a bit like the *ly* in the English word *halyard*. Melpa also has three laterals: dental /l̪/ (made with the tongue between the teeth), velar /ɬ/ (with the tongue raised at the back of the mouth), and flapped /l̆/ (where the tongue flaps against the tooth ridge). Both Kobon and Melpa also have an /r/ phoneme that contrasts with all of these laterals.

Perhaps the most complex Papuan phonological system, however, is found in Yele (or Yeletnye), the language of Rossel Island. In addition to a set of simple phonemes, Yele also has labialized, palatalized, prenasalized, and postnasalized consonants, plus in some cases coarticulated consonants as well. So in addition to simple /p/, there is labialized /p^w/, palatalized /p^y/, prenasalized /^{m}p/, postnasalized /p^m/, and coarticulated /^{t}p/ and /^{k}p/. And similar statements could be made about many other Yele consonants!

5.2.3. Prosodic Features

Many descriptions of Papuan languages do not mention stress, perhaps because it is often associated with tone, and it is difficult to find general patterns. In some languages, stress appears to be predictable, though there is a range of patterns. Waskia, for example, tends to stress the last syllable of a word, whereas Kewa prefers the first.

Waskia

/kadí/	'man'
/naúr/	'coconut'
/bagesán/	'it stays'
/namerukó/	'he must go'

Kewa[6]

/póna/	'cut'
/rúmaa/	'portion out'
/rógoma/	'clay'

In other Papuan languages, though, stress is not predictable, as the following examples from Koita illustrate.

Koita

/ómo/	'head'	/omó/	'adze'
/ɣúdi/	'digging stick'	/ɣudí/	'lime'
/ɣúma/	'path'	/ɣumá/	'axe'

Quite a number of Papuan languages have phonemic tone. Tone languages are mainly found in the central Highlands and in parts of the Morobe and Sepik provinces of Papua New Guinea, but they do occur in other parts of the Papuan region as well. Most Papuan tone languages contrast only high and low tones.

Pawaian

/sú/	'tooth'	/sù/	'ginger'
/yé/	'new'	/yè/	'ancestor'

Fore

/àsìyúwè/	'I stand up'	/àsìyùwè/	'I peel it'
/nàyà:né/	'my hair'	/nàyá:né/	'my kidney'

Foley (1986, 63) says that in many such languages tone is closely associated with the stress system, with high tone correlating with accented syllables, and that these are not, strictly speaking, tone languages.[7]

In some languages—especially in the Eastern Highlands of Papua New Guinea—tonal systems are more complex. These seem to be true tonal systems. The following words in Awa, which has four phonemic tones, illustrate this.[8]

Awa

/pǎ/	'fish'	rising tone
/nâ/	'taro'	falling tone
/ná/	'breast'	high tone
/nà/	'house'	low tone

5.2.4. Word Structure

Some Papuan languages have only open syllables. A number of these languages allow combinations of vowels, sometimes quite a few vowels appearing in sequence without any intervening consonant.

Toaripi

/pasisa/	'ladder'
/easo/	'fish spear'
/maeamariti/	'shame'
/eae/	'erroneously'

Mountain Koiari

/neinuvueabe/	'their mothers'
/neiniai/	'properly'
/saiamo/	'slow'
/ialelua/	'consequently'

Some Papuan languages that generally have open syllables (see the first two words in the example below), allow syllables to be closed with a nasal.

Buin

/itaka/	'freshwater shrimp'
/topituumoru/	'fish-killer'
/kuikuiŋ/	'driftwood'
/rempo/	'battle axe'

Probably the majority of Papuan languages allow fairly widespread consonant clustering. Words may end in a range of consonants.

Wahgi

/amŋa/	'yawn'
/okṣnaḷ/	'avoid'
/molmŋe/	'they were'
/eⁿḓzmo/	'waste?'
/kopṣⁿde/	'cut open'
/kaⁿḓẓIp/	'they saw'

Kamasau

/beryi/	'bean'
/torbiŋ/	'mouth harp'
/fraⁿgi/	'tomorrow'
/suⁿgrum/	'type of grass'
/surog/	'caterpillar'
/waⁿd/	'speech'

Reduplication is a much less common feature of Papuan than of Oceanic languages.

5.3. Australian Languages

In comparison with Oceanic and Papuan languages, Australian languages are probably of moderate phonological complexity. None of them has phonemic tone, for example, and in most stress is predictable, occurring on the first syllable of the word. Many have quite small vowel inventories, though a few Australian languages rival those of New Caledonia in their large number of vowels. Consonant inventories are neither small nor large.

5.3.1. Vowel Systems

Most Australian languages have just three vowel phonemes, though many of these also distinguish vowel length, for a total of six vowel contrasts.

i	u	i:	u:
	a		a:

Exceptions are generally of two kinds. First, there are a few languages in Central Australia that have only two vowel phonemes: Kaitij, for example, has just /i/ and /a/ (though each of these has a number of different pronunciations in different phonetic contexts). Second, some languages in the north and northwest have a four- or five-vowel system, for example, Alawa and Kunjen.

	Alawa			**Kunjen**	
i		u	i		u
e			e		o
	a			a	

But a few languages, especially those in the Cape York area, have developed complex vowel systems from what was probably an ancestral three-vowel system. One such system, that of Anguthimri, appears in appendix 3.

5.3.2. Consonant Systems

In discussing the consonants of Australian languages it is helpful to use two technical terms: **Apical** refers to sounds made with the tip of the tongue, and **laminal** describes sounds made with the blade of the tongue. Many

Australian languages distinguish apical and laminal stops and nasals, and many have two sets of apicals and two sets of laminals. Apicals include the apico-alveolar (tongue tip on the tooth ridge) consonants /d t n/ and the apico-postalveolar, or retroflex (tip on the roof of the mouth) consonants /ḏ ṭ ṇ/. Laminals occur as laminodentals (tongue blade on the teeth), namely /d̪ t̪ n̪/, and laminopalatals (blade on the roof of the mouth), /dʸ tʸ ñ/.

Australian languages generally have bilabial (/b p m/) and velar (/g k ŋ/) stops and nasals as well. Along the east coast, languages usually have only one lateral, but elsewhere they have two or more. Most Australian languages have two **rhotics**, or *r*-sounds. One is usually a retroflex semivowel /ṛ/ (rather like English *r*), and the other a flapped or trilled *r*.

Consonant inventories for four languages illustrate some general patterns. Wargamay is an example of an east-coast language, with no contrast between apicals or between laminals, and with one lateral. Kunjen is an eastern language with a laminal contrast but no apical contrast, and with one lateral. Wajarri, a western language, exhibits apical contrast but no laminal contrast, and has more than one lateral. Pitta-Pitta is a central Australian language that contrasts both apicals and laminals and has more than one lateral.

Wargamay

b	ḏ	d	g
m	ṇ	n	ŋ
		l	
		ṛ	
w		y	

Kunjen

p		t̪	t	tʸ	k
b		d̪	d	dʸ	g
	f	ð			γ
m		n̪	n	ñ	ŋ
			l		
			ṛ		
w				y	

Wajarri

p	t̪	t	ṭ	k
m	n̪	n	ṇ	ŋ
	ḻ	l	ḷ	
		r	ṛ	
w		y		

Pitta-Pitta

p	ṭ	t	ṭ	tʸ	k
m	ṇ	n	ṇ	ñ	ŋ
	ḷ	l	ḷ	λ	
		r	ṛ		
w				y	

Two other patterns emerge from an examination of the four consonant systems given above. First, contrast between voiceless and voiced stops, i.e., between /p t k/ and /b d g/, is not common, though it does occur in a minority of languages. Second, fricative phonemes are rare. Of the languages above, only Kunjen has fricative phonemes (/f ð γ/). (But in some languages stops like /b/ are pronounced as fricatives, say [f] or [v], in some phonetic contexts.)

5.3.3. Word Structure

Australian languages show remarkable similarity in the way in which consonant and vowel phonemes combine to form words. As in other Pacific languages, words of one syllable are extremely rare. Most words contain two syllables, some more than two. Words seldom begin with a vowel, and sequences of vowels are also rare. Two-consonant clusters are common in the middle of words, but not initially or finally. Words may end in either a consonant or a vowel. The typical pattern is CVC(C)V(C), and words of more than two syllables simply build on this pattern.

There are commonly restrictions on where consonants occur. Typically, laterals and rhotics do not occur in word-initial position, and stops do not occur finally. Rules also govern the formation of two-consonant clusters in medial position. Here are some examples from Bandjalang, showing the distribution of laterals, rhotics, and stops, as well as a limited range of medial two-consonant clusters (*rb, ñb, ŋb, mb*):

Bandjalang

/dʸa:dʸam/	'child'	/ba:baŋ/	'grandmother'
/burbi/	'koala'	/ŋu:ñba/	'snake'
/guluŋbay/	'flu'	/yalañ/	'tongue'
/dʸimbaŋ/	'sheep'	/bala:ya/	'die'

There are exceptions to these constraints. Anguthimri, mentioned above as an atypical Australian language for its vowel system, is exceptional in other ways as well. It contrasts voiceless and voiced prenasalized stops and possesses five fricative phonemes. It also has a phonemic glottal stop (see appendix 3). Besides these phenomena, Anguthimri has many monosyllabic words and allows word-initial vowels and consonant clusters. It does not, however, allow word-final consonants (except /w/ and /y/). Some examples:

Anguthimri

/pwe:ke/	'groper'	/pæŋa/	'elbow'
/kyabara/	'alligator'	/iɣiti/	'brown'
/ubu/	'red gum'	/baw/	'tooth'
/ḏwa/	'eye'	/dʳya/	'wing'

Reduplication is often used in Australian languages to form the plural of nouns and adjectives:

Dyirbal

| /bari/ | 'axe' | /baribari/ | 'axes' |
| /bulgan/ | 'big one' | /bulganbulgan/ | 'big ones' |

It sometimes has such other functions as intensity (Kalkatungu), diminution (Diyari), or unreality (Western Desert).

Kalkatungu

| /jagabi/ | 'listen' | /jagabijagabi/ | 'listen intently' |
| /buyud/ | 'hot' | /buyudbuyud/ | 'very hot' |

Diyari

| /kinṯala/ | 'dog' | /kinṯalakinṯala/ | 'puppy' |

Western Desert

| /wati/ | 'man' | /watiwati/ | 'child playing at being an adult' |

5.4. Orthographies

No Pacific languages were written before European contact,[9] and even today, not all Pacific languages are written. This usually means that no missionaries or linguists have done sufficient work on these languages to design an orthography. Languages in this category are found almost exclusively in Melanesia and Australia.

Many languages in Melanesia and Australia are used for a much narrower range of written purposes than are other Pacific languages: The main writers are probably linguists! One reason for this has to do with the relatively small numbers of speakers of these languages, and the fact that they generally write in a more widely understood language (English, French, or Melanesian Pidgin, for example).

5.4.1. General Issues

The Latin alphabet (in which English and most European languages are written) is universally applied to the writing of Pacific languages. Orthographies for most of the written languages of the Pacific were developed by Christian missionaries during the nineteenth and twentieth centuries, although linguists have also made their contributions.

In developing orthographies for Pacific languages, missionaries and linguists faced a number of problems that reliance on the spelling system of, say, English or French could not always resolve. The first of these, of course, is that the spelling systems of these two European languages are themselves not always consistent—or at least not transparently so. In English, for example, we now spell Fiji as *Fiji*, but earlier explorers wrote it as *Fejee* or *Feejee*; the French write it as *Fidji*. The "correct" Fijian spelling, however, is *Viti*.

There are also distinctive phonological features in Pacific languages that languages like English or French do not have. For these there is no "natural" orthographic representation. Two examples common to many parts of the region are (1) the contrast between short and long vowels and (2) the glottal stop phoneme. Different solutions were often found for these kinds of problems in different areas. For vowel length, the macron (as in *ā, ē*) has been used in many Polynesian languages, although double vowels (*aa, ee*) are used in others. The glottal stop has most often been indicated in Polynesia by a quotation mark (as in Hawai'i), though in some parts of Melanesia letters like *c* or *q*, which are not otherwise needed in the spelling system, have been used.

The problem with additional marks like apostrophes and macrons is that, because they are not perceived as "normal" letters, they are very often left out by people when they are writing the language.[10] For example, although Hawaiian has both the glottal stop and the distinction between long and short vowels, many people do not indicate either of these distinctions when they write Hawaiian. Thus the words /pau/ 'finished' and /pa:ʔu:/ 'lavalava, sarong' are often both written as *pau*, although a more accurate writing system (and the one recently officially re-endorsed) would write the word for 'finished' as *pau* and the word for 'lavalava' as *pāʻū*.

The problems have not only been technical, however. There are general principles on the basis of which a good orthography can be developed, but there is often a certain amount of choice even after the application of these scientific principles. For example, it makes equal scientific sense to write /a:/ as *ā*, as *aa*, or in a number of other ways (like *ah* in parts of Micronesia). Orthographic design in many parts of the Pacific has often revolved around these areas of choice, and reflects the fact that speakers of a language—and outsiders—have very strong feelings about how a language *ought* to be written, regardless of any scientific approach to the situation.

Factionalism of various kinds shows itself in spelling controversies all over the Pacific. There has been a long debate in Kiribati over whether to write *b'* and *m'* or *bw* and *mw* for the phonemes /bʷ/ and /mʷ/. The Nauruan Language Board is currently preparing a Nauruan dictionary in two different orthographies, pending a final decision on spelling. One of these systems derives from the Protestant Bible translation, while the other was developed by Catholics and endorsed by an earlier official body. In the spelling of Tok Pisin in Papua New Guinea before the Second World War, there were the following competitive orthographic decisions.[11]

	/g/	/ŋ/
Lutherans	g	ŋ
Catholics	g	ng
Methodists	q	g

There have also been other nonlinguistic factors at work. English and French, as international languages, have considerable prestige in the Pacific. Although linguists have their own phonetic symbols for sounds, many of these are not standard letters in the English or French writing systems—β ð θ ʔ ə ŋ, for example. Attempts to use letters like these to represent sounds in Pacific languages are often met with resistance by speakers of those languages, who don't want their languages to look "funny" in comparison with English or French.

Other problems are also related to the orthographies of the prestige languages. In general, a scientific approach to orthographic design requires that, wherever possible, each phoneme should be represented by a single letter.[12] Following this principle, the early missionaries used the single letter *g* to represent the phoneme /ŋ/ (the sound written *ng* in English *singer*) in a number of Polynesian languages: Pago Pago, the capital of American Samoa, for example, is pronounced /paŋopaŋo/. This principle was extended by Methodist and related missionaries to some other parts of Polynesia, to Fiji, and to certain areas in Melanesia.

But though this decision may follow scientific rationality, there is a conflict with the spelling system of English, where the letter *g* has a very different value. In Tongan, for example, original *g* was later changed to *ng*, since it was felt that Tongans learning English would be confused by the two different values of the letter *g* in these two languages. Many languages in Melanesia and Micronesia use *ng* for this sound, but this has led to problems of a different sort. On the one hand, English *ng* represents both the sound /ŋ/ as in *singer* and the sounds /ŋg/ as in *finger*, and outsiders often mispronounce words written in Pacific languages with this letter combination (Tonga frequently being pronounced by English speakers as if it were Tongga, for example). On the other hand, if *ng* is used for /ŋ/, then designers of writing systems are often forced to use the somewhat unsightly three-letter combination *ngg* to represent /ŋg/. There have, then, been a number of problems in the development of spelling systems in the Pacific, by no means all of them having to do with the nature of the languages.

5.4.2. Polynesia and Fiji

Because of their relatively simple phonological structures, the development of writing systems for the Polynesian languages has been a fairly straightforward matter. There have been different approaches to the velar nasal phoneme /ŋ/, written *g* or *ng*, and to long vowels, written with macrons or with double vowels. Sometimes even in the same language some writers have used macrons and some double letters, while others have ignored vowel length altogether: *Māori, Maaori,* and *Maori* have all had some currency in New Zealand, for example, though the first seems now to be the preferred spelling.

The designers of the Fijian writing system fairly consistently applied the one-phoneme-one-letter principle, although not without controversy.[13] In Fijian, the prenasalized stops /ᵐb ⁿd ᵑg/ have been written with the single letters *b, d,* and *q* rather than *mb, nd,* and *ngg*. According to the same principle, /ŋ/ is written as *g* and /ð/ as *c* (rather than the *ng* and *th* of English). Where vowel length is written, the macron is used, but many writers of Fijian ignore this feature.

5.4.3. Melanesia and Micronesia

In some parts of Melanesia, the early missionaries made similar kinds of decisions as those made for Fijian and Polynesian languages. In a number of languages in Vanuatu especially, *g* is used for /ŋ/, and in some *c* is used for /γ/. Additional single symbols were created to try to adhere to this principle, *p̃* and *m̃* being used to represent /pʷ/ and /mʷ/. Many of these languages, along with those of the Solomons, have only five vowels, which caused no problems. Vowel length (where it was recognized), however, was generally represented by doubling vowels.

Further west, in the New Guinea area, the Methodist traditions from Fiji and Polynesia had less influence, and orthography designers have generally kept fairy closely to English spelling, at least as far as consonants are concerned. In these languages, for example, the prenasalized stops /^{m}b ^{n}d ^{ŋ}g/ tend to be written *b, d,* and *g* in word-initial position (where the pre-nasalization is fairly weak), and *mb, nd,* and *ngg* in other positions. The velar nasal [ŋ] is usually written *ng,* although in some areas where the Lutheran church is strong, the letter ŋ is used. The occurrence of more than one lateral in Highlands languages has required the use of two letters to represent a single phoneme, like *tl, dl, gl,* and so on, in addition to simple *l,* while *gh* is frequently used for the velar fricative /ɣ/. In dealing with languages which have more than five phonemic vowels, both **digraphs** (two-letter combinations) and **diacritics** (additional marks like accents) have been used. Thus where there is a contrast between /i/, /ɪ/, and /e/ (as in English *seat, sit, set*), for example, these vowels are written *i, î, e;* or *i, ê, e;* or *ii, i, e.*

The complex nature of the consonant and vowel systems of most New Caledonian languages has forced linguists to use both diacritics and combinations of letters. The vowels of Xârâcùù, for example, are *a â ä e é è ê ë i î o ô ö u ù û ü,* and the long vowels are written by doubling these letters. Writing the consonant phonemes of Pije involves single letters (*p, m, h, w*), digraphs (*pw, ph, hm, hw*) and even **trigraphs**—combinations of three letters representing a single phoneme—like *phw, hmw, hny, hng.*

In Micronesia, digraphs are usually used to help represent complex vowel and consonant systems. A number of Micronesian languages use *oa* for /ɔ/ when this contrasts with /o/ (written *o*), and *h* is often used to mark long vowels: thus *i* represents /i/, while *ih* represents /iː/.[14] Digraphs and tri-graphs are also widely used in writing consonant phonemes. Carolinian, for example, distinguishes *bw, gh, mw, pw, rh, sch,* and *tch* from *b, g, m, p, r, s,* and *t.* Long consonants are usually represented by doubling the consonant (as in *ll* for long /lː/). In the case of digraphs, only the first letter is doubled (*mmw* represents long *mw*).

5.4.4. Australia

In general, the small number of vowel phonemes in Australian languages has not posed many problems for designers of orthographies. Long vowels have sometimes been written as double vowels, sometimes with a following *h;* thus /aː/ is written *aa* in some languages, but *ah* in others.

Decisions made about writing consonants vary, but a common pattern is to write retroflex sounds with a preceding *r,* dentals with a following *h,* and palatals with a following *y;* palatal stops are sometimes written *j.* In Gooniyandi, for example, the stop and nasal phonemes given on the left below are written with the letters on the right:

Gooniyandi

Phonemes						Letters					
b	ḍ	d	ḍ	dʸ	g	*b*	*th*	*d*	*rd*	*j*	*g*
m	ṇ	n	ṇ	ñ	ŋ	*m*	*nh*	*n*	*rn*	*ny*	*ng*

Similarly, multiple laterals are generally written *lh, l, rl,* and *ly* (or *lj*), while the two rhotics are generally written *r* and *rr*.

I have adopted these spelling conventions here and transliterated symbols in this way from sources that use phonetic symbols. Note, however, that there is pressure to spell Australian languages following English conventions. For example, the Bandjalang (/bañdʸalaŋ/) people now choose to write their language name *Bundjalung*, to avoid its possible mispronunciation as /bæñdʸəlæŋ/ by English speakers.

5.5. Summary

Pacific languages show a great diversity of phonological systems. Vocalically they range from Australian languages with just three short vowels to New Caledonian languages with seventeen short vowels. Consonant inventories can be very small and simple, or extremely large and complex. Some languages have phonemic tone, others do not. Some allow a great deal of consonant clustering; others allow none.

Various social issues surround and affect the development of orthographies for these languages. In the remainder of this book, I use the standard writing system, in italics, for each language from which I give examples. In the case of languages without a generally accepted writing system, I use a modified set of phonetic symbols, also in italics.

CHAPTER

6

Oceanic Languages: Grammatical Overview

6.1. Pronouns

I use the term "pronoun" fairly loosely. Oceanic languages generally have only one set of free pronouns, but they also have one or more sets of pronominal forms that are more or less bound to nouns, verbs, or other morphemes. While only the free forms might qualify as pronouns under a strict definition, I discuss the other forms here as well.

6.1.1. Person

Almost all Oceanic languages make a distinction between **inclusive first person**, referring to the speaker and the addressee or addressees ("I + you") and **exclusive first person**, referring to the speaker and some other individual or individuals ("I + he/she/it/they"). For example:

	Motu	Mono-Alu	Nakanamanga	Puluwat
Singular				
I	*lau*	*maha*	*kinau*	*ngaang*
you	*oi*	*maito*	*niigo*	*yeen*
he/she/it	*ia*	*eʻa*	*nae*	*yiiy*
Plural				
we:INC	*ita*	*maita*	*nigita*	*kiir*
we:EXC	*ai*	*maani*	*kinami*	*yáámem*
you	*umui*	*maang*	*nimu*	*yáámi*
they	*idia*	*relanaʻi*	*naara*	*yiir*

Exceptions to this general statement are found in a few languages that seem to have lost the inclusive/exclusive distinction. These include the five languages of the Siau family in the West Sepik Province of Papua New Guinea (Sera, Sissano, Ali, Tumleo, and Ulau-Suain), Kiribati, and possibly also one or two varieties of Fijian.

	Sissano	**Kiribati**
Singular		
I	*ya*	*ngngai*
you	*e*	*ngkoe*
he/she/it	*i*	*ngaia*
Plural		
we	*eit*	*ngaira*
you	*om*	*ngkamii*
they	*ri*	*ngaiia*

Very few Oceanic languages mark gender in pronouns. In all the examples above, the third person singular refers to male or female animates as well as to inanimates. Maringe (Isabel, Solomon Islands) is one of the few Oceanic languages that does have a gender distinction, though it differs from the English one. Female speakers use only one set of third person forms, but male speakers use two sets—one referring to males, and the other in all other cases.

Maringe

	Male speaker	**Female speaker**
he	*mana*	*naʿa*
she/it	*naʿa*	*naʿa*
they (males)	*mare*	*reʿe*
they (non-males)	*reʿe*	*reʿe*

Some languages in Melanesia have no third-person pronouns at all. Mari (Morobe Province, Papua New Guinea) is one such: It uses demonstratives (roughly translated, "this one," "those ones") instead of pronouns like "he/she/it" or "they."

6.1.2. Number

A three-way distinction between singular, dual, and plural number is perhaps the commonest pattern in Oceanic languages, the **dual** number referring to two and only two. This pattern is found in Polynesian languages and

Rotuman, as well as in many languages in Melanesia and Micronesia. For example:

	Yapese	Nakanai	A'jië	Samoan
Singular				
I	gaeg	eau	gènya	a'u
you	guur	eme	gèi	'oe
he/she/it	qiir	eia	ce	ia
Dual				
we two:INC	gadow	etalua	görru	tā'ua
we two:EXC	gamow	emilua	gövu	mā'ua
you two	gimeew	emulua	göu	'oulua
they two	yow	egirua	curu	lā'ua
Plural				
we:INC	gadaed	etatou	gèvé	tātou
we:EXC	gamaed	emiteu	gèrré	mātou
you	gimeed	emutou	gëvë	'outou
they	yaed	egiteu	céré	lātou

There are two common departures from this pattern. A number of languages in Melanesia and Micronesia show only a two-way distinction between singular and plural. The examples given in 6.1.1 above from Motu, Mono-Alu, and Nakanamanga (in Melanesia), and Puluwat and Kiribati (in Micronesia) illustrate this.

The other variation is quite common in Melanesia (including Fiji), though not elsewhere in the Pacific. It involves a four-way distinction, between singular, dual, trial or paucal, and plural. Some of these languages have a **trial** number, which refers to three and only three:

		Tolai	Anejom̃
Singular	he/she/it	ia	aen
Dual	they two	dir	aarau
Trial	they three	dital	aattaj
Plural	they (>three)	diat	aara

Others have a **paucal** number, which refers to a few (perhaps three to six or so), or to a small group in comparison with a larger group.[1]

		Paamese	Nadrau Fijian
Singular	he/she/it	kaie	i kwaya
Dual	they two	kailue	i kirau

| **Paucal** | they (a few) | *kaitelu* | *i kiratou* |
| **Plural** | they (many) | *kaile* | *i kira* |

6.1.3. Functions

The pronouns cited so far are known as **independent** pronouns. They may stand alone as the answer to a question and may also act as subject of a verb (though they often have an emphatic function in this usage). There are, however, other pronominal forms in many Oceanic languages, although they may not always be able to stand alone.

Most Oceanic languages, for example, have a separate set of **subject markers**, which are formally different from the independent pronouns. These subject markers mark the person and number of the subject and usually occur within the verb complex. In some languages they are preverbal particles, in others prefixes to the verb. In many of these languages, the independent pronoun is used in subject position only for emphasis. Contrast the following sentences in Lenakel:

Lenakel
I-es-ol-aan.
I-not-do-not
'I didn't do it.'

Io   i-es-ol-aan!
I   I-not-do-not
'*I* didn't do it!,' 'It wasn't *I* who did it!'

In both sentences, the person and the number of the subject are marked within the verb by the prefix *i-* 'I.' The first sentence, with no independent pronoun, is a neutral statement. In the second, however, emphasis is placed on the subject, 'I,' through the use of the independent pronoun *io*.

Below are some examples—in just singular and plural numbers—illustrating the formal difference between independent pronouns and subject markers. The Nehan and Fijian subject markers are free preverbal particles, while the Trukese ones are verbal prefixes.[2]

	Nehan		**Trukese**		**Fijian**	
	IND.	SUBJ.	IND.	SUBJ.	IND.	SUBJ.
Singular						
I	*ingo*	*ku*	*ngaang*	*wú-*	*o yau*	*au*
you	*inga*	*ko*	*een*	*ke-*	*o iko*	*o*
he/she/it	*git*	*ke*	*iiy*	*e-*	*o koya*	*e*

Plural

we:INC	*ingeg*	*ki*	*kiich*	*si-*	*o keda*	*da*
we:EXC	*ingam*	*king*	*áám*	*éwú-*	*o keimami*	*keimami*
you	*ingam*	*kung*	*áámi*	*wo-*	*o kemunī*	*nī*
they	*gisit*	*ka*	*iir*	*re-*	*o ira*	*ra*

Rather fewer Oceanic languages have formally distinct **object markers**, many using the independent pronoun in this role. Above, for example, we saw the use of the Lenakel independent pronoun *io* 'I' as an emphatic subject. This same form is also used in object position.

Lenakel

R-ɨs-aamh-aan   *io.*
he-not-see-not   me
'He didn't see me.'

Languages with distinct object pronouns are found in Melanesia and Micronesia. In some of these languages (like Anejom̃ in the example below) these are free forms, while in others (like Kiribati) they are suffixed to the verb.[3]

	Anejom̃		Kiribati	
	IND.	OBJ.	IND.	OBJ.
Singular				
I	*añak*	*ñak*	*ngngai*	*-ai*
you	*aek*	*yic*	*ngkoe*	*-iko*
he/she/it	*aen*	*yin*	*ngaia*	*-ia*
Plural				
we:INC	*akaja*	*caja*	*ngaira*	*-iira*
we:EXC	*ajama*	*cama*		
you	*ajowa*	*cowa*	*ngkamii*	*-ingkami*
they	*aara*	*ra*	*ngaiia*	*-iia, -i*

For more about the functions of both subject and object markers, see section 6.4.

Virtually all Oceanic languages also have a set of **possessive affixes** (normally suffixes) marking the person and number of the possessor. These differ from independent pronouns and subject markers (though they are frequently identical or similar to object markers). The grammar of possession in Oceanic languages is quite complex (refer to section 6.3 below). For example, the Fijian possessive suffix *-qu* 'my' is attached directly to certain types of possessed nouns (like *tama* 'father' in the example below), but when used with nouns of other types it is attached to a possessive marker or classifier (as with *vale* 'house').

Fijian

na	tama-*qou*	but	na	*no-qau*	*vale*
the	father-my		the	POSS-my	house
'my father'				'my house'	

These affixes are almost always suffixes. But in a few languages they occur as prefixes in some grammatical contexts.

Wayan Fijian

o	mna-*m*	but	*m-ulu*
the	mother-your		your-head
'your mother'			'your head'

A comparison between the singular and plural independent, object, and possessive pronouns in Anejom̃ and Kiribati is given below.

	Anejom̃			**Kiribati**		
	IND.	OBJ.	POSS.	IND.	OBJ.	POSS.
Singular						
I	*añak*	*ñak*	-k	*ngngai*	-ai	-u
you	*aek*	*yic*	-m̃	*ngkoe*	-iko	-m
he/she/it	*aen*	*yin*	-n	*ngaia*	-ia	-n(a)
Plural						
we:INC	*akaja*	*caja*	-ja	*ngaira*	-iira	-ra
we:EXC	*ajama*	*cama*	-ma			
you	*ajowa*	*cowa*	-mia	*ngkamii*	-ingkami	-mii
they	*aara*	*ra*	-ra	*ngaiia*	-iia, -i	-ia

It follows from all of this that, while some Oceanic languages have a pronoun system as simple as that of English, many have pronoun systems of considerable complexity. Table 5 lists the full set of independent, object, and possessive pronouns in Anejom̃, along with the three sets of subject markers used in the aorist, past, and inceptive tenses, to illustrate this complexity.

6.2. NOUNS AND NOUN PHRASES

The notion of parts of speech as we understand it in English, does not necessarily apply to Oceanic languages. While some Oceanic languages clearly distinguish nouns from other parts of speech in some formal or functional way, many others do not. The Fijian word *tagane*, for example, can function as a noun meaning 'man,' as a verb meaning 'to be male,' and as an adjective meaning 'male.'

Table 5. Anejom̃ Pronouns

	1. INC	1. EXC	2.	3.
Independent				
Singular	—	añak	aek, aak	aen, aan
Dual	akajau	ajamrau	ajourau	aarau
Trial	akataj	ajamtaj	ajoutaj	aattaj
Plural	akaja	ajama	ajowa	aara
Object				
Singular	—	ñak	yic, -c	yin, -n
Dual	cajau	camrau	courau	rau
Trial	cataj	camtaj	coutaj	ettaj
Plural	caja	cama	cowa	ra
Possessive				
Singular	—	-k	-m̃	-n
Dual	-jau	-mrau	-mirau	-rau
Trial	-taj	-mtaj	-mitaj	-ttaj
Plural	-ja	-ma	-mia	-ra
Subject (aorist)				
Singular	—	ek	na	et
Dual	tau	ekrau	erau	erau
Trial	taj	ettaj	ettaj	ettaj
Plural	ta	ekra	eka	era
Subject (past)				
Singular	—	kis	as	is
Dual	tus	eris	arus	erus
Trial	tijis	eris	atijis	etijis
Plural	eris	ekris	akis	eris
Subject (inceptive)				
Singular	—	ki	an	iñiyi
Dual	tu	ekru	aru	eru
Trial	tiji	etiji	atiji	etiji
Plural	ti	ekri	aki	eri

Fijian

E	lako	mai	na	*tagane*	oyā	(*tagane* = noun).
he	come	here	the	man	that	

'That man is coming.'

E	*tagane*	na	vuaka	oqō	(*tagane* = verb).
he	male	the	pig	this	

'This pig is male.'

E	mate	na	vuaka	*tagane*	(*tagane* = adjective).
he	die	the	pig	male	

'The boar died.'

In this and subsequent sections, when I use the word "noun," I am referring to *words functioning as nouns* in a particular context. For our purposes, then, *tagane* is a noun in the first Fijian sentence above, though not in the other two.

6.2.1. Form of the Noun

Nouns in Oceanic languages are generally invariable in form. That is, a noun does not change form to mark singular and plural, nor generally do nouns take prefixes and suffixes (apart from possessive affixes, discussed later). Fijian *vuaka* and Hawaiian *puaʻa*, for example, both mean 'pig' or 'pigs.'

In languages of this type, plurality is expressed either by a separate morpheme in the noun phrase (see 6.2.5) or by a subject or object marker in the verb complex. Often, a combination of strategies is used, as in the Vinmavis example below, in which the noun itself (*matoro* 'old man') remains invariable:

Vinmavis

Matoro	*i-fwelem.*
old:man	he-come

'The old man came.'

Matoro	*ar*	*at-fwelem.*
old:man	PL	they-come

'The old men came.'

There are, however, some exceptions to the generalization that nouns are invariable in form. First, in some languages of Polynesia and Melanesia, there is a small set of nouns referring to human beings that form the plural by a change in the position of stress or by partial reduplication, as in Motu, or by lengthening a vowel, as in Māori and Hawaiian.

	Singular	Plural
Motu		
tau	'man'	*tatau*
hahíne	'woman'	*háhine*
mero	'boy'	*memero*
kekéni	'girl'	*kékeni*
Māori		
tāngata	'man'	*tāngata*
tupuna	'ancestor'	*tūpuna*
tuahine	'sister'	*tuāhine*
Hawaiian		
luahine	'old woman'	*luāhine*
kahuna	'priest'	*kāhuna*
kupuna	'grandparent'	*kūpuna*

In Kiribati, vowel lengthening also occurs in nouns, but it indicates generic reference rather than plurality:

Kiribati

te tina	'(the) mother'	*tiina*	'mothers in general'
te ika	'(the) fish'	*iika*	'fish in general'
te ben	'(the) coconut'	*been*	'coconuts in general'
te bong	'(the) day'	*boong*	'days in general'
te biti	'(the) knife'	*biiti*	'knives in general'

In Rotuman, the long form of a noun (see 5.1.1 above) marks a noun as definite. Indefinite nouns occur in the short form.[4]

Rotuman

| *Famori* | *'ea.* |
| people | say |

'The people say.'

| *Famör* | *'ea.* |
| people | say |

'(Some) people say.'

There are also some languages, geographically and genetically fairly widespread, that mark plurality of nouns by a prefix or a suffix. Among these are the non-Oceanic languages Palauan and Chamorro:

	Singular	Plural
Palauan		
chad	'person'	*rę-chad*

kangkodang	'tourist'	*rę-kangkodang*
sęchel-ik	'my friend'	*rę-sęchel-ik*

Chamorro

estudiante	'student'	*man-estudiante*
pale'	'priest'	*mam-ale'*
saina	'parent'	*mañ-aina*

Some languages in Vanuatu have fairly complex pluralization strategies. In Sye, for example, there is a general plural prefix *ovn-*. (This varies slightly according to the following consonant.) Kinship terms without possessive suffixes (like *namou* 'mother') *may* take this prefix and also the suffix *-me*: they *must* take one of these. Kinship terms with possessive suffixes (like *asu-g* 'my husband' and *ma-n* 'her brother') must take the suffix *-me*, and may take the prefix *r(o)-*. Thus:

Sye

Singular		Plural
kuri	'dog'	*ovn-kuri*
nakeh	'axe'	*ov-nakeh*
neteme	'person'	*ovo-teme*
namou	'mother'	*ov-namou, namou-me, ov-namou-me*
asu-g	'my husband'	*asu-g-me, r-asu-g-me*
ma-n	'her brother'	*ma-n-me, ro-ma-n-me*

In Anejoñ, nouns beginning with *n* or *in* drop this in the plural. Nouns referring to humans must take a plural prefix *elpu-*; those referring to the higher animates may take this prefix; other nouns take no plural prefix.

Anejoñ

Singular		Plural
natañañ	'man'	*elpu-atañañ*
natimi	'person'	*elpu-atimi*
nepcev	'shark'	*elpu-epcev, epcev*
incai	'tree'	*cai*
inhat	'stone'	*hat*

Some Oceanic languages make no formal distinction between nouns and, say, verbs or adjectives. Those that do make this distinction (and also some that do not), have one or more **nominalizers**—morphemes that convert verbs or adjectives into nouns. Some examples are presented below.

Lenakel

aklha	'steal'	*i̱-aklha*	'thief'

| | | n-aklha-aan | 'theft, robbery' |
| | | k-aklha | 'house-breaking tool' |

Mokilese

karaja	'explain'	karaja-poa	'example'
wia	'make'	wia-poa	'construction'
woaroai	'to last'	woaroai-n	'duration'

Māori

kimi	'to seek'	kimi-hanga	'a search'
noho	'sit'	noho-anga	'seat'
inu	'to drink'	inu-manga	'a drink'

6.2.2. Articles

Articles are morphemes marking the class or reference of a noun. In English, the article *the* marks a noun as definite, while *a/an* marks it as singular indefinite; in French, *un* and *le* mark singular masculine nouns (indefinite and definite, respectively), while *une* and *la* mark singular feminine nouns.

Generally speaking, the languages of the New Guinea mainland and the islands of Papua, and those spoken in Vanuatu, have no articles.[5] Examples:

Manam

| Tamoata | roa | to'a | i-ti'in-i. |
| man | his:spouse | his:older:brother | he-show-her |

'The man showed his wife to his older brother.'

Kilivila

| E | seki | Kilagola | yena | guyau. |
| he | give | Kilagola | fish | chief |

'The chief gives Kilagola the fish.'

Sye

| Natmonuc | y-omonki | nacave. |
| chief | he:DISTANT:PAST-drink | kava |

'The chief drank (the) kava.'

Most of the remaining Oceanic languages—those of the islands to the northeast of New Guinea, the Solomon Islands, New Caledonia, Micronesia, Fiji, and Polynesia—do have articles, although there are some exceptions.

Fijian languages generally have two articles. In Standard Fijian, *o* is the **proper article** and is used before pronouns, proper nouns (names of specific people or places), and some kinship terms. *Na* is the **common article** and is used before other nouns that are definite in some sense.[6] Indefinite nouns (like *yaqona* in the second example below) are not marked by articles. Examples:

Fijian

E	*gunu-va*		*na*	*yaqona*	*o*		*Seru.*
he	drink-TRANS		the	kava	the:PERSONAL		Seru

'Seru is drinking the kava.'

E	*gunu*	*yaqona*	*o*		*Seru.*
he	drink	kava	the:PERSONAL		Seru

'Seru is drinking kava.'

Polynesian languages have a slightly larger number of articles. In Hawaiian, for example, the articles are:

Hawaiian

ka, ke[7]	definite article, singular: 'the'
nā	definite article, plural: 'the'
he	indefinite article: 'a'
a	personal article

Mokilese and Yapese provide illustrations of different kinds of Micronesian article systems. In Mokilese, a noun may occur with no article (or demonstrative). The reference is usually generic.

Mokilese

Mahnsang	*kin*	*wia*	*ahr*	*paj*	*in*	*pohn*	*suhkoa.*
bird	HABITUAL	make	their	nest	in	top	tree

'Birds build their nests in treetops.'

A	*koah*	*kak*	*wiahda*	*war?*
QUESTION	you	can	build	canoe

'Can you build canoes?'

When the reference is specific but indefinite—the addressee does not know which individual is being referred to—Mokilese nouns take as a suffix the appropriate numeral classifier (see 6.2.5 below) in the singular, and *-pwi* in the plural:

Mokilese

Ngoah	*kapang*	*lih-men*		*o.*
I	see	woman-CLASSIFIER		there

'I saw a woman there.'

Ngoah	*kapang*	*lih-pwi*		*o.*
I	see	woman-a:PL		there

'I saw women there,' or 'I saw some women there.'

When the reference is both specific and definite, the suffix -*o* (sometimes-*u*) is used.

Mokilese

Ngoah	*kapang*	*lih-o.*
I	see	woman-the

'I saw the woman.'

Yapese is similar to Fijian or the Polynesian languages, in that it has three articles, all of which come before the noun: *fa* definite, *ba* indefinite singular, and *ii*, which is used optionally before personal names.

Yapese

fa	*rea*	*kaarroo*
the	SG	car

'the car'

ba	*kaarroo*
a	car

'a car'

ii	*Tamag*	(or just *Tamag*)
the:PERSONAL	Tamag	

'Tamag (a man's name)'

Most languages of the Bismarck Archipelago and the Solomon Islands also have a small number of articles that precede the noun. Gender distinction is not uncommon. To'aba'ita, for example, has a common article *nga*, and two personal articles, *tha* (used with masculine names) and *ni* (used with feminine names).

To'aba'ita

nga	*'ai*	*lakoo*	*ki*
the	wood	this	PL

'the firewood'

ai	*tha*	*Gerea*
wife	the:MASCULINE	Gerea

'Gerea's wife'

maka	*ni*	*'Oina*
father	the:FEMININE	'Oina

'Oina's father'

The most complex article systems are those of New Caledonia. In these languages articles precede the noun and mark—among other features—

definiteness, number, and gender. Drehu has the following articles and article-like particles:

Drehu

la	definite, near speaker, visible
lai	definite, near addressee, visible
lo	definite, not present or visible
ketre	indefinite singular
xaa	indefinite non-singular
isa	'each'
itre, o	paucal
nöjei	plural
haa	collective

Cèmuhî has an even more complex system. Its articles distinguish gender—feminine and nonfeminine, which both treat the noun as a person or individual, as well as neuter, which treats the noun as a thing or idea); number—singular, dual, and plural; and reference—definite, indefinite, and neutral. (Neutral reference marks the noun as a noun without specifying whether it is definite or indefinite.)

Cèmuhî

		Neutral	Definite	Indefinite
Singular	Nonfeminine	pā	pàcɛ	pàli
	Feminine	ɛ̀	ɛ̀cɛ	ɛ̀gi
	Neuter	ā	ācɛ	āli
Dual	Nonfeminine	lūpwɔ	lūpwɔcɛ	lūpwɔli
	Feminine	lū	lū cɛ	lū li
Plural	Nonfeminine	lēpwɔ	lēpwɔcɛ	lēpwɔli
	Feminine	lē	lēcɛ	lēli
	Neuter	ni	cɛ	li, ili

6.2.3. Demonstratives

Demonstratives are words that locate the noun in space and/or time, generally with reference to the speaker and the addressee, though sometimes with reference to some other focus. English has a simple two-way distinction (between *this/these* and *that/those*), and this system is found in a few Oceanic languages in Melanesia.

Manam	**Maringe**	
ngae	*gne*	'this'
ngaedi	*gre*	'these'

| ngara | gno | 'that' |
| ngaradi | gro | 'those' |

Almost universal in Oceanic languages, however, is a *three-way* directional/locational/temporal distinction in demonstratives, corresponding to the three grammatical persons. The three categories are often referred to as **proximate**—near the speaker and corresponding to the first person (the speaker); **intermediate**—near the addressee and corresponding to the second person (the person spoken to); and **distant**—away from both speaker and addressee and corresponding to the third person (some other person or thing).

Some languages simply mark this distinction without specifying number:

Motu	**Fijian**	**Māori**	
ina	(o)qō	nei	PROXIMATE: 'this'
ena	(o)qori	na	INTERMEDIATE: 'this/that'
una	(o)yā	ra	DISTANT: 'that (yonder)'

Others, however, not only make the three-way contrast but also indicate singular and plural:

Nakanai	**Kiribati**	**Rotuman**		
aleie	aei	te 'isi	PROXIMATE:	'this'
ini	aikai	'i		'these'
alele	anne	ta 'a	INTERMEDIATE:	'this/that'
ene	akanne	'o		'these/those'
aleio	arei	tæe	DISTANT:	'that (yonder)'
unu	akekei	'ie		'those (yonder)'

There are further complications in some languages. To'aba'ita, for example, has not only a regular distant demonstrative *labaa*, but two others specifying vertical orientation: *loo* 'that, yonder and higher up,' and *fuu* 'that, yonder and lower down.' Anejom̃ possesses not only the three-way distinction noted above, but also has a set of **anaphoric** demonstratives, which mark a noun as having been previously referred to. Example:

Anejom̃
> niom̃ iyiiki
> house that
> 'that house (the one I was talking about before)'

In addition, Anejom̃ distinguishes number in demonstratives, and so has the following:

Anejom̃

	Singular	Dual	Plural
Proximate	*iniñki*	*erañki*	*ijiñki*
Intermediate	*enaanai*	—	*ijeknaa*
Distant	*enaikou*	*erañkou*	*ijeknaikou*
Anaphoric	*iyiiki*	*eraaki*	*ijiiki* (recent)
			ijekeñ (distant)

6.2.4. Adjectives

I mentioned earlier that there is often difficulty in rigidly assigning a word to a specific part of speech in Oceanic languages. This is especially apparent in the distinction, or lack of it, between verbs and adjectives.

Words that translate into English as adjectives generally have two functional possibilities in most Oceanic languages. First, they may occur within a noun phrase, almost always following the noun which they modify.

Fijian

na	*waqa*	*levu*
the	canoe	big

'the big canoe'

Samoan

'o	*le*	*teine*	*puta*
FOCUS	the	girl	fat

'the fat girl'

Second, and more frequently, adjectives function as **stative verbs**. That is, they function in the same way as other intransitive verbs (being marked for subject, tense, and so on), but they express a state rather than an action, with the subject being the experiencer of that state.

Fijian

E	*levu*	*na*	*waqa.*
it	big	the	canoe

'The canoe is big.'

Samoan

Ua	*puta*	*le*	*teine.*
STATIVE	fat	the	girl

'The girl is fat.'

Many languages in Melanesia, however, do have a category of adjectives that differs from the category of stative verbs, although both of these categories include words that would translate as adjectives. Lenakel, for example, has a set of stative verbs similar to those illustrated for Fijian and Samoan: *vit* 'good' and *esuaas* 'small' may function as adjectives, following the noun in a noun phrase:

Lenakel

R-ɨm-aamh	*nimwa*	<u>*v ɨ t*</u>	*ker.*
he-PAST-see	house	good	one

'He saw a good house.'

Kova	<u>*esuaas*</u>	*ka*	*r-ɨ s-apul-aan.*
child	small	that	he-not-sleep-not

'The small child is not asleep.'

They may also occur as the head of a verb complex, taking prefixes marking subject and tense aspect just like any nonstative verb (compare the behavior of *vit* and *esuaas* in the examples below with that of *aamh* 'see' and *apul* 'sleep' above).

Lenakel

Nimwa	*taha-n*	*r-ɨm-<u>vɨt</u>*	*akɨn.*
house	POSS-his	it-PAST-good	very

'His house was/used to be very nice.'

Kova	*ka*	*r-ɨs-<u>esuaas</u>-aan.*
child	that	he-not-small-not

'That child is not small.'

There is, however, a set of words that can only be adjectives, like *vi* 'new' and *ituga* 'foreign.' These also follow the noun in a noun phrase.

Lenakel

R-ɨm-ol	*nimwa*	<u>*vi.*</u>
he-PAST=make	house	new

'He built a new house.'

Nɨkava	<u>*ituga*</u>	*r-is-vɨt-aan.*
kava	foreign	it-not-good-not

'Alcohol (lit., foreign kava) is not good.'

Words in this category never function as stative verbs, and utterances like the following ones are unacceptable.

Lenakel

°*Nimwa*	*r-(ɨm)-<u>vi.</u>*
house	it-(PAST)-new

°Nĭkava	r-ĭs-<u>ituga</u>-aan.
kava	it-not-foreign-not

6.2.5. *Numerals and Quantifiers*

Two classes of words or morphemes relate to counting. **Numerals** are exact numbers in a counting system: one, two, three, four, and so on. Oceanic languages exhibit a range of numeral systems; the commonest are simple decimal (base 10) or quinary (base 5) systems, but there are variations on these systems, and other systems are also represented (see chapter 11 for a detailed discussion). **Quantifiers** are morphemes that mark grammatical number (singular, dual, plural) or express less mathematically exact quantities, like "some," "many," "few," "all," and so forth.

In many Oceanic languages, numerals and quantifiers function as stative verbs. The following Fijian examples illustrate this.

Fijian

E	*moce*	*na*	*gone.*
he	sleep	the	child

'The child slept/is sleeping.'

E	*dua*	*na*	*gone.*
he	one	the	child

'(There is) one child.'

Two features of such systems are (1) that a noun modified by a numeral occurs in what is effectively a relative clause in the sentence, and (2) that numerals above one usually take singular rather than plural subject markers.

Fijian

Erau	*moce*	*e*	*rua*	*na*	*gone.*
they:two	sleep	he	two	the	child

'The two children slept/are sleeping.'

Such systems are common in Polynesia and are also found in some languages in Melanesia.

Tahitian

'Ua	*hoʻi*	*mai*	*na*	*taʻata*	*ʻe*	*toru.*
PAST	return	here	the:PL	person	it:is	three

'Three people came back here.'

Anejom̃

> A   noup̃an is   ithii, is   amen a   natimi is   esej.
> at time   it:PAST one, it:PAST live   SUBJECT person PAST three
> 'Once upon a time, there were three people.'

In most other Oceanic languages—which tend to be those that distinguish adjectives from stative verbs (like Lenakel in 6.2.4 immediately above)—numerals and quantifiers function much like adjectives. That is, they occur within the noun phrase, not as stative verbs. For example:

Manam		**Lenakel**			
aine	rua	peravin	(mil)	kiu	
woman	two	woman	(DUAL)	two	
'two women'		'two women'			
ʻaleti	ʻoʻoʻo	neram	ituga	asuul	(miin)
white:man	many	people	foreign	many	(PL)
'many Europeans'		'many foreigners'			

This is perhaps the commonest pattern among the languages of Melanesia, and it is also found in a few Micronesian languages.

There are in many of these languages, however, vestiges of an earlier system in which the numerals were once stative verbs. Compare the Vinmavis and Lenakel numerals for two through five with the Proto Oceanic forms from which they originate.[8]

	Proto Oceanic	**Vinmavis**	**Lenakel**
'two'	°rua	iru	kiu
'three'	°tolu	itl	kisil
'four'	°vati	ifah	kuvir
'five'	°lima	ilim	katilum

Here we can see that the roots of the numerals have something in front of them: i in Vinmavis, k (+ vowel) in Lenakel. In Vinmavis, i- is a third person singular non-future verbal prefix, and in Lenakel k (+ vowel) is a third person non-singular verbal prefix. Many languages of this type may once have treated numerals as stative verbs, but over time the verbal prefix has become attached to the numeral, and the numeral has lost its verbal nature.

The third kind of system involves what are known as **numeral classifiers**. Some Micronesian languages have an elaborate system of these classifiers, and they are perhaps the best known representatives of this type, although such classifiers also occur in the Admiralty Islands languages. As Rehg says of Ponapean: "Every concrete noun in Ponapean belongs to one or more classes. When we use a numeral with a noun, an appropriate numeral classifier must be employed. More simply stated, the choice of the numeral system one uses is dependent upon what one is counting" (Rehg 1981, 125).

Here are three such numeral systems in Ponapean, with the forms of the numerals one through nine. The words in the second column are used with the word *mwutin* 'heap or pile of.' Those in the third column are used to count stalks of things. And those in the last column are used for counting slices or chips of something.

Ponapean

	'heaps of'	'stalks of'	'slices of'
1	*emwut*	*osop*	*edip*
2	*riemwut*	*riasop*	*riadip*
3	*silimwut*	*silisop*	*silidip*
4	*pahmwut*	*pahsop*	*pahdip*
5	*limmwut*	*limisop*	*limadip*
6	*wenemwut*	*wensop*	*wenedip*
7	*isimwut*	*isisop*	*isidip*
8	*walimwut*	*welisop*	*welidip*
9	*duwamwut*	*duwasop*	*duwadip*

Examples:

Ponapean

mwutin	*dihpw*	*pahmwut*
pile:of	grass	four-CLASSIFIER

'four piles of grass'

sehu	*pah-sop*
sugarcane	four-CLASSIFIER

'four stalks of sugarcane'

dipen	*mei*	*pah-dip*
slice:of	breadfruit	four-CLASSIFIER

'four slices of breadfruit'

As you can see from these examples, the numeral is made up of a morpheme representing the number itself (*sili-* 'three,' *pah-* 'four,' etc.), and a suffix, which is the classifier. Ponapean has *twenty-nine* such classifiers, which include the following (the first three being those exemplified above).

-mwut	used to count heaps or piles
-sop	used to count stalks
-dip	used to count slices, chips, or shavings of something
-pak	used to count times

-pit	used to count strips or strands of something
-mwodol	used to count small round objects
-pali	used to count body extremities
-pwoat	used to count long objects
-men	used to count animate beings

It has as well a general classifier *-u*, which can be used with a range of nouns.

These classifiers may also be used without any numeral, in which case they function as indefinite articles (compare section 6.2.2 in relation to Mokilese).

Ponapean

pwihk men		*tuhke*	*pwoat*
pig	CLASSIFIER	tree	CLASSIFIER
'a pig'		'a tree'	

Other languages in Micronesia with elaborate systems of numeral classifiers include Kiribati (with sixty-six classifiers), Ulithian (forty-three), Trukese, Nauruan, and Yapese. In contrast, Mokilese has only four classifiers and Marshallese only vestiges of a classifier system; Kosraean may have never had a classifier system at all. (See Bender and Wang [1985, 79] for a brief discussion of this.)

The languages of the Kilivila family in the Trobriand Islands in Papua New Guinea (Kilivila, Muyuw, and Budibud) have sets of classifiers like those of Ponapean, but they are used with other items in noun phrases as well (see section 6.2.6). Other Oceanic languages have numeral classifiers, but these systems are more limited than the Micronesian ones. Some Polynesian languages fall into this category. Tongan, for example, requires the classifier *toko* when numerals refer to persons or animals.

Tongan

ha	*kau*	*faifekau*	*'e*	*toko*	*fitu*
a	PL	minister	it:is	CLASSIFIER	seven
'seven ministers'					

Other quantifiers behave similarly. Compare the following Tongan phrase with the one above.

Tongan

ha	*kau*	*faifekau*	*'e*	*toko*	*fiha?*
a	PL	minister	it:is	CLASSIFIER	how:many
'how many ministers?'					

6.2.6. Noun Phrase Structure

As a general rule, articles (where they occur) precede the noun in a noun phrase in Oceanic languages, while adjectives and demonstratives follow the noun. The position of numerals and quantifiers is more variable. In some languages, these precede the noun, in others they follow it. In the examples below, the head noun is underlined to illustrate these patterns.

Labu

gwa	*kege*	*ànì*
canoe	small	one

'a small canoe'

hanô	*anamô*	*maipi*	*lene*
house	big	five	this

'these five big houses'

Banoni

na	*tavana*	*kota*
PL	person	all

'all people'

numa	*ghoom*	*bangana*	*bubu*
house	new	big	red

'the big new red house'

To'aba'ita

roo	*wela*	*loo*	*ki*
two	child	this	PL

'those two children'

nga	*fau*	*ba'ita*
the	stone	big

'a/the big stone'

Port Sandwich

naviis	*xavoi*	*minac*	*ngail*	*pwici*	*isa-n*	*rai*
bow	real	other	PL	all	POSS-his	only

'all his other real bows only'

Ponapean

pwutak	*reirei*	*sili-men-o*
boy	tall	three-CLASSIFIER-that

'those three tall boys'

Kiribati

teni-ua	*te*	*boki*	*akanne*
three-CLASSIFIER	the	book	those

'those three books'

Fijian

na	*wai*	*batabatā*
the	water	cold

'(the) cold water'

na	*vinivō*	*damudamu*	*oqō*
the	dress	red	this

'this red dress'

Tahitian

te	*mau*	*pōti'i*	*purotu*
the	PL	girl	beautiful

'the beautiful girls'

tē-ra	*ta'ata*	*'ino*
the-that	man	bad

'that bad man'

The Kilivila language has a system of classifiers similar to, but much richer than, the Bantu languages of Africa, with close to two hundred different classifiers altogether. Not only numerals, but also demonstratives and adjectives have to be attached to a classifier. The examples below illustrate the use of the classifiers *to* 'male humans' and *bwa* 'trees or wooden things.'

Kilivila

tau	*m-to-na*		*to-kabitam*	
man	this-CLASSIFIER-this		CLASSIFIER-intelligent	

'this intelligent man'

ma-bwa-si-na		*bwa-tolu*		*kai*
this-CLASSIFIER-PL-this		CLASSIFIER-three		tree

'these three trees'

6.3. Possessive Constructions

In virtually all Oceanic languages, the grammar of possession is more complex than it is in English (as mentioned briefly in chapter 2). In this discussion of possession we look first at those languages that most closely reflect the reconstructed Proto Oceanic system, then at major departures from this system.

6.3.1. Possessive Constructions Similar to Proto Oceanic

The languages most closely reflecting the original Proto Oceanic system of possession are found in parts of Island Melanesia, especially the more easterly parts of this region (including Fiji). These languages indicate whether possession is direct or indirect, and then discriminate between several different types of indirect possession.

In **direct possession**, the possessive pronoun is attached directly to the possessed noun. These constructions generally encode a semantic relationship between the possessor and the possessed noun that has been referred to as close, or subordinate, or **inalienable**. They most commonly imply that the possessor has little if any control over the *fact* of possession and are typically used with normally irremovable and integral parts of the body and of things, and with all or some kinship terms. For example:

Paamese

nati-n	*mete-n*
child-his/her	eye-his/her/its
'his/her child'	'his/her/its eye'

Fijian

na	tina-qu		na	ulu-qu
the	mother-my		the	head-my
'my mother'			'my head'	

In **indirect possession**, on the other hand, the possessive pronoun is not attached to the possessed noun, but rather to a separate morpheme that I refer to as a **possessive marker**. These constructions generally encode a relationship between possessor and possessed that can be called remote, or dominant, or **alienable**. They most commonly imply that the possessor has control either over the possession itself or at least over the fact of possession. Such constructions are typically used with items of disposable property, nominalized verbs of which the possessor is the underlying subject, and nouns that the possessor owns or controls in some way or another.

The languages with which I am dealing in this section have a small number of subclasses of indirect possession, each with its own possessive marker. Paamese and Fijian, for example, have the following markers.[9]

Paamese

aa-	food, passive
mo-	drink or for domestic use
so-	social relationship determined by law or custom
ono-	general, active

Fijian

ke-	food, passive
me-	drink
no-	general, active

Some examples:

Paamese

auh	aa-k		ipu	aa-m
yam	POSS:FOOD-my		loss	POSS:PASSIVE-your
'my yam (to eat)'			'your loss/disadvantage'	

oai	mo-m		aisin	mo-n
water	POSS:DRINK-your		clothes	POSS:DOMESTIC-his
'your water (to drink)'			'his/her clothes'	

meteimal	so-m		telai	ono-m
village	POSS:CUSTOM-your		axe	POSS:GENERAL-your
'your village'			'your axe'	

Fijian

na	ke-mu	madrai	na	ke-na	itukutuku
the	POSS:FOOD-your	bread	the	POSS:PASSIVE-his	report

'your bread (to eat)'   'his report (the one made about him)'

na	me-qu	bia	na	no-na	vale
the	POSS:DRINK-my	beer	the	POSS:GENERAL-his	house

'my beer (to drink)'   'his house'

When the possessor is a noun, what is known as a **construct suffix** (abbreviated here C:S) is often added to the possessed noun in a direct construction and to the possessive marker in an indirect construction. In Paamese, for example, the construct suffix is -*n*:

Paamese

mete-n	huli		kailu
eye-C:S	dog		DUAL

'the two dogs' eyes'

vakili	one-n		isei?
canoe	POSS:GENERAL-C:S		who

'whose canoe?'

The distinction between direct and indirect possession, and between the various types of indirect possession, depends partly on the semantics of the possessed noun and partly on the nature of the relationship between the possessor and the possessed. It follows, therefore, that at least some nouns may participate in more than one kind of possessive construction, depending on the nature of that relationship. For example:

Fijian

na	yaca-qu		na	no-qu	yaca
the	name-my		the	POSS:GENERAL-my	name

'my name'   'my namesake'

na	ke-na	niu	na	me-na	niu
the	POSS:FOOD-his	coconut	the	POSS:DRINK-his	coconut

'his coconut (meat, to eat)'   'his coconut (water, to drink)'

na	ke-mu	itaba	na	no-mu	itaba
the	POSS:PASSIVE-your	photo	the	POSS:GENERAL-your	photo

'your photo (the one taken of you)'   'your photo (the one you took or have)'

6.3.2. *Simplification of Indirect Possession*

One common departure from this original system, the loss of contrast between some or all of the half-dozen or so indirect possessive subtypes, is widespread in western Melanesia and occurs also in parts of Micronesia (for example, in Yapese and Kiribati). Many of the languages of New Guinea and Solomon Islands distinguish direct and indirect constructions, but have only two indirect possessive markers. One of these refers to food and drink (and often to items involved in producing or cooking food), and the other to all other alienable possessions. In Manam, the markers are *'ana-* (food and drink) and *ne-* (other):

Manam

mata-ng		*tama-gu*	
eye-your		father-my	
'your eye'		'my father'	

bang	*'ana-gu*	*suru*	*'ana-Ø*
taro	POSS:FOOD-my	soup	POSS:FOOD-his
'my taro'		'his soup'	

uma	*'ana-ng*	*'aula*	*'ana-gu*
garden	POSS:FOOD-your	fishhook	POSS:FOOD-my
'your garden'		'my fishhook'	

'usi	*ne-gu*	*mata*	*ne-da*
lavalava	POSS:GENERAL-my	custom	POSS:GENERAL-our:INC
'my lavalava'		'our custom'	

Other languages—distributed somewhat randomly throughout this area—simply contrast direct and indirect constructions, with no subclassification of indirect possession:

Sye

noru-g		*etme-n*	
hand-my		father-his	
'my hand'		'his/her father'	

nimo	*horu-g*	*nup*	*horo-m*
house	POSS-my	yam	POSS-your
'my house'		'your yam'	

Kiribati

tina-na		*kuni-u*	
mother-his		skin-my	
'his mother'		'my skin'	

a-na	*boki*	*a-u*	*ben*
POSS-his	book	POSS-my	coconut
'his book'		'my coconut'	

6.3.3. Development of Classifier Systems

By contrast, some Oceanic languages have developed a complex system of classifiers (similar to those discussed in relation to the numerals) to mark categories of indirect possession.[10] Many Micronesian languages fall into this category, as do a few in Melanesia (like Iaai in the Loyalty Islands).

Ponapean, like almost all Oceanic languages, distinguishes direct and indirect constructions:

Ponapean

moange-i	*nime-i*	*uhpw*
head-my	CLASSIFIER-my	coconut
'my head'	'my drinking coconut'	

Indirectly possessed nouns belong to a number of different classes in Ponapean, the members of each class usually having some semantic feature that distinguishes them from other nouns. **Possessive classifiers** mark the noun as belonging to a particular class, and possessive suffixes and the construct suffix are attached to these classifiers. There are more than twenty possessive classifiers in Ponapean, some of which are:

Ponapean

Classifier	Used with nouns referring to
kene-	edible things
nime-	drinkable things
sapwe-	land
were-	vehicles
kie-	things to sleep on
ipe-	things used as coverings
pelie-	peers, counterparts, opponents
mware-	garlands, names, titles
nah-	small or precious things, and people or things over which the possessor has a dominant relationship

There is also a general classifier *ah-*, which is used with nouns that do not fall into any other class. Examples:

Ponapean

ah-i seht	'my shirt'
ah-i pwutak	'my boyfriend'

ah-i mahi	'my breadfruit tree'
ah-i rong	'my news'

Many nouns may occur with more than one classifier, with slight semantic changes. So the noun *pwihk* 'pig' may be possessed with the dominant classifier *nah-*, the general classifier *ah-*, and the edible classifier *kene-*, each with different meanings:

Ponapean

nah-i pwihk	'my (live) pig'
ah-i pwihk	'my (butchered) pig'
kene-i pwihk	'my pork, my pig (as food)'

The system in Iaai is similar to that of Micronesian languages like Ponapean. Kinship terms, body parts, and certain other nouns closely related to the possessor are directly possessed.

Iaai

hinyö-k	*ba-n*
mother-my	head-his
'my mother'	'his/her head'
hwakeci-m	*i-fuuc-in*
custom-your	NOM-speak-his
'your custom'	'his/her way of speaking'

But there is also quite a large number of markers used in indirect constructions.

Iaai

a-	food
bele-	drink
hanii-	something caught (e.g., through hunting or fishing)
höne-	a contribution
hwa-	a noise
iie-	a piece of something to chew
ii-	land
dee-	a road
hnââ-	something done to one
anyi-	general (none of the above)

Examples include:

Iaai

anyi-k	*thaan*	*a-n*	*könying*
CLASSIFIER-my	chief	CLASSIFIER-his	taro
'my chief'		'his taro (to eat)'	

bele-n		*trii*	*hanii-ny*		*wââ*
CLASSIFIER-his		tea	CLASSIFIER-his		fish
'her tea (to drink)'			'his fish (which he caught)'		

There are also specific possessive markers in Iaai. These are derived from nouns and are used to indicate possession of those same (or related) nouns.

Iaai

umwö-k uma	'my house'
nuu-k nu	'my coconut tree'
huu-k hu	'my boat'
waii-k wai	'my reef'

6.3.4. Loss of Direct Constructions

A few languages in the New Guinea area, and Rotuman and all the Polynesian languages, have for the most part lost the distinction between direct and indirect constructions. Only indirect constructions are used.[11] In Labu, for example, there is only one set of possessive pronouns, and it is used with all nouns.

Labu

yê	*na*	*ana*	*yê*	*na*	*hanô*
you	your	mother	you	your	house
'your mother'			'your house'		

Rotuman has two indirect possessive-markers: *'e(n)*, used with possessed nouns that refer to food, drink, a person's turn at doing something, and with some nouns to do with contests and challenges, and *'o(n)*, used with all other nouns, including kinship terms and nouns referring to parts of things.

Rotuman

'e-n	*'a 'ana*	*'a 'an*	*'e*	*le*	*Fauholi*
POSS:FOOD-his	taro	taro	POSS:FOOD	the:PERSONAL	Fauholi
'his taro'		'Fauholi's taro'			

'o-n	*lele 'a*	*'o-n*		*'ala*
POSS:GENERAL-his	children	POSS:GENERAL-his		teeth
'his children'		'his teeth'		

'o-n	*'eap*	*'eap*	*'o*	*le*	*Fauholi*
POSS:GENERAL-his	mat	mat	POSS:GENERAL	the:PERSONAL	
					Fauholi
'his mat'		'Fauholi's mat'			

Almost all Polynesian languages (except Niuean and Takuu) have retained the dichotomy between inalienable (or subordinate) and alienable (or dominant) possession, but this is expressed by two different indirect constructions. Generally speaking, inalienable or subordinate possession is expressed by a possessive morpheme based on the vowel *o*, while alienable or dominant possession is expressed with the vowel *a*. For example:

Samoan

'o	*lo̱-'u*	*tama*	*'o*	*le*	*ulu*	*o̱*	*Tavita*
FOCUS	POSS-my	father	FOCUS	the	head	POSS	DAVID

'my father' | 'David's head'

'o	*la̱-'u*	*ta'avale*	*'o*	*le*	*naifi*	*a̱*	*Tavita*
FOCUS	POSS-my	car	FOCUS	the	knife	POSS	David

'my car' | 'David's knife'

Nukuoro[12]

to̱ -no	*potu*	*te*	*potu*	*o̱*	*Soan*
POSS-his	wife	the	wife	POSS	John

'his wife' | 'John's wife'

ta̱-na	*naivi*	*te*	*naivi*	*a̱*	*Soan*
POSS-his	knife	the	knife	POSS	John

'his knife' | 'John's knife'

As in most other languages we have looked at, there are many examples of the same noun being possessed in both constructions, with a concomitant semantic difference.

Nukuoro

to-ku	*ngavesi*	*ta-ku*	*ngavesi*
'POSS-my	box	'POSS-my	box

'my coffin' | 'my storage box'

to-no	*potopoto*	*ta-na*	*potopoto*
POSS-his	short	POSS-his	short

'his shortness (permanent condition)' | 'his shortness (temporary condition, as when hunched over)'

te kkai	*o*	*Vave*	*te kkai*	*a*	*Vave*
the story	POSS	Vave	the story	POSS	Vave

'Vave's story (told about him)' | 'Vave's story (that he tells)'

Niuean has lost even this distinction, using only *a-* forms in all cases:

Niuean

haa-ku	*ihu*		*haa-ku*	*fale*
POSS-my	nose		POSS-my	house
'my nose'			'my house'	

6.4. Verbs and the Verb Complex

I use the term **verb complex** to refer to a phrase consisting of a **verb**, which may be preceded and followed by **particles** of various kinds.[13] In some Oceanic languages, the verb itself is fairly simple in structure, but numerous particles may occur in a verb complex. In others, a verb may take quite a number of prefixes and suffixes, and the verb complex is usually simpler in structure.

6.4.1. General Structure of the Verb

It is common in many Oceanic languages for the verb to consist simply of the **verb root** (underlined in the next set of examples), with no prefixes or suffixes. This is particularly true of the Micronesian and Polynesian languages, but is also common in languages of Melanesia.

Nehan

A	*mahoh*	*ene*	*pak-e*		*rikin*	*wah*.
the	old	this	should-he:NONPAST		lie	rest

'This old man should lie down and rest.'

Toʻabaʻita

Nau	*ku*	*biʾi*	*fula*.
I	I	just:now	arrive

'I arrived just now.'

Aʻjië

Gö	*yé*	*vi*	*köyö*.
I	will	CONTINUOUS	play

'I am going to go on playing.'

Ponapean

Soulik	*kin*	*pirida*	*kuloak*	*isuh*.
Soulik	HABITUAL	get:up	clock	seven

'Soulik gets up at seven o'clock.'

Fijian

E	*lailai*	na	*vale*.
it	small	the	house

'The house is small.'

Rotuman

'Eap	ta	la	hoa'.
mat	the	FUTURE	take

'The mat will be taken.'

Māori

I	kai	te	*rangatira*.
PAST	eat	the	chief

'The chief ate.'

Languages of this type do, however, have a fairly small set of verbal prefixes and suffixes. The most frequently used prefixes mark causativity (see the Toʻabaʻita example below) and reciprocality (Aʻjië), while suffixes commonly mark the person and number of the object (Toʻabaʻita, Aʻjië), transitivity (Fijian), or the passive (Māori).

Toʻabaʻita

Nia	'e	faʻa-faalu-a	rabo'a.
he	he	CAUSATIVE-clean-it	bowl

'He cleaned the bowl.'

Aʻjië

Curu	vi-ya'-ru.
they:two	RECIPROCAL-hit-them:two

'They hit each other.'

Fijian

E	rai-ci	ira.
he	see-TRANS	them

'He saw them.'

Māori

Ka	pūhi-a	te	poaka	e	wai?
INCEPTIVE	shoot-PASSIVE	the	pig	by	who

'By whom was the pig shot?'

Grammatical features that are marked by particles in languages like these are marked by prefixes in another set of languages found mainly in Melanesia. In these languages, the verb root almost never occurs alone. When it does, it marks the (singular) imperative.

Lenakel

Amnuumw!
drink
'Drink (it)!'

In such languages, however, verbs typically take prefixes and suffixes marking subject, tense-aspect, and a range of other grammatical features. In the examples below, the verb root is underlined:

Manam

'U-lele-'ama.
you-look:for-us:EXC
'You looked for us.'

Ma'asi-lo   i-ngara-ngara.
ocean-in   he-CONTINUOUS-swim
'He is swimming in the ocean.'

Natu   i-laba-doi.
child   he-big-COMPLETIVE
'The child has grown up.'

Robu'a   i-ro-ro'a'-i-ramo-la.
rubbish   it-HABITUAL-throw-them-randomly-persistently
'He keeps throwing rubbish all over the place.'

Lenakel

R-im-kɨn   mun   akɨn.
he-PAST-eat   again   very
'He ate a lot again.'

K-n-ai-ami   ru   apus   am   nɨkom.
they-COMPLETIVE-PL-urinate   try   extinguished   just   fire
'They just tried to put the fire out by urinating on it.'

K-ɨm-am-ai-akar-atu-pn   kam   ilar   miin.
they-PAST-CONTINUOUS-PL-talk-   to   they   PL
   RECIPROCAL-there
'They (pl.) were talking to one another.'

K-ɨm-uɨni-uas   to   nahuto.
they-PAST-DUAL-say-together   to   crowd
'They were both talking at once to the crowd.'

6.4.2. Tense, Aspect, and Mood

Tense refers to the time of the action or state referred to by the verb. For example, in English one makes a basic tense distinction between past, present, and future. **Aspect** refers to the way in which the action is carried out or is seen to be carried out. English distinguishes completive, habitual, continuous, and punctiliar aspects in each tense.[14] In many languages, there are some markers of tense, some of aspect, and some that mark a combination of tense and aspect. Descriptions of these languages often refer to the **tense-aspect** system.

Some languages have tense systems similar to or simpler than that of English. For example, Fijian has only two markers of tense, *ā* 'past' and *na* 'future,' which are particles coming before the verb. The past tense marker is optional once the time has been established, as in the second example below:

Fijian

E	*ā*	*lako*	*mai*	*o*		*Jone.*
he	PAST	go	here	the:PERSONAL		John

'John came.'

E	*nanoa,*	*e*	*(ā)*	*lako*	*mai*	*o*	*Jone.*
on	yesterday,	he	(PAST)	go	here	the:PERSONAL	John

'John came yesterday.'

E	*na*	*lako*	*mai*	*o*		*Jone.*
he	FUTURE	go	here	the:PERSONAL		John

'John will come.'

Rotuman has only one tense-marker, *la* (sometimes *tæla*), which marks the future. The non-future is unmarked.

Rotuman

Ia	*ʻea*	*ia*	*la*	*leum.*
he	say	he	FUTURE	come

'He says he will come.' or 'He said he would come.'

Tɔn	*ta*	*sun-ʻia.*
water	the	hot-STATIVE

'The water is (now) hot.'

Fā	*ta*	*leume-a.*
man	the	come-COMPLETIVE

'The man has already come.'

Other languages have more complex tense systems than that of English. Lenakel, for example, distinguishes four non-future tenses:

Lenakel

n-<u>ak</u>-ol	'you do it'
n-<u>i</u>m-ol	'you did it'
n-<u>n</u>-ol	'you have done it'
n-<u>ep</u>-ol	'you did it (after you did something else)'

A future prefix, *t-*, can be used in combination with two of the tense prefixes above to produce two different future tenses.

Lenakel

<u>t</u>-n-<u>ak</u>-ol	'you will do it soon'
<u>t</u>-n-<u>ep</u>-ol	'you will do it some time later'

In yet other languages, tense is not really marked at all. Let us consider what Rehg (1981, 268) has to say about Ponapean:

> Ponapean may be described as a **tenseless** language. This is not to say that in Ponapean it is impossible to express notions of time. . . . What is meant by saying that Ponapean is tenseless is that it expresses considerations of time in a way different from English. Rather than using a tense system to signal time relations, Ponapean employs what we will call an **aspect system**. The basic difference between these two systems is this: in a tense system, **when** an event occurred is important; in an aspect system, the **time contour** of the event is crucial.

This idea of a *time contour* can be clarified by looking at four aspects marked in Ponapean:

1. **Habitual** aspect is marked by the preverbal particle *kin*: this implies that the action is or was a customary or habitual one, which is or was done regularly.
2. **Continuous** aspect (Rehg calls this "durative"), marked by reduplicating the verb, signals that the action or state of the verb is carried out or takes place over some length of time.
3. **Completive** aspect, marked by the suffix *-ehr*, indicates that the action has reached or is on the way to reaching some kind of conclusion or completion.
4. **Irrealis** aspect, marked by the preverbal particle *pahn*, implies that the action is not complete or realized (often it corresponds to a future tense in other languages).

Some examples:

Ponapean

Soulik	<u>*kin*</u>	*kang*	*rais.*
Soulik	HABITUAL	eat	rice

'Soulik eats rice.'

Soulik	<u>*kang*</u>-*kang*	*rais.*
Soulik	CONTINUOUS-eat	rice

'Soulik is eating rice.'

Soulik	*kang*-<u>*ehr*</u>	*rais.*
Soulik	eat-COMPLETIVE	rice

'Soulik has eaten rice.'

Soulik	<u>*pahn*</u>	*kang*	*rais.*
Soulik	IRREALIS	eat	rice

'Soulik will eat rice.'

A verb may also occur without any of these aspect markers, as in:

Ponapean

Soulik	*kang*	*rais.*
Soulik	eat	rice

'Soulik is eating rice,' 'Soulik ate rice,' etc.

This simply indicates that Soulik was involved in eating rice. No time is specified, although this can of course be included if it is necessary:

Ponapean

Soulik	*kang*	*rais*	*nan*	*sounpar*	*samwalahro.*
Soulik	eat	rice	on	year	last

'Soulik ate rice last year.'

Soulik	*kang*	*rais*	*met.*
Soulik	eat	rice	now

'Soulik is eating rice now.'

Ponapean illustrates the use of an aspect rather than a tense system. As I mentioned above, however, many Oceanic languages have particles or affixes that mark both tense and aspect. Here is the list of Māori tense-aspect particles:

Māori

ka	inceptive	Beginning of a new action
i	past	Action in the past
kua	completive	Action (fairly recently) completed
kia	desiderative	Desirability of an action
me	prescriptive	Action should take place
e	non-past	Present or future (when used with *ana* following the verb, indicates incomplete or continuous action)

| *kei* | warning | 'Don't' or 'lest' |
| *ina* | conditional | 'If' or 'when' |

Examples:

Māori

| *Ka* | *takoto* | *te* | *tamaiti* | *ka* | | *moe.* |
| INCEPTIVE | lie | the | child | INCEPTIVE | | sleep |

'The child lay down and slept.'

| *Kua* | *mate* | *ta-ku* | *hoa.* |
| COMPLETIVE | die | POSS-my | friend |

'My friend has died.'

| *Me* | *hoki* | *te* | *tamaiti* | *ra* | *ki* | | *te* | *kāinga.* |
| PRESCRIPTIVE | return | the | child | that | to | | the | home |

'That child should go home.'

| *E* | *haere* | *ana* | | *te* | *wahine* | *ki* | *te* | *moana.* |
| NONPAST | go | CONTINUOUS | | the | woman | to | the | sea |

'The woman is going to the sea.'

Kia	*āta*	*kōrero*	*tātou*	*kei*	*rongo mai*	*a-ku*		*hoa.*
DESIDE-	careful	talk	we: INC	LEST	hear	here	POSS:PL-my	friend
RATIVE								

'We should talk quietly lest my friends hear.'

A final set of examples, from Nakanamanga, illustrates a different feature, the concept of mood, and shows a pattern of root-initial consonant alternation that is found in a few areas within Oceanic (particularly central Vanuatu and the Morobe Province of Papua New Guinea). **Mood** (sometimes referred to as **modality**) does not relate so much to time as to actuality. An actual state or event is said to be in the **realis** mood, while a nonreal or non-actual state or event is in the **irrealis** mood. Realis often refers to something that happened, is happening, or will definitely happen, whereas irrealis refers to something that only might take place. Oceanic (and other) languages differ in the treatment of negatives. In some languages, the negative is in the realis mode (because it actually did not happen); in others, it is in the irrealis mode, because the action was not real.

Nakanamanga has a set of preverbal particles marking tense-aspect. Some of these are used in realis mood, others in irrealis mood. It is also one of the many central Vanuatu languages in which there is alternation between some initial consonants of verbs. Verbs with initial *v, w, k,* and *r* retain these consonants in irrealis mood, but change them to *p, p̃, g,* and *t,* respectively, after any preverbal particle. (The verb root is underlined in the examples.)

Nakanamanga

Irrealis mood			Realis mood		
a	*ga*	*vano*	*e*		*pano*
I	INTENTIONAL	go	he		go
'I'm going'			'he goes'		
e	*pe*	*rogo*	*e*	*poo*	*togo*
he	CONDITIONAL	hear	he	COMPLETIVE	hear
'if he hears'			'he has heard'		

6.4.3. Subject

Most Oceanic languages mark the person and the number of the subject somewhere in the verb complex—either as a prefix to the verb, or as a preverbal particle.[15] In some cases, a single morpheme marks both person and number:

Paamese

Na-mūmon   *alok.*
I-make:it   pudding
'I made the pudding.'

Ro-mūmon   *alok.*
we:INC-make:it   pudding
'We (inclusive) made the pudding.'

Ma-mūmon   *alok.*
we:EXC-make:it   pudding
'We (exclusive) made the pudding.'

Kiribati

E   *ata-ai.*
he   know-me
'He knows me.'

A   *ata-ai.*
they   know-me
'They know me.'

In other languages, person and number are marked by separate morphemes:

Lenakel

<u>N</u>-ak-am-kɨn   *menuk*   *ua*?
you-PRESENT-CONTINUOUS-eat   chicken   or
'Are you (singular) eating chicken?'

<u>N</u>-ak-am-<u>ia</u>-kɨn   *menuk*   *ua*?
you-PRESENT-CONTINUOUS-DUAL-eat   chicken   or
'Are you two eating chicken?'

<u>N</u>-ak-am-<u>ar</u>-kɨn   *menuk*   *ua*?
you-PRESENT-CONTINUOUS-PL-eat   chicken   or
'Are you (plural) eating chicken?'

In a number of languages in Melanesia, the marking of tense-aspect or mood is combined with the marking of the subject's person and number in a single morpheme. Manam, for example, has two sets of subject prefixes to verbs, one used in realis mood and the other in irrealis mood:

Manam

	Singular			**Plural**	
	Realis	Irrealis		Realis	Irrealis
1	*u-*	*m-*	1 INC	*ta-*	*ta-*
2	*ʻu-*	*go-*	1 EXC	*ʻi-*	*ga-*
3	*i-*	*nga-*	2	*ʻa-*	*ʻama-*
			3	*di-*	*da-*

For example:

Manam

Eu   *i-mate.*
dog   it:REALIS-die
'The dog died.'

Eu   *nga-mate*   *ʻana.*
dog   it:IRREALIS-die   likely
'The dog's going to die.'

In languages like these, the subject marker occurs whether the subject is a full noun phrase or a pronoun, and whether that subject is expressed in the sentence or not. By contrast, languages in western Polynesia use preverbal subject-marking pronouns only when the subject is a pronoun:

Tongan

Naʻe	*ʻalu*	*ʻa*	*e*	*tangata.* (noun phrase subject)
PAST	go	SUBJECT	the	man

'The man went.'

Naʻa	*ne*	*ʻalu.* (pronoun subject)
PAST	he	go

'He went.'

Samoan

Ua	*sau*	*le*	*aliʻi.* (noun phrase subject)
COMPLETIVE	come	the	chief

'The chief has come.'

Ua	*ʻou*	*sau.* (pronoun subject)
COMPLETIVE	I	come

'I have come.'

Languages in eastern Polynesia have lost this preverbal subject-marking system altogether:

Tahitian

ʻUa	*tāpū*	*te*	*vahine*	*ʻi*	*te*	*vahie.* (noun phrase subject)
PAST	cut	the	woman	OBJECT	the	wood

'The woman cut the wood.'

ʻUa	*tāpū*	*vau*	*ʻi*	*te*	*vahie.* (pronoun subject)
PAST	cut	I	OBJECT	the	wood

'I cut the wood.'

6.4.4. Object and Transitivity

Most Oceanic languages have suffixes that mark a verb as **transitive**—that is, as having an object.

Nakanamanga

A	*ga*	*munu.*
I	INTENTIONAL	drink

'I'll drink.'

A	*ga*	*munu-gi*	*noai*	*naga.*
I	INTENTIONAL	drink-TRANS	water	that

'I'll drink that water.'

Fijian

E	*bulu.*
he	bury

'He/she/it is buried.'

E	*bulu-t̲-a*	*na*	*benu.*
he	bury-TRANS-it	the	rubbish

'He/she buried the rubbish.'

There are a number of features of the marking of transitive and object. The first is the form of the transitive suffix. In many languages this is simply *-i*:

Anejom̃

Adap̃o-i	*upni*	*yin*	*aak!*
cover-TRANS	good	him	you

'Cover him up well!'

In other languages, however, the transitive suffix is *-Ci*, where *C* is a **thematic consonant**. This consonant (1) is not present when the root occurs by itself, (2) *is* present when the suffix is added, and (3) is different with different verbs. Look at the following Fijian intransitive and transitive verbs (the transitive is in the form used before a pronoun or proper noun).

Fijian

Intransitive	Transitive	
bulu	*bulu-ti*	'bury'
rai	*rai-ci*	'see'
tuku	*tuku-ni*	'tell'
kaci	*kaci-vi*	'call'
viri	*viri-ki*	'throw at'
kila	*kila-i*	'know'

As you can see from the examples, the form of the suffix (which is sometimes simply *-i*) is unpredictable. One simply has to learn that *bulu*, for example, takes *-ti*, but *rai* takes *-ci*.[16]

The second feature is that many Oceanic languages in fact have two transitive suffixes, the first deriving from Proto Oceanic °-*i* and the second from °-*aki* or °-*akini*. This second suffix is sometimes called the **applicative**. It often refers to the instrument with which the action is carried out, the reason for performing the action, or some other more indirect transitive notion. In the Fijian examples below, I have used the form of the suffix that incorporates a third person singular object *-a*. In Fijian, *-Ci-a* becomes *-Ca*, and *-Caki-a* becomes *-Caka*. In some cases the thematic consonant is the same in both suffixes.

Fijian

Transitive		Applicative	
cici-va	'run for it'	*cici-vaka*	'run with it'
cabe-ta	'ascend it'	*cabe-taka*	'ascend with it'
oso-va	'bark at it'	*oso-vaka*	'bark because of it'
uso-ra	'poke it'	*uso-raka*	'poke with it'

In other cases, the thematic consonants are different.

Fijian

Transitive		Applicative	
kaki-a	'scrape it'	*kaki-taka*	'scrape with it'
yaqa-va	'crawl to it'	*yaqa-taka*	'crawl with it'
masu-ta	'pray to it'	*masu-laka*	'pray for it'
tala-a	'send him'	*taka-vaka*	'send it'

Mention of the Fijian third person singular object suffix -*a* brings us to a third feature, the specific marking of object. Marking the object's person and number within the verb complex is less common than marking subject or transitivity. For example, although in Lenakel separate prefixes mark both the person and the number of the subject, and although some verbs take a transitive suffix, the object is not marked in the verb complex at all. Even pronominal objects occur as free forms.[17]

Lenakel

> *R-ɨm-eiua-in*   *mun*   <u>*iik*</u>.
> he-PAST-lie-TRANS   again   you
> 'He lied to you again.'

A large number of languages, however, do mark the person and the number of the object within the verb complex, either with a suffix to the verb (as in Manam and Kiribati) or as a postposed verbal particle (as in Fijian):

Manam

> *Bang*   *u-naghu-sereʻ-<u>i</u>*.
> taro   I:REALIS-pierce-split-it
> 'I split the taro by piercing it.'

Kiribati

> *E*   *ata-<u>a</u>*   *tama-u*.
> he   know-him   father-my
> 'He knows my father.'

Fijian

E	ā	rai-ci	*irau*	na	yalewa.
he	PAST	see-TRANS	them:two	the	woman

'He saw the two women.'

Generally, if a language has transitive and object suffixes, both occur suffixed to the verb in that order.[18]

Ulithian

Yule-*mi*-*ya*	cale	lee!
drink-TRANS-it	water	this

'Drink this water!'

Xa-*si*-*ya*	doxo	cale	laa!
carry-TRANS-it	here	water	that

'Bring that water here!'

In other languages, the object suffix occurs when the object is a pronoun, but not when it is a noun or noun phrase.

Nakanamanga

A	ga	munu-*gi*-*a*.
I	INTENTIONAL	drink-TRANS-it (pronoun object)

'I'll drink it.'

A	ga	munu-*gi*	noai	naga.
I	INTENTIONAL	drink-TRANS	water	that (noun object)

'I'll drink that water.'

6.4.5. The Passive

Only a small number of Oceanic languages contrast active and passive voice. A couple of Micronesian languages mark the passive by means of a suffix to the verb (e.g., Kosraean -*yuhk*). The example below contrasts an active sentence with the corresponding passive one.

Kosraean

Tuhlihk	sacn	tuhlakihn	pinsuhl	nuhtih-k	ah.
child	that	snatch	pencil	CLASSIFIER-my	the

'That child snatched my pencil.'

Pinsuhl	nuhtih-k	ah	tuhlakihn-*yuhk*	(sin	tuhlihk	sacn).
pencil	CLASSIFIER-my	the	snatch-PASSIVE	(by	child	that)

'My pencil was snatched (by that child).'

Most languages of eastern Polynesia have a passive. This is usually marked
by the suffix *-Cia*, where *C* once again represents a thematic consonant.[19]
Examples:

Hawaiian

Ua		*'ai*	*ka*	*mākaʻi*	*i*	*ka*	*poi.*
COMPLETIVE		eat	the	policeman	OBJECT	the	poi

'The policeman ate the poi.'

Ua		*'ai-ia*	*ka*	*poi*	*(e*	*ka*	*mākaʻi).*
COMPLETIVE		eat-PASSIVE	the	poi	(by	the	policeman)

'The poi was eaten (by the policeman).'

Māori

I	*inu*	*te*	*tangata*	*i*	*te*	*wai.*
PAST	drink	the	man	OBJECT	the	water

'The man drank the water.'

I	*inu-mia*	*te*	*wai*	*(e*	*te*	*tangata).*
PAST	drink-PASSIVE	the	water	(by	the	man)

'The water was drunk (by the man).'

Tahitian

'Ua	*hohoni*	*te*	*uri*	*'i*	*te*	*tamaiti.*
PAST	bite	the	dog	OBJECT	the	boy

'The dog bit the boy.'

Ua	*hohoni-hia*	*te*	*tamaiti*	*('et*	*e*	*uri).*
PAST	bite-PASSIVE	the	boy	(by	the	dog)

'The boy was bitten (by the dog).'

In examples of the passive given so far, I have put the agent in paren-
theses. In these languages a passive sentence may occur with or without
an agent.

Tahitian

'Ua	*hohoni-hia*	*te*	*tamaiti*	*'e*	*te*	*uri.*
PAST	bite-PASSIVE	the	boy	by	the	dog

'The boy was bitten <u>by the dog</u>.' (agent specified)

'Ua	*hohoni-hia*	*te*	*tamaiti.*
PAST	bite-PASSIVE	the	boy

'The boy was bitten.' (no agent specified)

Very few languages in Melanesia have a passive. Those that do are spoken in the western Solomons. In these languages, only the passive *without* agent is permitted. Indeed, in Roviana at least, the passive is used only when the agent is generic or is not recoverable from the context.

Roviana

Seke-a	*sa*	*tie*	*sa*	*siki.*
hit-it	the	man	the	dog

'The man hit the dog.'

Ta-seke	*sa*	*siki.*
PASSIVE-hit	the	dog

'The dog was hit.'

6.4.6. The Causative and the Reciprocal

A very widespread **causative** prefix in Oceanic languages whose form derives from Proto Oceanic °*paka-* expresses the notion that the subject makes or causes the action of the verb to happen. The causative can convert a stative or an intransitive verb into a transitive one.

Fijian

E davo-r-a.
he lie-TRANS-it
'He lay on it.'

E	*vaka-davo-r-a.*
he	CAUSATIVE-lie-TRANS-it

'He made him/her/it lie down.'

Further examples of this function are:

Manam

Dang	*i-aʻa-gita-i.*
water	he-CAUSATIVE-hot-it

'He heated the water.'

Roviana

Lopu	*va-mate*	*tie*	*si*	*rau.*
not	CAUSATIVE-die	person	SUBJECT	I

'I didn't kill anybody.'

Mokilese

Lih-o	*ka-loau-i*		*mwingeh-u.*
woman-the	CAUSATIVE-be:cooked-TRANS		food-the

'The woman made sure the food was cooked.'

West Futuna

Ne-i	*faka-sara*	*aia*	*ta*	*vetoka.*
PAST-he	CAUSATIVE-be:open	he	the	door

'He opened the door.'

The causative prefix often has a number of other functions in these languages. One common one is to form ordinal or multiplicative numerals from cardinal numerals, which are stative verbs.[20]

Kiribati

teniua	'three'	*ka-teniua*	'third'
nimaua	'five'	*ka-nimaua*	'fifth'

Samoan

lua	'two'	*faʻa-lua*	'twice'
tolu	'three'	*faʻa-tolu*	'three times'

There is also a widespread **reciprocal** prefix deriving from Proto Oceanic **paRi-*, that marks both reciprocality (the subjects perform the action on each other) and often also mutual, common, united, or concerted action. The following pair of examples illustrates reciprocality.

Fijian

E	*loma-ni*	*koya.*
he	love-TRANS	she

'He loves her.'

Erau	*vei-loma-ni.*
they:two	RECIPROCAL-love-TRANS

'They (two) love each other.'

The next examples show concerted action.

Fijian

Era	*butu-k-a.*
they	tread-TRANS-it

'They trod on it.'

Era	*vei-butu-yak-a.*
they	CONCERTED-tread-TRANS-it

'They trampled it all over.'

Samoan has taken this one step further. There the reciprocal prefix *fe-*, in addition to normal reciprocal functions, has also come to mark some verbs as having plural subjects (perhaps deriving from the idea of united or concerted action).

Samoan

Singular	Plural	
aʻa	*fe-aʻa*	'kick'
inu	*fe-inu*	'drink'
fefe	*fe-fefe*	'be afraid'
tagi	*fe-tagi-si*	'cry'
oso	*fe-oso-fi*	'jump'

6.4.7. The Structure of the Verb Complex

In some Oceanic languages, the verb root may take a fairly large number of verbal affixes, but the verb complex usually contains relatively few particles. Languages of this type are mainly found in Melanesia, though not all Melanesian languages fit this pattern. There is no clear correlation between the morphological complexity of the verb and the geographical location or genetic affiliation of the language.

In other languages—especially those of Polynesia, Micronesia, Fiji, and some parts of Melanesia—the verb is simpler morphologically. The verb complex usually contains a number of particles, marking tense, aspect, and various other adverbial features.

This difference can best be illustrated by looking at a couple of verb complexes in two languages: Fijian, which uses a range of preverbal and postverbal particles, and Lenakel, which relies heavily on affixes. The Fijian examples below are from Schütz (1985), while the Lenakel sentences are translations of these. The verb root is underlined in each example.

Fijian

E	*sā*	*qai*	<u>*tau*</u>-*r-a*	*mai.*	
she	ASPECT	then	bring-TRANS-it	here	

'Then she brought it here.'

Eratou	*sā*	<u>*lako*</u>	*vata*	*sara*	*yani.*
they:few	ASPECT	go	together	intensive	there

'They (few) went off there together.'

E	*ā*	<u>*wili*</u>-*k-a*	*tale.*	
he	PAST	read-TRANS-it	again	

'He read it again.'

Lenakel

R-ep-<u>os</u>-i-pa.
she-then-take-TRANS-here
'Then she brought it here.'

K-ɨm-hal-<u>vɨn</u>-uas.
they-PAST-TRIAL-go:there-together
'They (three) went off there together.'

R-ɨm-<u>avhi</u>-in   mun.
he-PAST-read-TRANS   again
'He read it again.'

One further complication in Oceanic languages, as in members of many other language families around the world, is that a single verb complex may consist of more than one verb, through a process known as **verb serialization**. Usually, the same participants (like subject and, if a verb is transitive, object) are involved with each verb in the series. The following examples illustrate simple intransitive serialization. Each serialized verb is underlined.

Roviana

Totoso	*<u>ene</u>*	*<u>nuguru</u>*	*<u>la</u>*	*ghami* . . .
when	walk	enter	go	we:EXC

'When we walked in . . .'

<u>Turu</u>	*<u>saghe</u>*	*<u>pule</u>*	*<u>mae</u>*	*si*	*rau.*
stand	rise	return	come	SUBJECT	I

'I stood back up.'

In a transitive sentence, transitivity or an object's features are usually marked only once. In the following example, note that the transitive suffix appears not on the first verb in the series (the transitive verb *seke* 'hit'), but on the last verb (the intransitive verb *mate* 'die').

Roviana

Lopu	*<u>seke</u>*	*<u>mate-i</u>*	*rau*	*pa*	*lima-gu.*
not	hit	die-TRANS:them	I	with	hand-my

'I didn't kill them with my hands.'

Paamese is a language in which negation is marked by a discontinuous affix (see 6.5.4 below), that is, a verb in the negative must take both the prefix *ro-* and the suffix *-tei.*

Paamese

Ni-<u>ro</u>-kan-<u>tei</u>   *ouh.*
I:FUTURE-not-eat-not   yam
'I will not eat the yam.'

In serial constructions in Paamese, the first verb in the series takes the prefix *ro-*, while the last verb takes the suffix *-tei*:

Paamese

Ni-<u>ro</u>-kan   *v̄s-<u>tei</u>*   *ouh.*
I:FUTURE-not-eat   try-not   yam
'I will not try to eat the yam.'

6.5. Sentences

English normally requires sentences to contain (at least) one verb, but Oceanic languages do not. Below I follow Krupa (1982) in distinguishing between **verbal sentences** and **nominal sentences**.

6.5.1. Nominal Sentences

Nominal sentences have no verb. They consist of a subject and a predicate (sometimes referred to as a topic and a comment about that topic), but the predicate is usually a noun phrase specifying a person, thing, place, and so on. In languages in which the subject normally precedes the verb in a verbal sentence (see below), the subject/topic comes before the predicate/comment in nominal sentences:

Subject	**Predicate**

Tolai
Iau   *mamati.*
I   from:here
'I am from here.'

Motu
Ia   na   *tau bada-na.*
he FOCUS   man big-SG
'He is a big/elderly man.'

Toʻabaʻita
Thata-mu   *ni*   *tei?*
name-your   the:PERSONAL who
'What is your name?'

Mokilese
Pediro	*kahdilik-men.*
Pediro	Catholic-CLASSIFIER

'Pedro is a Catholic.'

Rotuman
Ia	*gagaja-t.*
he	chief-a

'He is a chief.'

In languages in which the verb normally precedes the subject (see below), the predicate in a nominal sentence comes before the subject.

Predicate			**Subject**	

Yapese
		Subject	
Chitamngii-g		*Tamag.*	
father-my		Tamag	

'Tamag is my father.'

Roviana
Vineki	*zingazingarana*	*si*	*asa.*
girl	light:skinned	SUBJECT	she

'She is a light-skinned girl.'

Fijian
Na	*ke-na*	*i-liuliu*	*na*	*kānala.*
the	POSS-its	NOM-lead	the	colonel

'The colonel is its leader.'

Tongan
Ko	*e*	*faiako*	*au.*
FOCUS	a	teacher	I

'I am a teacher.'

Māori
He	*kātiro*	*ātāhua*	*a*	*Mārama.*
a	girl	beautiful	the:PERSONAL	Mārama

'Mārama is a beautiful girl.'

Kiribati, in which the verb comes first in a verbal sentence, apparently allows either subject + predicate or predicate + subject with little if any difference in meaning.

Kiribati

Te	beritititenti	ngaia. (subject + predicate)
the	president	he

'He is the president.'

Ngaia	te	beritititenti. (predicate + subject)
he	the	president

'He is the president.'

The translations of all these sentences contain some form of the verb "to be," which is used in equational sentences ("He is the president."), in some kinds of locational sentences ("I am from here."), and so on. Many Oceanic languages have no such verb, expressing equational and locational sentences as nominal sentences.

6.5.2. Accusative and Ergative Languages

In discussing the structure of verbal sentences in Pacific languages (Oceanic and other), we need to introduce a distinction between accusative structures and ergative structures.[21] English, for example, is a wholly **accusative** language. The subjects of transitive and intransitive verbs are marked in the same way, but the object of a transitive verb is marked differently.

For example:

1. *She is sleeping.*
2. *She saw the man.*
3. *The man saw her.*

Sentences (1) and (2) are intransitive and transitive, respectively. Both have *she* as subject. In sentence (3), the form of the object is *her*, not *she*.

The majority of Oceanic languages are accusative languages. In the following examples, the subject is underlined:

Anejom̃

Et	amjeg	*a*	*natam̃añ*	*iyii*.
he	sleep	SUBJECT	man	that

'That man is sleeping.'

Et	ecta-i	natam̃añ	iyii	*a*	*kuri*.
he	see-TRANS	man	that	SUBJECT	dog

'The dog saw that man.'

Et	ecta-i	kuri	*a*	*natam̃añ*	*iyii*.
he	see-TRANS	dog	SUBJECT	man	that

'That man saw the dog.'

Southwest Tanna

Kɨmlu	*i-ɨmn-la-gɨn.*
we:two:EXC	we-PAST DUAL-afraid

'We (two) were afraid.'

K ɨ mlu	*i- ɨ mn-la-hai*	*pukah.*
we:two:EXC	we-PAST-DUAL-stab	pig

'We (two) stabbed the pig.'

Pa	*l- ɨ mn-hai*	*amlu?*
who	he-PAST-stab	us:two:EXC

'Who stabbed us (two)?'

In Anejoṁ, the subject of intransitive and transitive sentences is marked with a preceding *a*, while the object is unmarked. In Southwest Tanna, the subject pronoun in both intransitive and transitive sentences is the same in form (*kɨmlu* 'we two EXC'), but it is *amlu* as the object of a transitive verb. In both languages, the subject is marked by its position in the sentence—at the end in Anejoṁ, at the beginning in Southwest Tanna.

Some Oceanic languages, however, have **ergative** structures. In these structures, the subject of a transitive verb, called the **agent**, is marked in one way (by the **ergative case**), while the subject of an intransitive verb (the **subject**) and the object of a transitive verb (the **object**) are marked differently by the **absolutive case**.

Look at the following examples from Samoan. In the first—intransitive—sentence, the subject is underlined, while in the second and third—transitive—sentences, the agent is underlined.

Samoan

Sa	*ma'i*	*le*	*fafine.*
STATIVE	sick	the	woman

'The woman is sick.'

Na	*mana'o-mia*	*le*	*fafine*	*e*	*le*	*tama.*
PAST	want-TRANS	the	woman	ERGATIVE	the	child

'The child wanted the woman.'

E	*salu-ina*	*e*	*le*	*fafine*	*le*	*fale.*
PRESENT	sweep-TRANS	ERGATIVE	the	woman	the	house

'The woman sweeps the house.'

In Samoan, the absolutive case is unmarked: *le fafine* 'the woman' is subject of the intransitive verb in the first sentence, and object of the transitive verb in the second. In the second and third sentences, however, *le tama* 'the child' and *le fafine* are subjects of the transitive verb and are marked as such by the ergative marker, *e*.

Note a similar pattern in Motu. *Morea* is unmarked in the first two sentences, where it is subject of the intransitive verb and object of the transitive verb, respectively. But when it occurs as subject of the transitive verb, as in the third example, it is marked by the following ergative marker *ese*.

Motu

Morea	*e-mahuta.*		
Morea	he-sleep		
'Morea is sleeping.'			

Boroma	*ese*	*Morea*	*e-ala-ia.*
pig	ERGATIVE	Morea	he-kill-it
'The pig killed Morea.'			

Morea	*ese*	*boroma*	*e-ala-ia.*
Morea	ERGATIVE	pig	he-kill-it
'Morea killed the pig.'			

6.5.3. Basic Structure of Verbal Sentences

Different Oceanic languages have different basic phrase orders. The order of subject, object, and verb within the simple verbal sentence varies from language to language.

SV(O) Languages

In the majority of Oceanic languages, the subject (whether it is a pronoun or a noun phrase) precedes the verb in both intransitive and transitive clauses. In transitive clauses, the object follows the verb. This order is found in most languages of island Melanesia (including many of the Polynesian Outliers), as well as in nearly all languages of Micronesia. For example:

Subject		**Verb**		**Object**

Nakanai

E	*pusi*	*tetala*	*eia*	*parakukuru.*	
the	cat	his	it	black	
'His/her cat is black.'					

E	*Baba*		*kue-a*		*la paia.*
the	Baba		hit-it		the dog
'Baba hit the dog.'					

Labu

Ase	*eme?*
who	come:PAST

'Who came?'

Êmaha	*mô-sôhô*	*hanô.*
we:EXC	we:EXC-build	house

'We built the house.'

To'aba'ita

Nau	*kwa-si*	*mata'i.*
I	I-not	sick

'I am not sick.'

Kini	*'e*	*ngali-a*	*redio.*
woman	she	take-it	radio

'The woman took the radio.'

Paamese

Mail	*he-to.*
Mail	he:DISTANT-bald

'Mail is going bald.'

Letau kail	*a-mūmo-n*	*alok.*
woman PL	they-make-TRANS	pudding

'The women made/are making the pudding.'

Lenakel

Nakankɨp	*r-ɨm-am-apul.*
Nakankɨp	he-PAST-CONTINUOUS-sleep

"Nakankɨp was sleeping."

Pehe	*r-n-os*	*nau*	*ka?*
who	he-COMPLETIVE-take	knife	that

'Who has taken that knife?'

Ponapean

Lamp-o	*pahn*	*pwupwidi.*
lamp-that	FUTURE	fall

'That lamp will fall down.'

Kidi-e	*ngalis*	*Soulik.*
dog-this	bite	Soulik

'This dog bit Soulik.'

S(O)V Languages

While the Oceanic languages of much of the mainland of Papua New Guinea, particularly the southern part, also prefer subject + verb order in intransitive sentences, in transitive sentences the preferred order is subject + object + verb.[22]

Subject		Object	Verb
Motu			
Morea			*e-mahuta.*
Morea			he-sleep
'Morea is sleeping.'			
Morea	*ese*	*boroma*	*e-ala-ia.*
Morea	ERGATIVE	pig	he-kill-it
'Morea killed the pig.'			
Maisin			
Pita-ka			*i-maa-matu.*
Peter-TOPIC			he-CONTINUOUS-sleep
'Peter is asleep.'			
Tamaate-seng		*sikoo-ka*	*ti-fune-si.*
men-ERGATIVE		pig-TOPIC	they-cut-it
'The men cut up the pig.'			

Verb-Initial Languages

Languages whose rules demand that the verb complex come first in the sentence are found in various parts of the Oceanic area.[23] Anejom̃ in Vanuatu, many New Caledonian languages, a few languages in Micronesia, and most Polynesian languages (especially those of the Polynesian Triangle) are verb-initial languages. In some of these languages, the normal order is verb + object + subject.

Verb		Object	Subject
Anejom̃			
Ek	*hag*		*añak.*
I	eat		I
'I am eating.'			

Is	*ecet*	*Deto*	*a*	*Tosei.*
PAST	see	Deto	SUBJECT	Tosei

'Tosei saw Deto.'

Iaai

A	*me*	*walak*	*wanakat.*
he	CONTINUOUS	play	child

'The child is playing.'

A	*me*	*kot*	*wanakat*	*thaan.*
he	CONTINUOUS	hit	child	chief

'The chief is smacking the child.'

Kiribati

E	*a*	*mataku*	*Itaia.*
he	CONTINUOUS	watch	Itaia

'Itaia is watching.'

E	*tenaa*	*Itaia*	*te*	*kirii.*
it	bite	Itaia	the	dog

'The dog bit Itaia.'

In others verb + subject + object is the norm.

Verb	**Subject**	**Object**

Yapese

Bea	*mool*	*Tamag.*
PRESENT	sleep	Tamag

'Tamag is sleeping.'

Kea	*guy*	*Tamag*	*Tinag.*
he	see:her	Tamag	Tinag

'Tamag saw Tinag.'

Māori

I	*kai*	*te*	*rangatira.*
PAST	eat	the	chief

'The chief ate.'

I	*inu*	*te*	*tangata*	*i*	*te*	*rongoa.*
PAST	drink	the	man	OBJECT	the	medicine

'The man drank the medicine.'

Tahitian

'Ua   tāmā'a   te   vahine.
PAST   eat   the   woman
'The woman has eaten.'

'Ua   tāpū   te   vahine   'i   te   vahie.
PAST   cut   the   woman   OBJECT   the   wood
'The woman cut the wood.'

Flexibility of Phrase Order

To some extent, all Oceanic languages, like most other languages in the world, allow some flexibility in basic phrase order. In English, for example, emphasis or contrast can be laid on the object by moving it to sentence-initial position: Compare *I just can't stand that fellow* with *That fellow I just can't stand.*

In Oceanic languages, it is generally possible to focus attention on any noun phrase by moving it to the beginning of the sentence. In some languages, there is a pause (marked in the examples below by a comma) or a special focusing morpheme after this phrase. The first set of examples is from languages that are normally verb-initial. The focus is on the subject:

Subject	**Verb**		**Object**

A'jië

Më'u,   wè,   na   kani.
yam,   FOCUS,   it   grow
'As for the yam, it's growing well.'

Iaai

Wanakat,   a me   walak.
child,   3SG CONTINUOUS   play
'As for the child, he/she is playing.'

Mā'ori

Ko   Wahieroa   kua   moe   i   a   Kura.
FOCUS   Wahieroa   COMPLETIVE marry   OBJECT   the:PERSONAL Kura
'Wahieroa [not someone else] has married Kura.'

The next couple of examples show focus on the object.

Object				Verb	Subject

Anejom̃

Nev-atimi	*iyii*	*na*	*ecta-i*	*aek?*
which-man	that	you	see-TRANS	you

'Which man was it that you saw?'

Object	Subject	Verb

Fijian

E	*dua*	*na*	*qito*	*levu*	*keimami*	*ākī-tak-a.*
it	one	the	game	big	we:EXC:PL PAST	do-TRANS-it

'It's a big game we played.'

The examples below are from normally subject-initial (either SVO or SOV) languages, with attention focused on the object.

Object	Subject	Verb

Nakanai

La	*paia taume,*	*eau*	*kama*	*hilo-a.*
the	dog your,	I	not	see-it

'As for your dog, I haven't seen it.'

Toʻabaʻita

Niu	*neʻe ki na*	*ku*	*ngali-a*	*mai.*
coconut	this PL FOCUS	I	carry-it	here

'It was these coconuts that I brought.'

Motu

Boroma	*Morea ese*	*e-ala-ia.*
pig	Morea ERGATIVE	he-kill-it

'The pig, Morea killed it.'

Lenakel

Nimwa	*aan*	*nimataag-asuul*	*r-im-atakin.*
house	that	wind-big	it-PAST-destroy

'That house was destroyed by the cyclone.'

The following extract from a Banoni story (Lincoln 1976, 229) shows how discourse features influence word order in these languages. The noun phrase we are interested in is *natsu-ri* 'their child.'

Banoni

Vi	*natsu-ri*	ke		*vakekariana*	*me-ria*
then	child-their	COMPLETIVE		play	with-them

'Their child was playing with

na	*dzoko*	na	*kanisi. Vi*	*ka*		*teviri*	*na-ria*
the	child	the	some then	COMPLETIVE		eat	POSS-their

some youngsters. But they ate

borogho	ke		*kota,*	*ke*		*tai-ma*	*natsu-ri.*
pig	COMPLETIVE		all,	COMPLETIVE		come-here	child-their

'all the pork (before) their child came.'

The story is about a man and his wife cooking pork. When their child (*natsu-ri*) is introduced into the story, it is obviously in focus. It comes before the verb of which it is the subject (*ke vakekariana* 'he was playing'). Once the child has been introduced, however, there is no necessity to focus on the child again. In the last clause in the above example, *natsu-ri* follows the verb of which it is the subject (*ke tai-ma* 'he came').

In some Oceanic languages, however, this variability in phrase order is a requirement of grammar. Tolai, for example, has SV(O) in most sentence types, but V(O)S in stative sentences. Compare examples 1 and 2 with examples 3 and 4.

Tolai

	Subject		**Verb**		**Object**
1.	A *pap*		*i*	*pot.*	
	the dog		it	come	

'The dog came.'

2.	*Iau gire*		*ra*	*pap.*	
	I see		the	dog	

'I saw the dog.'

	Verb		**Object**	**Subject**	
3.	*I*	*ga*	*buka*	*ra*	*evu*	*rat.*
	it	FAR:PAST	full	the	two	basket

'Two baskets were filled.'

4.	*I*	*ga*	*tup*	*dir*	*a*	*vinarubu.*
	it	FAR:PAST	tire	them:two	the	fight

'The fight tired them.'

Rotuman also has SV(O) as its normal order, but this can change to VS in certain kinds of intransitive sentences (e.g., imperatives). Compare the first two examples below with the last one.

Rotuman

Subject		Verb	Object	
Fā	*ta*	*joni-en.*		
man	the	run:away-he:STATIVE		

'The man ran away.'

Subject	Verb	Object	
Iris	*tauɔki-a*	*fuag*	*ta.*
they	repair-TRANS	breach:in:wall	the

'They are repairing the breach (in the wall).'

Verb	Subject
Leum	*'æe!*
come	you

'(You) come!'

6.5.4. Negation

There is some variety in the ways in which negation is marked in Oceanic languages. The most widespread pattern is for negation to be marked by a preverbal negative particle:

Manam

Tamoata	*tago*	*nga-te-a.*
man	not	he:IRREALIS-see-me

'The man will not see me.'

Banoni

Ma	*to*	*tai*	*no,*	*Ken*	*ma*	*to*	*tai.*
IRREALIS	not	go	you,	Ken	IRREALIS	not	go

'If you don't go, Ken won't go either.'

Nakanamanga

A	*ko*	*taa*	*munu.*
I	INCOMPLETE	not	drink

'I haven't drunk yet.'

A'jië

Céré	_daa_	të	ka'u.
they	not	still	big

'They are not big yet.'

Kiribati

E	_aki_	kiba	te	moa.
it	not	fly	the	chicken

'The chicken didn't fly.'

Nukuoro

Ia	e	_te_	hano
he	PRESENT	not	go

'He is not going.'

Tongan

Na'e	_'ikai_	'alu	'a	Siale.
PAST	not	go	SUBJECT	Siale

'Siale didn't go.'

In a considerable number of Oceanic languages, negation is marked by a **discontinuous morpheme**. Two separate particles must both occur, but they are separated by some other elements (compare French _Je suis malade_ 'I am sick,' with _Je ne suis pas malade_ 'I am not sick'). Generally, one of these particles occurs before the verb and the other after it.

Raga

Ran	_hav_	gita-u	_tehe_.
they:COMPLETIVE	not	see-me	not

'They didn't see me.'

Rotuman

Taunæ'	ta	_kat_	sok	_ra_.
meeting	the	not:NON-FUTURE	happen	not

'The meeting did not take place.'

Taunæ'	ta	_kal_	sok	_ra_.
meeting	the	not:FUTURE	happen	not

'The meeting will not take place.'

West Futuna

A	tata	ni	_se_	kauna	_ma_	avau	ki	ta	skul.
the	parent	PAST	not	send	not	me	to	the	school

'My parents didn't send me to school.'

Special mention must be made of the Lewo language of Epi Island, Vanuatu, which is probably unique in the world in requiring (in some grammatical contexts) a *triple* marking of negation:

Lewo

<u>Pe</u>	ne-pisu-li	<u>re</u>	Santo	<u>poli</u>.
not	I-see-try	not	Santo	not

'I've never seen Santo.'

Sa-na	puruvi	lala	<u>pe</u>	ka-la	kinan-ena	<u>re</u>	si	<u>poli</u>.
POSS-his	brother	PL	not	POSS:FOOD-their	eat-NOM	not	again	not

'His brothers didn't have any more food.'

In languages with complex verbal morphology, the negative is often marked by a verbal affix rather than by a particle. In a number of cases (like Paamese and Lenakel below), this affix is a discontinuous morpheme, incorporating a prefix and a suffix to the verb:

Motu

B-<u>asi</u>-na-ita-ia.
FUTURE-not-I-see-it
'I won't see it.'

Paamese

Inau	*na-<u>ro</u>-mesai-<u>tei</u>.*
I	I-not-sick-not

'I am not sick.'

Lenakel

Wusuaas	*ka*	*r-is-ho-<u>aan</u>*	*peravin*	*taha-m.*
boy	the	he-not-hit-not	woman	POSS-your

'The boy didn't hit your wife.'

Other Oceanic languages mark negation with a negative word that comes at the beginning of the clause or sentence but is not part of the verb complex. Discontinuous marking also occurs in some of these languages (Rapanui in the examples below).

Tahitian

<u>Aita</u>	*te*	*ta'ata*	*'i*	*hohoni-hia*	*'e*	*te*	*'uri.*
not	the	man	COMPLETIVE	bite-PASSIVE	by	the	dog

'The man was not bitten by the dog.'

Māori

Kāhore	*ngā*	*wāhine*	*e*	*kōrero*	*ana.*
not	the:PL	woman	NONPAST	talk	CONTINUOUS

'The women are not talking.'

Rapanui

Ina	*matou*	*kai*	*maʻa*	*i*	*te*	*vānaga*	*Magareva.*
not	we: EXC	not	know	OBJECT	the	language	Mangareva

'We ourselves don't know the Mangareva language.'

In some Oceanic languages the negative is marked by a negative verb. The first Southwest Tanna sentence below is in the affirmative, and the verb (*asim* 'to garden') takes subject and tense prefixes.

Southwest Tanna

Magau	*l-ɨmn-asim*	*niɨv.*
Magau	he-PAST-garden	yesterday

'Magau worked in the garden yesterday.'

In the negative equivalent of this sentence, person and tense marking occurs on the negative verb **apwah**, and the verb **asim** is nominalized.

Southwest Tanna

Magau	*l-ɨmn-apwah*	*n-asim-ien*	*niɨv.*
Magau	he-PAST-not	NOM-garden-NOM	yesterday

'Magau did not work in the garden yesterday.'

Fijian behaves similarly with the negative verb *sega*.

Fijian

E	*sega*	*na*	*kākana.*
it	not	the	food

'There is no food.'

Au	*sega*	*ni*	*kilā*	*na*	*vosa.*
I	not	that	know:TRANS:it	the	language

'I don't know the language.'

6.5.5. Prepositional and Postpositional Phrases

A **preposition** comes before a noun phrase and specifies that phrase's relationship to the verb or to other phrases in the sentence. Typically, prepositions mark relationships like location, time, instrument, cause, and so on. A **prepositional phrase**, therefore, is a noun phrase introduced by a preposition.

Most Oceanic languages have a small, closed set of prepositions. To'aba-'ita and Samoan are typical:

To'aba'ita

'i	location, direction
ni	purpose, instrument
mala	'like, as'
'ana	instrument, goal, comparison

Samoan

i	location, direction toward, instrument, cause
ma	comitative, 'with'
mā, mō	beneficiary, 'for' (the *a/o* distinction paralleling that of possessives)
mai	ablative, 'from'

In the examples below, the prepositional phrases are underlined.

To'aba'ita

Thaina-mare'a		*'e*	*nii*	*'i*	*luma*.
mother-our:two:EXC		she	be	in	house

'Our mother is in the house.'

Kasi-a	*'oko*	*'ena*	*'ana*	*nini*	*'ena*.
cut it	rope	that	with	knife	that

'Cut the rope with the knife.'

Samoan

Ua	*sau*	*le*	*tama*	*ma*	*se*	*'au-fa'i*.
STATIVE	come	the	boy	with	a	bunch-banana

'The boy is coming with a bunch of bananas.'

'O	*Malia*	*oleā*	*moe*	*i*	*le*	*pō*.
FOCUS	Maria	FUTURE	sleep	in	the	night

'Maria will sleep in the evening.'

As if to compensate for the fairly small number of basic prepositions, most of these languages make considerable use of **compound prepositions**. A compound preposition (underlined in the examples below) is composed of a general preposition plus a noun (often a body part) for greater specificity.

Toʻabaʻita

Ka	takalo-a	gano	fuu		ʻi maa-na	biʻu	fuu.
he:then	scatter-it	soil	that	in	face-its	house	that

'Then he scattered the soil in front of the house.'

ʻOno	ʻi	ninima-ku.
sit:down	at	side-my

'Sit down beside me.'

Ni	ʻOina	ʻe	nii	ʻi	laa	luma.
the:FEMININE	ʻOina	she	be:located	in	inside	house

'Oina is inside the house.'

Although the languages of Polynesia and Micronesia and the majority of the languages of Melanesia use prepositions, many of the languages of the New Guinea mainland and the nearby offshore islands use **postpositions** to mark the same kinds of grammatical functions. As the name implies, a postposition comes *after* the noun phrase to which it refers rather than before it. This kind of phrase is known as a **postpositional phrase**. There is a very strong correlation among the world's languages between SOV basic sentence order and postpositions. Within Oceanic as well, the languages that have postpositions are usually also those in which the object comes before the verb.

Below are the postpositions of Manam and Sinagoro. The last two Manam forms are suffixes; the Sinagoro forms are **clitics**, suffixed to the last word in the noun *phrase*, whatever its grammatical category.

Manam

zaiza	comitative, 'with'
ʻana	cause
ane, oti, ono	instrument
boʻana	'like, as'
-lo	location
-o	'on'

Sinagoro

ai	location, 'in, at'
na	instrument, ablative
γoti	accompaniment
γana	direction toward

Below are some examples in these two languages of sentences containing postpositional phrases.

Manam

Roa-gu	*uma-lo*	*i-malipi-lipi.*
wife-my	garden-in	she-work-CONTINUOUS

'My wife is working in the garden.'

Tanepwa	*zaiza*	*'i-pura.*
chief	with	we:EXC-come

'We came with the chief.'

Sinagoro

Au	*ɣe-ɣu*	*koko-na*	*a-kwari-a-to.*
I	POSS-my	axe-with	I-hit-it-PAST

'I hit it with my axe.'

Kila	*na*	*kwayalu*	*baraki-na-ɣana*	*ɣio*	*piu-a-to.*
Kila	ERGATIVE	dog	old-SG-toward	spear	throw-it-PAST

'Kila threw a spear toward the old dog.'

As with their preposition-using relatives, many of these languages have compound postpositions, like the following in Sinagoro:

Sinagoro

numa	*gabule-na-ai*
house	underneath-its-at

'under the house'

numa	*muli-na-ai*
house	back-its-at

'behind the house'

mimiga	*potiati-ai*
hole	gone:through-at

"through the hole"

6.6. Similarities and Differences

Oceanic languages exhibit a number of areas of similarity, but also many areas of difference. Given the period of time in which many of these languages have been developing separately from their relatives, the quite large degree of similarity is perhaps more surprising than the differences.

CHAPTER

7

Papuan Languages: Grammatical Overview

The seven hundred or so Papuan languages of the Pacific belong to a number of distinct and apparently unrelated families. For this reason alone, it is much more difficult to make grammatical generalizations about them than about the Oceanic languages treated in chapter 6. I attempt here to give a very general feel for the diversity of Papuan languages, focusing specifically on differences between them and Oceanic languages. The interested reader is referred to Foley's excellent survey of these languages (Foley 1986).

7.1. Pronouns

Pronoun systems vary widely among Papuan languages, but in general they are not so complex as Oceanic systems. Many Papuan languages distinguish only singular and plural (sometimes only in some persons, like Kuman in the examples below). Some languages in Irian Jaya do not even do this. They simply distinguish person, though they usually have a special plural morpheme preceding or following (like *king-* in Manem):

	Manem	**Kuman**	**Koita**
Singular			
I	*ga*	*na*	*da*
you	*sa*	*ene*	*a*
he/she/it	*angk*	*ye*	*au*
Plural			
we	*king-ga*	*no*	*no*
you	*king-sa*	*ene*	*ya*
they	*king-angk*	*ye*	*yau*

Some Papuan languages, however, have a dual as well as a plural number in pronouns:

	Wiru	**Alamblak**
Singular		
I	*no*	*nan*
you	*ne*	*nin*
he/she/it	*one*	*rër*
Dual		
we two	*tota*	*nën*
you two	*kita*	*nifɨn*
they two	*kita*	*rëf*
Plural		
we	*toto*	*nëm*
you	*kiwi*	*nikëm*
they	*kiwi*	*rëm*

The Wiru examples show another not uncommon feature of Papuan pronouns, conflation of non-singular second and third persons.

A number of Papuan languages distinguish gender in pronouns, most commonly in the third person singular, but occasionally in other persons as well. Note the following singular pronouns in Abelam:

Abelam

I	*wnə*	
you masculine	*mə*	*nə*
you feminine	*ñə*	*nə*
he	*də*	
she	*lə*	

Very few Papuan pronominal systems distinguish inclusive and exclusive first person. Nimboran in Irian Jaya is one language that makes this distinction, though it does not distinguish singular and plural:

Nimboran

io	I, we inclusive
ngo	I, we exclusive
ko	you (singular and plural)
no	he, she, it, they

The Papuan languages of Solomon Islands also have the inclusive/exclusive distinction. All of them distinguish gender in the third person, and some languages do so in other persons as well. They also mark dual and in some cases trial number. The most complex of these pronoun systems is that of Baniata (see table 6).

Table 6.   Baniata Independent Pronouns

	Unspecified[a]	Masculine	Feminine	Neuter
Singular				
1	*eei*			
2	*noe*			
3		*zo*	*vo*	*na, ño*
Dual				
1INC		*be*	*bebe*	
1EXC		*eere*	*eerebe*	
2		*bere*	*berebe*	
3		*sere*	*robe*	*rede*
Trial				
1INC		*meno*	*menu*	
1EXC		*eebeno*	*eebenu*	
2		*mebeno*	*mebenu*	
3		*nomo*	*numo*	*nafi*
Plural				
1INC	*memo*			
1EXC	*eebo*			
2	*mebo*			
3		*mo*	*mo*	*no*

[a] Gender is not distinguished in these persons and numbers.

Many Papuan languages mark person and number of subject (and, less often, object) by verbal affixes, usually suffixes, but sometimes prefixes. Interestingly, a number of languages make more distinctions in these affixes than they do in free pronouns. Kuman is one such language:

Kuman

	Independent pronouns	Subject suffixes
Singular		
I	*na*	*-i*
you	*ene*	*-n*
he/she/it	*ye*	*-uw*

Dual

we two	—	*-bugl*
you two	—	*-bit*
they two	—	*-bit*

Plural

we	*no*	*-mun*
you	*ene*	*-iw*
they	*ye*	*-iw*

Kuman (1) contrasts dual and plural in the subject pronoun suffixes; (2) like Wiru, it conflates non-singular second and third persons in the subject suffixes. Neither of these features appears in the independent pronouns.

Bilua, on the other hand, has subject prefixes. One small class of verbs marks the object by prefixes, but most verbs take object suffixes. Here are the singular forms of these pronouns (along with the independent pronouns).

Bilua

		Subject	Object	
	Independent	**Prefixes**	**Prefixes**	**Suffixes**
I	*anga*	*a-*	*l-*	*-l*
you	*ngo*	*ngo-*	*ng-*	*-ng*
he	*vo*	*o-*	*v-*	*-v*
she	*ko*	*ko-*	*k-*	*-k*

7.2. Nouns and Noun Phrases

7.2.1. Noun Class Systems

Many Papuan languages, especially those in the central north of the mainland of New Guinea, have elaborate noun class systems. While a language like French, for example, grammatically distinguishes two genders (masculine and feminine), and a language like German three (masculine, feminine, and neuter), Abuʻ, the language I use to exemplify this system in Papuan languages (Nekitel 1986), has *nineteen* different noun classes. These classes are based on a combination of semantic and phonological factors. So while class 1 contains nouns referring to males and class 2 nouns referring to females, class 5 (which contains such diverse nouns as the words for "song," "leg," "sago," "vine," and "tooth") is distinguished by the fact that the singular form ends in *h* while the plural ends in *lih*.

What is of interest in these systems is that other words in a clause that relate to a noun—the verb of which it is subject, adjectives, demonstratives, and so on—are all marked morphologically to indicate that they refer to a noun of a particular class. The word order in the examples below is /noun + demonstrative + adjective + verb/. The class marker is underlined in each case.[1]

Abu‘

Noun	Dem.	Adj.	Verb	
Aleman	ana	afuni	n-ahe‘	'This good man went.'
Alemam	ama	afumi	m-ahe‘	'These good men went.'
Numata‘	au‘a	afu‘i	kw-ahe‘	'This good woman went.'
Numatawa	awa	afuweri	w-ahe‘	'These good women went.'
Aul	ala	afuli	l-ahe‘	'This good eel went.'
Akuh	akuha	afukuhi	h-ahe‘	'These good eels went.'
Bahiataf	afa	afufi	f-ahe‘	'This good river fish went.'
Ihiaburuh	aha	afuhi	h-ahe‘	'This good butterfly went.'

7.2.2. Articles and Demonstratives

Articles are virtually nonexistent in Papuan languages. As far as demonstratives are concerned, some Papuan languages show the three-way distinction common to Austronesian languages.

Koita

o	PROXIMATE:	'this'
e	INTERMEDIATE:	'this, that'
vire	DISTANT:	'that'

Other Papuan languages are more like English, with a two-way contrast in demonstratives between proximate (near the speaker) and distant (not near the speaker). Barai, though closely related to Koita, is one such language, but the demonstrative situation is complicated by the fact that other aspects of the location of the noun referred to are also incorporated into the system.

Barai

Proximate	Distant	
ig-	ij-	general
—	gar-, gur-	to the side
—	gam-	down at an angle
—	gaf-	up at an angle
—	gum-	straight down
—	guf-	straight up

In languages with strongly developed noun class systems, the demonstratives usually incorporate a marker of the class membership of the noun referred to. The earlier examples from Abu‘ illustrate this.

7.2.3. Noun Phrase Structure

Although there are exceptions, in general the noun phrase in Papuan languages has the head noun first and all modifying and descriptive words following. Below are a few examples, with the head noun underlined in each case.

Koita

ata	_ahu_	_inuhati_	_vire_
man	old	all	that

'all those old men'

Daga

gutut	_otu_	_ame_	_uiwa_
story	little	that	last

'that last little story'

Abuʿ

ba-kuh	_a-kuha_	_bia-kuh_	_afu-kuhi_
stick-CLASS	this-CLASS	two-CLASS	good-CLASS

'these two good sticks'

Enga

akáli	_épé_	_kitúmende_	_dúpa_
man	good	four	those

'those four good men'

7.3. Possessive Constructions

Possessive constructions are less complex in Papuan languages than in Oceanic languages. Many Papuan languages simply mark a noun as being possessed, with none of the various subtypes found in Oceanic languages. In Koita, for example, the noun possessed is preceded by the independent pronoun and takes the suffix -*Ce*, where the thematic consonant varies depending on the noun to which it is suffixed.

Koita

_di_	_hete-re_		_di_	_ava-ɣe_
I	chin-POSS		I	mouth-POSS

'my chin'   'my mouth'

_di_	_vaiɣa-de_		_di_	_muni-ve_
I	spear-POSS		I	stone-POSS

'my spear'   'my stone'

Other Papuan languages show a distinction between alienable and in-alienable nouns rather like that of the simplest systems in Oceanic. In Daga, for example, kinship nouns take possessive suffixes.

Daga

ne   *goani-na*
I   younger:sibling-my
'my younger sibling'

nu   *mama-nu*
we   father-our
'our father'

Other nouns do not take these possessive suffixes, but are followed instead by an independent pronoun plus a possessive marker.

Daga

ne   *anu-t*   *ne-ga*
I   thing-NOM   I-POSS
'my thoughts'

nu   *dugup*   *nu-ga*
we   clan   we-POSS
'our clan'

7.4. Verbs and the Verb Complex

7.4.1. Person and Number; Tense and Aspect

The majority of Papuan languages mark person, number, and sometimes noun class of the subject, as well as tense-aspect and related categories by suffixes to the verb stem. In many cases, this leads to complex strings of suffixes, with concomitantly complex morphophonemics. This complexity can also mean that a clause, or indeed a whole sentence, may consist only of a verb. In the following examples from widely separated languages, the verb root is underlined.

Magi

<u>Oni</u>-la-es-a.
go-IMPERFECTIVE-PRESENT-he
'He is going.'

<u>Oni</u>-bi-ava-i!
go-CONDITINOAL-you:two-IMPERATIVE
'You two go!'

<u>Oni</u>-sa-ʻa-i-dei.
go-FUTURE-I-IMPERATIVE-short:time
'I will go now for a short time.'

Wahgi

Na-<u>pi</u>-s-a-mbił-mo?
not-hear-CLASSIFIER-FUTURE-two-QUESTION
'Will you two not hear?'

<u>No</u>-n-a-mb-ua?
eat-CLASSIFIER-FUTURE-they-QUESTION
'Can they eat?'

Na-<u>no</u>-tang-e-r-ind.
not-eat-HABITUAL-COMPLETIVE-CLASSIFIER-I
'I do not always eat.'

Abelam

<u>wʌ-kʌ</u>-wtə-kwʌ.
talk-FUTURE-I-NONPAST
'I will talk.'

gəra-kʌ-ñ ə nə-gwʌ.
cry-FUTURE-you: FEMININE-NONPAST
'You (fem.) will cry.'

<u>kʌ</u>-kʌ-wtə-kwʌ-y
eat-FUTURE-I-NONPAST-not:FUTURE
'I will not eat.'

There are Papuan languages, however, in which at least some of the grammatical information is carried by prefixes rather than suffixes. In the following examples from Yimas, the verb root is again underlined.

Yimas

yan   na-ka-<u>kumprak</u>-asa-t
tree   OBJECT:CLASS-I-broken-CAUSATIVE-COMPLETIVE
'I broke the tree.'

ka-n-<u>wa</u>-n
likely-he-go-PRESENT
'He's likely to go.'

antɨ-ka-<u>wa</u>-ntut
might-I-go-FAR:PAST
'I would have gone.'

An almost bewildering variety of tense-aspect situations may be marked in the verbs of Papuan languages. Let us take Korafe as an example. Korafe verbs take one of a number of tense-aspect suffixes:

Korafe

-e	present
-are	future
-ete	immediate past (something that happened today)
-imuta	very near past (something that happened yesterday)
-a	recent past (something that happened before yesterday, but not very long ago)
-ise	far past
-erae	habitual

These tense-aspect markers are followed by suffixes marking the subject's person and number, and then by a further set of suffixes marking mood—indicative (statements), interrogative (yes-or-no questions), question (information questions), hortative, subjunctive, and imperative. The verb root is underlined in the examples.

Korafe

Y-are-s-a.
go-FUTURE-you-STATEMENT
'You will go.'

Re-da   y-are-s-i?
what-to   go-FUTURE-you-QUESTION
'Where will you go?'

Y-a-s-a.
go-RECENT:PAST-you-STATEMENT
'You went (recently).'

Re-da   y-a-s-i?
what-to   go-RECENT:PAST-you-QUESTION
'Where did you go (recently)?'

A further feature of the verb in Papuan languages is that complex morphophonemic processes are involved. It is often difficult to break down what follows a verb into its component suffixes. Here are a few examples from Kuman:

Kuman

Underlying form		Surface form
/pit-i-ka-a/	>	*prika*
hear-I-REALIS-STATEMENT		
'I hear.'		

/kumbt-uw-ka-a/   >   *kumbrukwa*
twist-it-REALIS-STATEMENT
'It twists.'

/ne-kit-mbugl-ka-a/   >   *nekulka*
eat-not-we:two-REALIS-STATEMENT
'We two didn't eat (it).'

/kan-nagl-mba-t-a/   >   *kanaglmbra*
see-FUTURE-hopefully-EMPHATIC-STATEMENT
'(I) will hope to see it.'

7.4.2. *Adjunct and Serial Constructions*

Adjunct and serial constructions, a feature of many Papuan languages, can be introduced by examples from Kuman. Look first at the following sentences (the relevant morphemes are underlined).

Kuman

Bugla	*kinde*	*su ŋgwa.*
pig	bad	it:hit

'The pig is sick.'

Ambai	*giglaŋge*	*duŋgwa.*
girl	song	she:say

'The girl is singing.'

These two sentences are examples of what are called **adjunct constructions**, in which the verb of the sentence is preceded by a morpheme of some other word class, usually a noun or an adjective, which is known as an **adjunct**. Some other examples in Kuman are:

Kuman

ka	*di*	*gaugl*	*ere*
word	say	laughter	do
'say'		'laugh'	

kai	*ere*	*nigl*	*pai*
tears	do	water	lie
'cry'		'wash (self)'	

Serial constructions are similar but not identical to adjunct constructions, as illustrated in the following examples.

Kuman

Ye	mbo	<u>mbat</u>	<u>narukwa</u>.
he	sugarcane	cut	he:give

'He cut sugarcane for me.'

Ye	komboglo	<u>ake</u>	suŋgwa.
she	stone	hold	she:hit

'She hit it with a stone.'

In serial constructions, the final verb is preceded by one or more other verbs. Some more examples include:

Kuman

di	te		di	pre	
say	give		say	perceive	
'tell'			'ask'		
si	bogl		si	gogl	
hit	cut		hit	die	
'sew'			'kill'		
ere	kan		pre	pol	si
do	see		perceive	undo	hit
'try'			'understand'		

In all of these cases, what other languages often view as a single state or event and express by a single verb is broken up into components. For example, the sentence *Ye komboglo ake suŋgwa* is idiomatically translated 'She hit it with a stone,' but is more literally 'She held a stone and hit it.' In the more literal translation, the two components of *holding* the stone and *hitting* something with it are separated.

While many Papuan languages, like Kuman, make quite frequent use of adjunct and serial constructions, "the closely related Kalam and Kobon are the most remarkable in applying this idea in the most thoroughgoing fashion. . . . Kalam immediately strikes one as a language in which the speakers are excessively specific in their description of events" (Foley 1986, 113). An example like the following one gives an idea of just how specific these languages can be.

Kalam

Yad	am	mon	pk	d	ap	ay-p-yn.
I	go	wood	hit	hold	come	put-COMPLETIVE-I

'I fetched firewood.'

While the sentence "translates" as 'I fetched firewood,' the act of fetching is broken down into its components in Kalam. What the Kalam speaker is saying is something like 'I went and chopped wood and got it and came and put it.'

In languages with these kinds of constructions, the number of actual verbs is often much smaller than in other languages. "Kalam has under 100 verb stems and, of these, only about twenty-five are commonly used" (Foley 1986, 115). The Kalam sentence above shows five verbs in a serial construction. Other serial constructions in Kalam include the following. (The hyphen after the last element indicates where subject and tense suffixes occur.)

Kalam

nb	*nŋ-*		*ag*	*tk-*	
consume	perceive		sound	sever	
'taste'			'interrupt'		
pwŋy	*md*	*ay-*	*d*	*am*	*yok-*
poke	stay	put	take	go	displace
'fix (by insertion)'			'get rid of'		

Kalam also uses adjunct constructions to a great degree.

Kalam

wdn	*nŋ-*		*tmwd*	*nŋ-*
eye	perceive		ear	perceive
'see'			'hear'	
kwnk	*g-*		*joŋb*	*tmey* *g-*
saliva	do		mouth	bad do
'spit'			'whine'	
ywg	*ñ-*		*mnm*	*ag* *ñ-*
lid	give		speech	sound give
'put a lid on'			'confide'	

7.5. Sentences

7.5.1. Simple Sentences

Any generalization about word order in Papuan languages would state that they tend to be verb-final languages. The order of the core constituents is SV in intransitive clauses and SOV in transitive clauses.[2]

Subject	**Object**	**Verb**

Barai

Bu	*bajae*	*fiad-ia.*
they	body	pain-they
'They (i.e., their bodies) are in pain.'		

Fu	*mave*	*kana-e.*
he	pig	hit-PAST

'He hit the pig.'

Wahgi

Na		*wo-tang-n-al.*
I		come-HABITUAL-CLASS-I:will

'I will always come.'

Na	*mokine*	*no-tang-ind.*
I	food	eat-HABITUAL-I:have

'I always ate food.'

Anggor

Songgo		*borə me-fe-o.*
fowl:egg		broke-change-it:S

'The wildfowl egg broke.'

Nindou	*ai*	*songgo*	*borəma-r-ea-ndə.*
man	he	fowl:egg	broke-TRANS-it:S-it:O

'The man broke the wildfowl egg.'

Grand Valley Dani

Ap		*nik-k-e.*
man		eat-REALIS-he

'The man ate.'

Ap	*palu*	*na-sikh-e.*
man	python	eat-FAR:PAST-he

'The man ate the python.'

While in many languages this is the usual order, in others word order is not significant for indicating functions like subject or object. Many Papuan languages "may be regarded as free word-order languages. Although the verb is usually positioned clause-finally, this rule is rigid only in some languages. In a great many Papuan languages, peripheral nominals such as locatives or temporals commonly occur after the verb. . . . The general impression of clause structure in Papuan languages in comparison to English is its overall looseness" (Foley 1986, 168).

Foley illustrates this statement using Yimas. The following sentence follows "standard" Papuan SOV order:

Yimas

Subject	Object	Verb
Pay-um	*nar-mang*	*na-mpu-tay*.
man-CLASS:PL	woman-CLASS:SG	her-they:MASCULINE-see

'The men saw the woman.'

Each noun is marked as belonging to a particular noun class, and the verb takes prefixes corresponding to the noun class of the object and the subject, in that order. In the verb *namputay* in the sentence above, *na-* marks a third-person singular object of the human female noun class, and *mpu-* marks a third-person plural subject of the human male noun class. The verb *namputay* on its own means 'They (male human) saw her (human).' Consequently, it is clear which noun is subject and which is object without relying on word order. The following Yimas sentences also mean 'The men saw the woman.'

Yimas

Narmang payum na-mpu-tay.   (object-subject-verb)
Payum na-mpu-tay narmang.   (subject-verb-object)
Narmang na-mpu-tay payum.   (object-verb-subject)

Nominal sentences are far less common in Papuan languages than in Oceanic languages, as many Papuan languages have existential verbs, often more than one. Kuman, for example, has three: *yoŋgwa* is used when the subject is inanimate, *paŋgwa* with animate and inanimate subjects that are in a specific place, and *molkwa* with animate or inanimate subjects whose existence is being declared.

Kuman

Di	*ta*	*yoŋgwa.*
axe	a	it:be

'There is an axe.'

Usi	*gagl*	*mina*	*paŋgwa.*
cigarette	bag	in	it:be:in:that:place

'There are cigarettes in the bag.'

Togoi	*ta*	*molkwa.*
snake	a	it:exist

'There is a snake.'

Many of the languages of the Highlands are similar to Kuman. Huli, for example, has three existential verbs, Sinasina four, and Enga seven (Piau 1981).

An extreme case is Anggor in the Sepik, with *eighteen* verbs roughly translating "be." What is important is the shape of the object, its location, and its posture (Litteral 1981, 128). So before choosing the appropriate verb, one needs to know if the subject is masculine or feminine, elongated or bunched up, inside something else or not, in a horizontal or vertical plane, hanging on something, stuck to something, and so on. Some of the Anggor existential verbs are:

Anggor

amar-	be sitting on or inside
anəngg-	be standing on
enggor-	be lying, on a low plane
anangg-	be lying, on a high plane
apeningg-	be attached flat to
apaiyar-	be attached and curling around
apuiyar-	used only of liquids
ahetar-	be hanging from a protrusion

This is not to say that there are absolutely no verbless sentences in Papuan languages. They do occur, in both subject-predicate and predicate-subject orders.

	Subject		**Predicate**

Koita

Ata	*bera*	*yaga-uhu-gera.*
man	a	house-in-the

'A man is in the house.'

Kuman

Yuŋgu-n	*awe?*
house-your	where

'Where is your house?'

	Predicate	**Subject**

Daga

Ne	*tata-na*	*ge.*
I	older:sibling-my	you

'You are my older sibling.'

7.5.2. Peripheral Cases

Peripheral cases—relations other than subject and object—are generally marked by postpositions or suffixes in Papuan languages. More concrete spatial notions tend to be expressed by postpositions.

Kuman

> *Kagl-e*   *mina*   *yoŋgwa.*
> foot-her   on   it:be
> 'It is on her foot.'

> *Komboglo*   *pagl*   *siŋga.*
> stone   with   I:hit
> 'I hit it with a stone.'

Kewa

> *Ada*   *ru-para*   *pá-lua.*
> house   inside-to   go-I:FUTURE
> 'I will go inside the house.'

> *Ada*   *rolo-para*   *pá-lua.*
> house   underneath-to   go-I:FUTURE
> 'I will go under the house.'

But "the more basic case relations are expressed directly," usually by suffixes (Foley 1986, 93):

Kuman

> *Mokona*   *gagl-e*   *krika.*
> greens   bag-in   I:pack
> 'I put the greens in the bag.'

> *Ye*   *nigl-e*   *molkwa.*
> he   water-at   he:be:there
> 'He is at the river.'

Kewa

> *Ada-para*   *pá-lua.*
> house-to   go-I:FUTURE
> 'I will go home.'

> *Ní-na*   *méáá-ria.*
> I-for   get-he:PAST
> 'He got it for me.'

Many Papuan languages have a very wide range of morphemes marking peripheral case relations. Koita, which uses clitics to mark these relations, is a good example.

Koita

-ɣe	'to (rivers)'
-va	'to (things)'
-ɣasina	'to (persons)'
-he	'at'

-da, -na	'on, to'
-ɣore	'with (accompaniment), singular'
-ruta	'with (accompaniment), plural'
-ɣahara	'for'
-ni	'for'
-ɣa, -ma	'with (instrument)'
-ka	partitive
-Ce	possessive (includes thematic consonant)

Some examples:

Koita

vani   be-he
time   some-at
'sometimes'

di   dehiye-he
I   back-at
'behind me'

a-ɣore
you-with
'with you'

idi   umuka-va
tree   root-to
'near the tree'

7.5.3. Complex Sentences

I discuss one syntactic feature of complex sentences in Papuan languages, **switch reference**, briefly here. This feature is typical of most groups of Papuan languages (and is also found, for example, in a number of Amerindian language groups), but it is rare in the Pacific.

The following examples from Enga illustrate what I am going to talk about. First, here are some basic verbs.[3]

Enga

Baá   p-é-á.
he   go-PAST-he
'He went.'

Baa-mé   kalái   p-i-á.
he-ERGATIVE   work   do-PAST-he
'He worked.'

Nambá   p-é-ó.
I   go-PAST-I
'I went.'

In each case the verb takes a suffix marking the tense and another marking the subject's person and number.

When two or more clauses are put together to form a complex sentence, the last verb in the clause (**final verb**) retains this subject-tense marking, but the other verbs (**medial verbs**) do not. Rather, they incorporate a suffix indicating whether the subject of the verb is the same as, or different from, the subject of the following verb. Look now at the following Enga examples:

Enga

Baa-mé   *pá-o̱*   *kalái*   *p-i-á.*
he-ERGATIVE   go-SAME:SUBJ   work   do-PAST-he
'He went and worked (at the same time).'

Nambá   *p-e-ó-pa̱*   *baa-mé*   *kalái*   *p-i-á.*
I   go-PAST-I-DIFF:SUBJ   he-ERGATIVE   work   do-PAST-he
'I went and he worked.'

In both of these sentences, the final verb, 'do,' has the suffix marking subject and tense, but the verb preceding it does not. In the first example, the verb *pá* 'go' takes the suffix -*o*, which indicates that the subject of this verb is the same as the subject of the next one, and the actions happened at the same time. In the second case, the verb 'go' (now with the form *p*) takes both tense and subject markers *and* the suffix -*pa*, which indicates that the subject of the next verb is going to be different from the subject of this verb. This is what is meant by switch-reference.

Languages with switch-reference systems are generally a little more complex than I have shown. For example, in the first sentence we find the suffix -*o*, which marked the verb as having the same subject as the next one and indicated that the actions of the two verbs were roughly simultaneous. If the second action occurred after the first, however, we would have to use the suffix -*(a)la* rather than -*o*. Here are some suffixes found on Enga medial verbs:

Enga

-*o*	same subject, simultaneous action
-*(a)la*	same subject, sequential action
-*pa*	different subject, simultaneous or sequential action
-*nya*	same subject, next verb expresses purpose or desire
-*ní-mi*	same subject, next verb expresses intense desire

Some other Papuan languages have even more complex switch-reference systems.

Languages with switch-reference systems generally have no, or few, conjunctions. The information that is carried by conjunctions in most Austronesian languages—and in languages like English—is carried by the switch-reference verbal suffixes.

8

Australian Languages: Grammatical Overview

In attempting to make generalizations about the structure of the two hundred or so languages of the Australian continent, we have to remember that many of them have disappeared virtually without trace, while many others became extinct after only a small amount of linguistic work—and that little usually the effort of linguistically untrained people—was done on them. To some extent any general statement about Australian languages is an extrapolation from the languages for which we have reasonable amounts of data and an educated reanalysis of those languages recorded by amateurs in the last century.[1]

8.1. Pronouns

Almost all Australian languages distinguish at least three numbers in pronouns—singular, dual, and plural—though a few have a trial or a paucal as well. About half the languages of Australia have an inclusive/exclusive distinction, like nearly all Oceanic languages, while the rest (like most Papuan languages) do not. There appear to be no geographical correlates of these different systems. They are scattered fairly randomly across the continent.

Below are examples of the two most common types of pronoun systems.[2]

	Wargamay	**Wajarri**
Singular		
I	*ngayba*	*ngaja*
you	*nginba*	*nyinta*
he/she/it	*nyunga*	*palu*

Dual

we two	*ngali*		we two INC	*ngali*
			we two EXC	*ngalija*
you two	*nyubula*			*nyupali*
they two	*bula*			*pula*

Plural

we	*ngana*		we INC	*nganyu*
			we EXC	*nganju*
you	*nyurra*			*nyurra*
they	*jana*			*jana*

In many Australian languages, the third person "pronouns" are not really pronouns at all, especially in the singular, but rather demonstratives, with a meaning something like "this one" or "that one" as opposed to "he/she/it".

Apart from languages with two or four numbers, there are some other variations in these general patterns. Pitta-Pitta, for example, distinguishes between masculine and feminine in the third person singular. In addition, all third person pronouns have to take a locational suffix, so the full range of third person pronouns is:

Pitta-Pitta

	Singular		Dual	Plural
	'he'	'she'	'they two'	'they'
Near	*nhuwayi*	*nhanpayi*	*pulayi*	*thanayi*
General	*nhuwaka*	*nhanpaka*	*pulaka*	*thanaka*
Far	*nhuwaarri*	*nhanpaarri*	*pulaarri*	*thanaarri*

Lardil is one of a number of languages in which non-singular pronouns take different forms depending on the relationship between the people involved. One set is used for people of the same generation or two generations apart, the other for people who are one or three generations apart. Here are the dual pronouns:

Lardil

	Same generation or two generations apart	One or three generations apart
we two INC	*ngakurri*	*ngakuni*
we two EXC	*nyarri*	*nyaanki*
you two	*kirri*	*nyiinki*
they two	*pirri*	*rniinki*

Pronouns generally vary in form according to case, that is, their function in the sentence. These case suffixes are usually the same as those for nouns.

As well as the free or independent pronouns discussed above, many Australian languages also have a set of bound pronouns, which must be attached to some other constituent in the sentence. Bound pronouns typically mark subject or object, and they are often attached to verbs:

Western Desert

pu-ngku-<u>rna</u>-<u>nta</u>
hit-FUTURE-I-you:OBJECT
'I will hit you.'

pu-ngku-<u>rni</u>-<u>n</u>
hit-FUTURE-me-you:SUBJECT
'You will hit me.'

In some languages bound pronouns are attached to an **auxiliary**—a special word in the sentence whose main function is to carry these suffixes—rather than to the verb. In the Walmajarri example below, the verb is *yi-* 'give,' but the bound pronouns are attached to the auxiliary *ma-*.

Walmajarri

Yi-nya	*ma-rna-ny-pilangu-lu*	*kakaji.*
give-PAST	AUXILIARY-we:EXC:PL-to:you:two-DUAL:O-PL:S	goanna

'We gave the goanna to you two.'

8.2. Nouns and Noun Phrases

In Australian languages, nouns are sometimes reduplicated to mark plurality or other features. The major feature of interest in the morphology of nouns in Australian languages, however, is the marking of case.

8.2.1. Case Marking

In most Australian languages, a noun phrase must take a suffix indicating its function in the sentence. Pronouns also take these case-marking suffixes.

Yidiny illustrates the kinds of case-marking systems common in Australian languages.[3] It marks a number of cases, as listed below. (Different forms of the same case marker occur after different noun-final phonemes. See the discussion of Wargamay on pp. 189–190 below for an example of this.)

Yidiny

absolutive	Ø
ergative	*-nggu, -du, -bu, -ju*

locative, allative, instrumental	-la, -da, -ba, -ja
ablative, causal	-mu, -m
dative	-nda
purposive	-gu
causal	-mu, -m
aversive	-jida, -yida
possessive	-ni

The absolutive case marks the subject of an intransitive verb and the object of a transitive verb. The ergative case marks the agent (the subject of a transitive verb).

Yidiny

Wagaal-_du_   mujam   wawa-l.
wife-ERGATIVE   mother:ABSOLUTIVE   look:at-PRESENT
'(My) wife is looking at Mother.'

The locative, allative, and ablative cases have to do with direction and location. **Locative** refers to the location, **allative** marks direction toward, and **ablative** marks direction from.

Yidiny

Mujam   gali-ng   digarra-_mu_.
mother:ABSOLUTIVE   go-PRESENT   beach-ABLATIVE
'Mother is going from the beach.'

Here are some examples of some of the other case suffixes:

Yidiny

Yingu   gurnga   mangga-ng   waguja-_nda_.
this:ABSOLUTIVE kookaburra: laugh-PRESENT   man-DATIVE
                ABSOLUTIVE
'This kookaburra is laughing at the man.'

Mujam   dubuurrji   wuna-ng   minya-_m_.
mother:ABSOLUTIVE   full:up   lie-PRESENT   meat-CAUSAL
'Mother is lying down satiated with meat.'

Yingu   waguuja   garba-ng   bama-_yida_.
this:ABSOLUTIVE man:ABSOLUTIVE   hide-PRESENT   people-AVERSIVE
'This man is hiding for fear of the people.'

The **possessive** case suffix -ni marks the possessor. A noun with this suffix also takes the case suffix of the possessed noun (since it functions like an adjective describing that noun):

Yidiny

Wagal-ni-nggu	*gudaga-nggu*	*mujam*	*baja-l.*
wife-POSS-ERGATIVE	dog-ERGATIVE	mother:	bite-PRESENT
		ABSOLUTIVE	

'(My) wife's dog is biting Mother.'

Case markers in Australian languages play the same kind of role as prepositions or postpositions in other languages of the Pacific. They indicate various kinds of grammatical relations between a noun phrase and the verb or between the noun phrase and another noun phrase. Because of this, Australian languages have no prepositions or postpositions.[4]

Nouns in Australian languages may also take other suffixes, referred to as **derivational suffixes**. Dyirbal illustrates some typical kinds of nominal suffixes.

Dyirbal

-jarran	plural
-garra	one of a pair
-manggan	one of a group
-mumbay	'all'
-barra	'belonging to a place'
-bila	comitative, 'with'
-ngarru	similative, 'like, as'

For example:

Dyirbal
gambil-barra
tablelands-belonging:to
'tablelands people'

mijiji-garra
white:woman-one:of:pair
'a white woman and someone else'

Morphophonemic changes are common when suffixes are added to nouns and verbs. Two patterns are particularly widespread. First, in many languages the initial consonant of some suffixes changes according to the final phoneme of the root to which it is suffixed. In Wargamay, for example, the ergative suffix has (at least) five forms.

Wargamay

-nggu after a vowel	*bari-nggu*	'stone'
-ndu after *l*	*maal-ndu*	'man'
-dyu after *ny*	*munyininy-dyu*	'black ant'

| -du after n, rr | gururr-du | 'brolga' |
| -bu after m | walam-bu | 'tick' |

Second, in some languages there is **vowel copying**. The vowel of a suffix mimics the final vowel of the root to which the suffix is attached. For example, Anguthimri has an ergative suffix on nouns of the form -gV, with the vowel repeating the final vowel of the root.

Anguthimri

Root		**Ergative**
kyabara	'crocodile'	kyabara-ga
βüyi	'ashes'	βüyi-gi
ku	'stick'	ku-gu

8.2.2. Noun Classes

Quite a number of Australian languages, especially in the northern part of the continent, have a gender or noun class system. Nouns belong to one of a number of classes, determined partly at least on a semantic basis. The class membership of a noun may be marked on the noun by an affix (a prefix in some languages, a suffix in others) or a particle, and it is often also marked on adjectives and other modifiers referring to the noun. In prefixing languages, the noun class membership of subjects or objects may also be marked in the verb.

Tiwi has a noun class system rather like that of French. Nouns are either masculine or feminine. Inherently masculine or feminine nouns may not be overtly marked as such, but other nouns often take a suffix. (What is inherently masculine or feminine is, of course, culturally defined: Crocodiles, for example, are thought of as masculine, [some] crabs as feminine.)

Tiwi

Masculine		**Feminine**	
tini	'male person'	tinga	'female person'
matani	'male friend'	matanga	'female friend'
kirijini	'boy'	kirijinga	'girl'

In Tiwi, adjectives, demonstratives, and possessives have to agree with the class membership of the noun they refer to:

Tiwi

Masculine		**Feminine**	
arikula-ni	yirrikipayi	arikula-nga	kiripuka
big-MASCULINE	crocodile	big-FEMININE	crab
'a big crocodile'		'a big crab'	

ngi-nanki	*kirijini*	*angi-nanki*	*pilimunga*
MASCULINE-this	boy	FEMININE-this	road
'this boy'		'this road'	
ngini-wutawa	*alawura*	*angi-wutawa*	*pulagumoka*
MASCULINE-they	boss	FEMININE-they	female:dog
'their boss'		'their bitch'	

Yanyuwa has sixteen noun classes, each one marked by a prefix that occurs also with adjectives and numerals. (The class marker is underlined in each example below.)

Yanyuwa

rra-muwarda	*rra-walkurra*	*rra-jakarda*
FEMININE-canoe	FEMININE-big	FEMININE-many
'many big dugout canoes'		
na-lungundu	*na-walkurra*	*na-jakarda*
ARBOREAL-shelter	ARBOREAL-big	ARBOREAL-many
'many big bark shelters'		
ma-murala	*ma-walkurra*	*ma-jakarda*
FOOD-wild:cucumber	FOOD-big	FOOD-many
'many big wild cucumbers'		
narnu-yabi	*narnu-arrkula*	
ABSTRACT-good	ABSTRACT-one	
'one good thing'		
nya-yabi	*nya-arrkula*	
MASCULINE-good	MASCULINE-one	
'one good man/boy'		

The last two examples show how noun class prefixes can occur even without an accompanying noun. The class marker makes the referent clear.[5]

8.2.3. Modifiers to Nouns

Demonstratives

Australian languages have no articles, but they do have a number of demonstratives referring to spatial relations. The complexity of the demonstrative system varies from language to language. Here are the demonstratives in three Australian languages.

Gumbaynggir

yaam	'this, these, here'
yarang	'that, those, there'

Yaygir

adyi, ngadyi	'this, these, here'
ila, yila	'here'
dyaadyi	'there (not too far away)'
alaara, yalaara	'there (a long way off)'

Djapu

dhuwai	'this, these, here'
dhuwali	'that, those, there (nearby)'
ngunha	'that, those, there (a long way off)'
ngunhi	anaphoric, 'the one we are talking about'

Adjectives

Adjectives behave like nouns in many ways. They take the same case suffixes and very often occur as the head of a noun phrase. (In these examples from Gumbaynggir, the ergative suffix takes the forms -*du* and -*dyu*.)

Gumbaynggir

Niiga-du	*barway-dyu*	*buwaa-ng*	*giibar*	*dyunuy*.
man-ERGATIVE	big-ERGATIVE	hit-PAST	child:O	small:O

'The big man hit the small child.'

Barway-dyu	*buwaa-ng*	*dyunuy*.
big-ERGATIVE	hit-PAST	small:O

'The big one hit the small one.'

8.2.4. Noun Phrase Structure

The tendency in Australian languages is for possessives and demonstratives to precede the head noun in the noun phrase, while adjectives follow it. The following examples illustrate this tendency. (The head noun is underlined in each case.)

Pitta-Pitta

nganya-ri	*murra*	*wima*
I-POSS	stick	big

'my big stick'

Guugu Yimidhirr

nambal	*warrga-al*
stone	big-with

'with a big stone'

Yukulta

rtathinta	*pirwanta*	<u>*ngawu*</u>	*pirtiya*
that	their	dog	bad

'that nasty dog of theirs'

This is, however, only a tendency. As with other areas of grammar in Australian languages, word order in the noun phrase is usually relatively free. In the Gumbaynggir sentence (repeated from the previous section) the adjectives follow the noun.

Gumbaynggir

Niiga-du	<u>*barway-dyu*</u>	*buwaa-ng*	*giibar*	<u>*dyunuy*</u>.
man-ERGATIVE	big-ERGATIVE	hit-PAST	child:O	small:O

'The big man hit the small child.'

But either or both *could* precede the noun in a noun phrase, yielding these possibilities:

Gumbaynggir

<u>*Barway-dyu*</u>	*niiga-du*	*buwaa-ng*	*giibar*	<u>*dyunuy*</u>.
big-ERGATIVE	man-ERGATIVE	hit-PAST	child:O	small:O

'The big man hit the small child.'

<u>*Barway-dyu*</u>	*niiga-du*	*buwaa-ng*	<u>*dyunuy*</u>	*giibar*.
big-ERGATIVE	man-ERGATIVE	hit-PAST	small:O	child:O

'The big man hit the small child.'

This freedom of order sometimes extends beyond the phrase: "Not only can words occur in any order in a phrase and phrases in any order in a sentence, [but] in addition words from different phrases may be freely scattered through a sentence" (Dixon 1980, 442). Look first at the following sentence:

Wargamay

Yibi-yibi	*ngulmburu-* *nggu*	*wurrbi-* *bajun-du*	*buudi-lganiy*	*malan-gu*.
child-PL	woman- ERGATIVE	big-very- ERGATIVE	take-CONTINUOUS	river-to

'The very big woman is taking the children to the creek.'

In this sentence, the adjective *wurrbi-bajun-du* 'very big' immediately follows the noun *ngulmburu-nggu* 'woman,' and it also clearly refers to it, because both adjective and noun are marked with the ergative suffix

194   CHAPTER 8

(morphophonemically -*nggu* and -*du*). Because of this, other orders are possible. The same sentence could be said:

Wargamay

Ngulmburu-nggu buudi-lganiy malan-gu yibi-yibi wurrbi-bajun-du.
woman-   take-   river-to child-PL big-very-
ERGATIVE   CONTINUOUS   ERGATIVE
'The very big woman is taking the children to the creek.'

Here the noun subject *ngulmburu-nggu* 'woman' is separated from its modifying adjective *wurrbi-bajun-du* 'very big' by the verb, the allative phrase, and the object.

8.3. Possessive Constructions

One case suffix added to nouns and pronouns in many Australian languages is a possessive suffix.

Djapu

djamarrkurli   *Milyin-gu*
children   Milyin-POSS
'Milyin's children'

ngarra-ku-ny   *dhuway-'mirringu-ny*
I-POSS-EMPHATIC husband-kinship-EMPHATIC
'my husband'

Many Australian languages also distinguish between alienable and inalienable possessive constructions. Alienable possession is marked by the possessive suffix, as in the examples above, and is used with all possessed nouns except parts of wholes. The part-to-whole relationship uses an inalienable construction in which there is no specific marking. Possessed and possessor nouns are just put one after the other, in that order.

Djapu

Dharpu-ngal *ngarra-n* *dhandurrung-dhu* *gatapanga-y.*
pierce-   I-OBJECT horn-ERGATIVE buffalo-ERGATIVE
COMPLETIVE
'The buffalo's horn has pierced me.'

Rluku *ngarra* *gara-thi-n.*
foot I   spear-INCHOATIVE-COMPLETIVE
'My foot has been speared.'

8.4. Verbs and the Verb Complex

In the verb system, a major grammatical difference exists between Pama-Nyungan languages and those of the rest of Australia. The Pama-Nyungan languages are nonprefixing: They use suffixes exclusively to mark verbal categories like tense, aspect, and the like. Many of the languages of Arnhem Land and the Kimberleys use both prefixes and suffixes.

8.4.1. Verbs in Pama-Nyungan Languages

The general structure of the verb in nonprefixing languages is root + (derivational suffixes) + inflection. There may be one or more derivational suffixes following a root, and there will definitely be an inflectional suffix.

Derivational Suffixes

Some derivational suffixes convert a transitive verb into an intransitive one, or an intransitive verb into a transitive one. Others mark continuous, habitual, and other aspects of the verb, as well as expressing meanings for which other languages often use adverbs.

Below are some examples of a number of derivational suffixes in two languages, Pitta-Pitta and Wargamay. In each case, only the verb root (plus derivational suffix) is given; the final hyphen means that a tense-aspect inflection needs to be added.

Pitta-Pitta

kathi-	'climb'	*kathi-la-*	'put up'
mari-	'get'	*mari-la-*	'get for'
mirrinta-	'scratch'	*mirrinta-mali-*	'scratch self'
ngunytyi-	'give'	*ngunytyi-mali-*	'exchange'
thatyi-	'eat'	*thatyi-li-*	'want to eat'
thatyi-	'eat'	*thatyi-linga-*	'going to eat'
rtinpa-	'run'	*rtinpa-ma*	'run around'
thatyi-	'eat'	*thatyi-yarnrta-*	'eat while walking along'

Wargamay

baadi-	'cry'	*baadi-ma-*	'cry for'
dyinba-	'spear'	*dyinba-ma-*	'spear with'
mayngga-	'tell'	*mayngga-ba-*	'tell each other'
dyuwara-	'stand'	*dyuwara-bali-*	'be standing'
bimbiri-	'run'	*bimbiri-yandi-*	'run away'

Inflectional Suffixes

Inflectional suffixes to verbs mark tense (or tense-aspect). They often mark a verb as being imperative or as occurring in a subordinate clause. Most Australian languages, like Latin, have more than one **conjugation** or **conjugational class** of verbs. Verbs in the same conjugation take the same suffixes, but verbs in another conjugation take a different set of suffixes, and there is no semantic explanation for why a particular verb belongs to a particular conjugational class.

To illustrate both the idea of conjugations and the kinds of grammatical functions they mark, here are some data from the Atampaya dialect of Uradhi, which has four conjugations (labeled I, II, III, and IV):

Uradhi

	I	II	III	IV
past	*-γal, -kal*	*-n*	*-ñ*	*-n*
present	*-ma*	*-al*	*-ña*	*-ø*
future	*-maŋka*	*-awa*	*-ñaŋka*	*-ŋka*
imperative	*-ði, -ṭi*	*-ri*	*-yi*	*-γu*

For the verb roots *wa-* 'burn,' *rima-* 'twirl,' *lapu-* 'blow,' and *ruŋka-* 'cry,' which belong to conjugations I, II, III, and IV, respectively, the verb forms in each tense are:

Uradhi

	I	II	III	IV
	'burn'	'twirl'	'blow'	'cry'
past	*wa-γal*	*rima-n*	*lapu-ñ*	*ruŋka-n*
present	*wa-ma*	*rima-al*	*lapu-ña*	*ruŋka*
future	*wa-maŋka*	*rima-awa*	*lapu-ñaŋka*	*ruŋka-ŋka*
imperative	*wa-ði*	*rima-ri*	*lapu-yi*	*ruŋka-γu*

8.4.2. Verbs in Prefixing Languages

Verbs in the prefixing languages of Australia have a quite different, and usually more complex, structure. I take the Wunambal language as an example here.

In Wunambal, there are two classes of verbs, which I call I and II. There appears to be no good semantic explanation as to why any particular verb belongs to one class rather than the other. In class I verbs, features of the subject are marked by a prefix, but features of the object are marked by a suffix. In class II verbs, prefixes mark both subject and object.

Class I verbs begin with one of the prefixes marking person of the subject (and, if third person, noun class membership).[6]

Wunambal

ng-	first person
g-	second person
b-, w-, m-, a-, n-, nj-	third person, different noun classes

The number of the subject is variously marked: Non-singular is marked by a prefix, but specifically dual and trial subjects take an additional suffix. For example:

Wunambal

gu-r̲-wanban	*gu-r̲-wanban-miya*
you-NON:SG-fall	you-NON:SG-fall-DUAL
'you (pl.) fall'	'you two fall'

Some tense-aspects and moods are marked by prefixes, others by suffixes.

Wunambal

gu-nu̲-ma	*gu-ma-ya*
you-not-come	you-come-FUTURE
'you didn't come'	'you will come'

For class I verbs, the object's person and number are indicated by a suffix.

Wunambal

ba-nbun-bun-wuru	*ba-nbun-bun-ngu*
he-spear-PRESENT-them	he-spear-PRESENT-it
'he spears them'	'he spears it'

Class II verbs have much the same tense-aspect marking system as class I verbs. The difference lies in the fact that the object's person and number are marked by prefixes (underlined in the examples below), which precede the subject prefixes.

Wunambal

gu̲-nga-nbun	*gu̲-r̲-nga-nbun*
you:OBJECT-I-hit	you:OBJECT-PL-I-hit
'I hit you'	'I hit you (pl.)'
bu̲-r̲-nga-nbun	*bu̲-r̲-nga-ru-nbun*
him-PL-I-hit	him-PL-I-PL-hit
'I hit them'	'we hit them'

Both classes of verbs also have a set of derivational suffixes along the lines of those found in nonprefixing languages.

8.4.3. The Verb Complex

So much semantic information is contained in the verb itself, especially because of the system of derivational suffixes, that the verb complex in
Australian languages often consists of no more than the fully inflected verb.
(Numerous examples of this have been given in preceding sections.) But a
verb complex may include adverbs or locative demonstratives, as in:

Gumbaynggir
> *Birmading*   *yilaaming.*
> run:PAST   here:PAST
> '(She) ran over here.'

> *Mudang*   *giduudaming*   *yaraang*   *yilaa.*
> unable:PAST   on:sand:PAST   there   near:speaker
> '(He) was unable to go on the sand here.'

8.5. Sentences

8.5.1. Nominal Sentences

Equational, stative, and locational sentences generally have no verb in
Australian languages. The most common order is subject + predicate.

Subject	**Predicate**

Wajarri
> *Pakarli*   *maparnpa.*
> man   sorcerer
> 'The man is a sorcerer.'

> *Warla*   *parnti.*
> egg   good
> 'The egg is good.'

> *Kuwiyari*   *marta-ngka.*
> goanna   rock-on
> 'The goanna is on the rock.'

Anguthimri
> *Angu*   *rtalawati.*
> I   red
> 'I am red.'

> *Ma*   *ngu-tyana.*
> man   clothes-without
> 'The man is naked.'

8.5.2. Verbal Sentences

In discussing the structure of verbal sentences in Oceanic languages, I introduced the distinction between accusative and ergative structures. Most Australian languages have ergative structures, so that the subject of a transitive verb (the **agent**) is marked differently from the subject of an intransitive verb. The subject of a transitive verb is in the ergative case, that of an intransitive verb in the absolutive case. The object of a transitive verb is also in the absolutive case.

Look at the following examples from Wargamay.

Wargamay

Subject/Agent	Object	Verb
Maal		*gagay.*
man:ABSOLUTIVE		go
'The man is going.'		
Maal-ndu	*ganal*	*ngunday.*
man-ERGATIVE	frog:ABSOLUTIVE	see
'The man is looking at the frog.'		
Ganal-ndu	*maal*	*ngunday.*
frog-ERGATIVE	man:ABSOLUTIVE	see
'The frog is looking at the man.'		

In Wargamay, the absolutive case is unmarked, so the noun *maal* 'man' appears as *maal* when it is the subject of an intransitive verb (as in the first sentence), and also when it is the object of a transitive verb (as in the third one). The ergative case is marked by one of a number of suffixes (cf. 8.2.1, above), one of which is *-ndu*. When *maal* 'man' or *ganal* 'frog' is the agent (the subject of a transitive verb), as in the last two sentences, it must take the ergative suffix.

In many Australian languages, however, pronouns behave differently from nouns in marking subjects and objects. Look now at the following set of sentences:

Wargamay

Subject/Agent	Object	Verb
Ngali		*gagay.*
we:two		go
'We two are going.'		
Ngali	*ganal*	*ngunday.*
we:two	frog:ABSOLUTIVE	see
'We two are looking at the frog.'		

Ganal-ndu	*ngali-nya*	*ngunday.*
frog-ERGATIVE	we:two-OBJECT	see

'The frog is looking at us two.'

These sentences show that, although the noun *ganal* 'frog' behaves erga-tively, the pronoun *ngali* 'we two' behaves accusatively. It has the same form (*ngali*) when it is subject either of an intransitive or a transitive verb, but a different form (*ngali-nya*) when it is the object of a transitive verb. In this respect it behaves exactly like its equivalent *we/us* in English. Australian lan-guages like Wargamay that treat nouns and pronouns differently are re-ferred to as **split-ergative** languages.[7]

Because Australian languages clearly mark the case or function of noun phrases in a sentence by affixes to the noun phrase (as in Wargamay), by af-fixes to the verb, or in both of these ways, it is obvious from looking at a noun phrase what its function in a sentence is. Because of this, "the order of words and phrases can, in most Australian languages, be extraordinarily free; it has little or no grammatical significance. A preferred order can usu-ally be perceived. . . .But there can be unlimited deviation from this pre-ferred order, dictated partly by discourse considerations ('topic,' and the like) and partly by the whim of the speaker" (Dixon 1980, 441).

Where there is a preferred word order, it is usually subject + verb in in-transitive sentences, and agent + object + verb in transitive sentences, as in the Wargamay examples above. Object + agent + verb, however, is just as frequent. Both versions of this Wargamay sentence are acceptable:

Wargamay

Agent	**Object**	**Verb**
Ganal-ndu	*ngali-nya*	*ngunday.*
frog-ERGATIVE	we:two-OBJECT	see

'The frog is looking at us two.'

Object	**Agent**	**Verb**
Ngali-nya	*ganal-ndu*	*ngunday.*
we:two:OBJECT	frog-ERGATIVE	see

'The frog is looking at us two.'

This is possible because (1) it is clear from the suffix *-ndu* that *ganal-ndu* 'frog' is the agent, and (2) it is also clear from the suffix *-nya* that *ngali-nya* 'us two' is the object.

Other phrases are also relatively free as far as their order is concerned, sometimes occurring before the verb and sometimes after it. It is rare, how-ever, for the verb to occur in sentence-initial position. In the following ex-amples the verb complex is underlined.

Bandjalang

Mali-yu	*ngagam-bu*	*yalany-dyu*	*giyay*	<u>*bunybeh-la*</u>.
the-ERGATIVE	dog-ERGATIVE	tongue-with	salt	lick-PRESENT

'The dog is licking salt with its tongue.'

Yidiny

Waguuja-nggu	*wagal*	<u>*bunja-ng*</u>	*banggaal-da*.
man-ERGATIVE	wife	hit-PRESENT	axe-with

'The man hit his wife with an axe.'

Wajarri

Yamaji-lu	*kuka*	*marlu*	*ngura-ki*	<u>*kangkarni-manya*</u>.
man-ERGATIVE	meat	kangaroo	camp-to	bring-PRESENT

'A man is bringing kangaroo meat to the camp.'

Australian languages do not have a passive construction, but they do have something similar. In accusative languages, the original object in an active sentence becomes the subject of the passive sentence, and the original active subject is either moved to a peripheral phrase (*The man chopped down the tree* > *The tree was chopped down by the man*), or deleted altogether (*The tree was chopped down*). Some Australian languages have what is called an **antipassive**. Look first at the following normal ergative Dyirbal sentence:

Dyirbal

Object		**Agent**		**Verb**
Bala	*yugu*	*banggul*	*yara-nggu*	*gunba-n*.
it	tree	he:ERGATIVE	man:ERGATIVE	cut-PAST

'The man was cutting the tree.'

In the antipassive, the agent (*banggul yara-nggu* 'the man') becomes the subject of what is now an intransitive verb, and the object (*bala yugu* 'the tree') becomes a peripheral phrase—in this case, a dative phrase. The verb is also marked differently. Here is the antipassive form of the sentence above:

Dyirbal

Subject		**Verb**	**Dative**	
Bayi	*yara*	*gunbal-nga-nyu*	*bagu*	*yugu-gu*.
he	man	cut-ANTIPASSIVE-PAST	it:DATIVE	tree-DATIVE

'The man was cutting the tree.'

Note that the translations of the two sentences are the same. Dixon says that, in Dyirbal at least, "a regular transitive sentence and its antipassive correspondent . . . have the same basic meaning and differ only in emphasis, rather like an active and its corresponding passive in English" (Dixon 1980, 449). Like the peripheral agent in a passive sentence, the peripheral dative phrase in an antipassive sentence can be deleted.

Dyirbal

Subject		Verb
Bayi	*yara*	*gunbal-nga-nyu.*
he	man	cut-ANTIPASSIVE-PAST

'The man was cutting.'

A small group of languages, mainly in Arnhem Land, the Pilbara region, and the Kimberleys in the northwest of the continent, offer exceptions to these generalizations. They are accusative, not ergative, in structure; the preferred order is frequently SVO (though OVS is also common); and some have a passive. Lardil illustrates these languages' structure.

Lardil

Subject	Verb	Object/Other
Pirngen	*rikur.*	
woman	cry	

'The woman is crying.'

Subject	Verb	Object/Other
Pirngen	*rnethakun*	*rtang-an.*
woman	hit	man-OBJECT

'The woman hit the man.'

Subject	Verb	Object/Other
Rtangka	*rnethakun*	*pirngen-in.*
man	hit	woman-OBJECT

'The man hit the woman.'

Subject	Verb	Object/Other
Rtangka	*rneyikun*	*pirngen-in.*
man	hit:PASSIVE	woman-OBJECT

'The man was hit by the woman.'

But these languages are in the minority, and most Australian languages adhere to the ergative model.

PART THREE

The Social
and Cultural Context

9

Languages in Contact

Languages are normally not spoken in totally isolated communities. People speaking one language usually come into contact, either occasionally or on a more regular basis, with speakers of one or more other languages, and the smaller the society that speaks a particular language, the greater is the likelihood of their being in contact with outsiders. This social contact very often has both major and minor linguistic effects.

9.1. The Social Context of Language Contact

9.1.1. Peaceful Contact between Settled Societies

One common kind of social contact between different language communities in the Pacific is that between relatively equal and settled societies. In many parts of the region, for example, marriage regulations require a man to marry a woman from outside his own clan and community. This practice of exogamy often means that husband and wife speak different languages. Where a number of men in the same village choose wives from the same outside community, a foreign-language enclave will form, at least temporarily, in the village. Since women have the primary responsibility for looking after younger children, those children will often grow up hearing two languages spoken in the home. The women may not much influence the way the men speak, but they do influence how their children speak. These children often end up incorporating some aspects of their mothers' language into their own.

A second kind of peaceful contact involves regular trade. There are numerous cases in the Pacific where, for example, people of a coastal village trade with inland villagers—the former supplying fish and other marine produce, the latter vegetables and other non-maritime commodities. Such a situation occurred in Central Papua, where the coastal Motu traded with the inland Koita and Koiari people. Many words for maritime concepts in Koita are originally Motu words, while the Motu have taken into their language Koita words for non-maritime things.

9.1.2. Peaceful Contact Involving Travel

Not all trade takes place between sedentary peoples; it may also involve some or all of the parties traveling considerable distances. In the western Pacific, for example, anthropologists have documented such large-scale trading complexes as the *hiri* of the Gulf of Papua, the *kula* of the islands of the Milne Bay area, and the *moka* of the highlands of Papua New Guinea. A great deal of long-distance trade in all kinds of commodities seems to have occurred in nearly every part of Australia and the Pacific.

Such trading expeditions, of course, bring people speaking different languages together, at least for short periods, and also often bring new things and ideas into at least one of the societies involved. In such cases, **borrowing** or **copying** often takes place. That is, the society into which something new is introduced often takes the word for that thing from the language of those introducing it. This is how English acquired such words as *alcohol, curry, tomato, pasta, tapioca, sago*, and hundreds of others.

Migration—either temporary or permanent—also brings people speaking different languages together. Temporary migration, at least in the Pacific, generally means that people leave their home area to work in towns or on plantations or ships for a period of time and then return home, often bringing with them new things and ideas—along with the words for them in some other language. Permanent migration involves long-term settlement in a new area, often because of overcrowding or sociopolitical problems at home, or because of natural disasters like volcanic eruptions. A smallish community speaking one language may live in the middle of a larger community speaking a different language, and the potential exists for each language to influence the other.

The whole of the Pacific region was settled from its western extremes, and Australia was probably settled from the north. Some of these migrants would have been the first people to settle a particular area, while others would have come into contact with descendants of the original settlers. In more recent times, not only have rural people moved into urban areas, but whole communities have been relocated: Mission stations all over the region, government settlements in Australia, and the resettlement of the

Banabans on Rabi Island in Fiji represent three such cases. There have also been significant movements of populations from Micronesia and Polynesia into the United States and New Zealand (see chapter 2). All of these situations bring languages into contact, with various degrees of closeness.

9.1.3. Conquest, Colonization, and Conversion

Politico-military takeovers by one society of another represent a less peaceful kind of social and linguistic contact. Once again, the Pacific abounds in examples, of which the Tongan domination of the Lau group in Fiji and the warlike Orokaiva and Mailu in Papua New Guinea, who enslaved conquered peoples, are three. As with the Norman conquest of England a thousand years ago, these takeovers produced dramatic changes in language, as the conquered peoples were forced to learn their conquerors' language to survive.

European and Asian colonization of Australia and the Pacific represents a more recent, but thoroughgoing, example of politico-military conquest. The Spanish, Dutch, Germans, French, and Japanese, as well as English speakers from a number of nations, have all made incursions into the region over the last four centuries, French and English currently being the dominant metropolitan languages in the Pacific. These outsiders introduced new forms of government and education, brought in a vast number of new technological items and social customs, and were responsible for the establishment of plantations and urban centers. English and French have been the major languages of government, education, and inter- and intraregional communication, and are looked on in many parts of the Pacific as *the* prestige languages. Because of both the attitudes toward these two European languages and the new concepts introduced by Europeans, English and French have had a considerable influence on most Pacific languages.

The founding of missions preceded colonization in some cases, and followed it in others. This process could be viewed as a conquest of a different kind—the displacement of traditional religious systems in favor of western Christian beliefs and religious practices, as missionaries aimed for a conquest of the souls and minds of aboriginal Australians and Pacific Islanders. The establishment of churches and schools, as well as the more or less successful abolition of some traditional customs, resulted in the introduction of new words for new concepts—in some cases even new ways of speaking, as formal prayers and hymns were developed.

In multilingual Melanesia particularly, missions were responsible for setting up certain vernaculars as church languages, for example, Tolai,

Gedaged, Yabêm, Kâte, Dobuan, Suau, and Wedau in Papua New Guinea, Roviana in Solomon Islands, and Mota in Vanuatu. Faced with a multiplicity of languages in a relatively small area, missionaries often chose one language as the language of the mission, requiring speakers of neighboring and usually related languages to use the chosen language in religious contexts. This practice has helped create a complex situation in which both European and Pacific church languages influence other languages in the region.

9.2. The Linguistic Effects of Contact

9.2.1. Lexical Change

Virtually all languages borrow or copy words from other languages. English is an excellent example, as it has taken in thousands of words from very diverse sources. In the Pacific, the influence of both local and intrusive languages on other Pacific languages has led to the incorporation of new words into those languages.

Speakers of the non-Polynesian languages of Southern Vanuatu, who have probably been in the area for well over two thousand years, came into contact with speakers of the Polynesian language West Futuna about a thousand years ago. These immigrant Polynesians introduced their neighbors to kava-drinking and refined their maritime skills, especially those involving deep-sea fishing. The words below are West Futuna loans into Kwamera, a Tanna language, suitably adapted to Kwamera's phonological and grammatical structure (Lynch 1994, 1996):

Kwamera Loans from West Futuna

	Kava terminology		
Kwamera		West Futuna	
n*i*kava	'kava'	kava	
tapuga	'chief's kava'	tapuga	
tamafa	'ritual spitting of kava'	taumafa	
nafunu	'food eaten after drinking kava'	fono	
akona	'drunk'	kona	
taporoka	'kind of canoe-shaped kava bowl'	ta poruku	'kind of canoe'
nafáu	'kava strainer'	fao	'coconut branch used as a kava strainer'

Maritime terminology

Kwamera		West Futuna
tira	'mast'	*shira*
nɨkiatu	'outrigger boom'	*kiato*
kwan-metau	'fishhook'	*metao*
takwarau	'prevailing wind'	*tokorau*
tafra	'whale'	*tafora*
tataua	'barracuda'	*tatao*
tagarua	'sea snake'	*tagaroa*

Trukese provides a good example of the influence of succeeding colonial powers. Much of western and central Micronesia was under Spanish control from the late seventeenth century until the Spanish-American War in 1898, when Guam was ceded to the United States, and the rest of Spain's possessions went to Germany, which had already colonized the Marshall Islands to the east. Japan succeeded Germany at the outbreak of World War I, and the United States succeeded Japan at the end of World War II. The influence of each of these colonial languages can be seen in borrowed words in Trukese (Goodenough and Sugita 1980):

Trukese

antiyos	'fishing goggles'	<	Spanish *anteojos*
koopwure	'corrugated iron'	<	Spanish *cobre* 'copper'
paatere	'priest'	<	Spanish *padre*
kiiwúfer	'suitcase'	<	German *Koffer*
kkumi	'rubber'	<	German *Gummi*
maak	'money'	<	German *Mark* (monetary unit)
kooyeng	'playground'	<	Japanese *kōen* 'park'
osiroy	'baby powder'	<	Japanese *oshiroi*
ramúne	'marbles'	<	Japanese *ramune*
miniyon	'million'	<	English *million*
pinakpwoot	'blackboard'	<	English *blackboard*
sekit	'jacket'	<	English *jacket*

Samoan is a good example of missionary influence on a language. Many new words came into it from the biblical languages Greek, Latin, and Hebrew:

Samoan

peritome	'circumcise'	<	Greek *peritome*
agelu	'angel'	<	Greek *angelos*

ti'āpolo	'devil'	<	Greek *diabolos*
sātauro	'cross'	<	Greek *stauros*
'aila	'deer, gazelle'	<	Hebrew *'ayyal*
'oreva	'vulture'	<	Hebrew *'orebh* 'raven'
'urosa	'bear'	<	Latin *ursus*

9.2.2. Semantic Change

Contact may also bring about changes in the meanings of existing words in a language. This may involve expanding the meaning of a word to refer to something newly introduced. For example, Fijian *dakai* originally meant 'bow (for shooting),' and Lenakel *kopwiel* means 'stone,' but both have taken on the additional meaning 'gun, rifle.' In Ponapean, *sakau* originally referred only to kava, but now it refers to any intoxicating beverage. *Nting* meant 'to tattoo' in Ponapean but now also means 'to write.'

Semantic change may also involve narrowing the meaning of a word. Lenakel *niko* originally meant both 'canoe' and 'moiety' (since it was believed that the first members of the two moieties arrived on the island in two different canoes). But the form *kenu* (from English via Bislama) is now the common word for 'canoe' and for most Lenakel speakers, *niko* now means only 'moiety.'

9.2.3. Phonological Change

When a language takes in words from another language, it often adapts them to its own phonology. The English words *restaurant, miracle, prince, royal,* and *court,* for example, all derive from French, but they are not pronounced as the French pronounce them: They have been adapted to English phonological patterns. Sometimes, however, the copying of words from one language into another may bring about a change in the phonological system of the borrowing language, either through the introduction of a totally new sound, or through the reorganization of the existing sounds in a language.

Dyirbal, for example, is typical of many Australian languages, in that the phoneme /l/ is not permitted at the beginning of words. However, the introduction of words like *lada* 'ladder' and *laymun* 'lemon' from English has brought about a change in the phonological structure of Dyirbal, which now permits word-initial /l/.

Motu originally had no contrast between the sounds [t] and [s]: [s] occurred before [i] and [e], while [t] occurred before other vowels. English words copied into Motu originally fit this pattern.[1]

Motu

[sesi]	'shirt'
[makesi]	'market'
[sini]	'tin'
[tupu]	'soup'
[topu]	'soap'

Due to the persistent influence of English, however, younger generations now pronounce these words as follows:

Motu

[seti]	'shirt'
[maketi]	'market'
[tini]	'tin'
[supu]	'soup'
[sopu]	'soap'

What has happened here is that the distribution of [s] and [t] has changed, and there is now contrast between them.

In addition to changing the distribution of existing sounds in a language, contact may also lead to the introduction of a new sound. Samoan, for example, originally had an *l* but no *r*. As the result of contact with other languages, however a number of words with *r* have been introduced:

Samoan

'Aperila	'April'	<	English
'areto	'bread'	<	Greek *artos*
'ario	'silver'	<	Tahitian *ario*
faresaio	'pharisee'	<	Greek *farisaios*
misionare	'missionary'	<	English
'oreva	'vulture'	<	Hebrew *'orebh* 'raven'
rosa	'rose'	<	English
teropika	'tropics'	<	English
'urosa	'bear'	<	Latin *ursus*

9.2.4. Grammatical Change

Finally, contact between languages may also bring about changes in grammatical structure. Polynesian Triangle languages are normally verb-initial (see chapter 6):

Tahitian

Verb		Subject		Object		
'Ua tāpū		*te*	*vahine*	*'i*	*te*	*vahie.*
PAST	cut	the	woman	OBJECT	the	wood

'The woman cut the wood.'

Polynesian Outlier languages, however, are much more flexible, allowing both VSO and SVO orders, with SVO probably being more common:

Nukuoro

Verb		Subject	Object	
Ne	*kake*	*ia*	*te*	*nui.*
PAST	climb	he	the	coconut

'He climbed the coconut.'

Subject	Verb		Object	
Ia	*ne*	*kake*	*te*	*nui.*
he	PAST	climb	the	coconut

'He climbed the coconut.'

This has almost certainly come about at least in part from contact with neighboring non-Polynesian languages, which are almost exclusively SVO.

A similar change seems to have occurred on the mainland of New Guinea. The original Oceanic languages spoken there almost certainly had verb + object order (whether SVO or VOS is a matter of some discussion, but is irrelevant here). Then they came into contact with Papuan speakers, for whom SOV was the basic order, and this contact led to a change in the Oceanic languages' word order, from SVO (or VOS) to SOV. (Some examples of languages with this order were given in chapter 6.)

Let us look at one more example, this time from the Papuan language Yimas:

> The formation of a negative verb from a positive one in Yimas is a complicated affair, involving alteration of the form and the position of certain verbal affixes. Many younger speakers do not know this method of negation, but negate a verb by merely placing a particle *ina* before it. This is clearly a borrowing from Tok Pisin *i no* [= PREDICATE MARKER + NEGATIVE], but these speakers were totally unaware of its origin, regarding it as a native Yimas word until I pointed out its similarity to the Tok Pisin negative. (Foley 1986, 40)

9.3. Three Case Studies

Direct and indirect inheritance of vocabulary in Rotuman, borrowing as a result of word taboo in Australia, and contact between Austronesian and Papuan languages in northwest New Britain are three cases illustrating the effects of language contact.

9.3.1. Rotuman

The Rotuman vowel system has undergone some interesting developments (chapter 5). But Rotuman is also a language where contact has led to a complex situation for the historical-comparative linguist.

> Rotuman words exhibit two sets of correspondences with proto-forms. . . . I propose to speak of directly [set I] and indirectly inherited words [set II] rather than inherited and loan words in order to emphasize that *all* of the words with etymologies were once part of a language ancestral to Rotuman in the comparativist's sense. Some of them however re-entered Rotuman from a collateral related language after undergoing changes other than those which affected forms which had remained continuously in the Rotuman line. (Biggs 1965, 389–390)

I am concerned here exclusively with the development of some of the consonants in Rotuman.

What appears to have happened in Rotuman is this. The original settlers would have brought with them a version of Proto Central Pacific (PCP). Over time, some of the consonants changed their pronunciation, with the result that the following regular developments can be identified (Biggs' directly inherited, or Set I, correspondences).[2]

PCP	°*v*	°*p*,°*b*	°*t*	°*d*	°*r*	°*dr*	°*l*	°*k*	°*g*	°*?*
Rotuman (Set I)	*h*	*p*	*f*	*t*	*r*	*t*	*l*	*?*	*k*	ø

Some examples of this set of sound correspondences are given below:

Proto Central Pacific		Rotuman (Set I)
°*vitu*	'seven'	*hifu*
°*kuli*	'skin'	*?uli*
°*?atu*	'line, row'	*afu*
°*viri*	'plait'	*hiri*

Subsequent to the original settlement of Rotuma, there seem to have been at least two later "invasions" by people speaking languages different from but related to pre-Rotuman. These invasions resulted in fairly large-scale borrowings of vocabulary. Biggs (1965, 411) sums up the situation as follows: "It is clear that Rotuman has borrowed extensively from a related language or languages. . . . Rotuman traditions are definite in associating at least two occupations of their island with the Samoa-Tonga area, particularly the islands of Savai?i [in Samoa] and Niuafo?ou [in Tonga]." The languages of the invaders had made somewhat different changes to the Proto Central Papuan consonant inventory. Of Biggs' corpus of Rotuman words with known etymologies, 38 percent belong to Set I (as above), but 29 percent belong rather to the set of indirectly inherited correspondences (Set II), which are given below along with Set I for comparison.[3]

PCP		°*v*	°*p,*°*b*	°*t*	°*d*	°*r*	°*dr*	°*l*	°*k*	°*g*	°*?*
Rotuman (Set I)		*h*	*p*	*f*	*t*	*r*	*t*	*l*	*?*	*k*	*ø*
Rotuman (Set II)	*f*	*p*		*t*	*t*	*r, ø*	*r*	*r*	*k*	*k*	*?*

Here are some examples of words containing Set II correspondences; in each case, the expected, but non-occurring, Set I form is given as well (marked with a double asterisk).

Proto Central Pacific		**Rotuman (Set II)**
°*viti*	'spring up'	*fiti* (expected Set I °°*hifi*)
°*tuki*	'pound'	*tuki* (expected Set I °°*fu?i*)
°*kolo*	'desire'	*koro* (expected Set I °°*?olo*)
°*robe*	'overhang'	*ope* (expected Set I °°*rope*)

In some cases the same word has come into the language twice, first directly (Set I) and later indirectly (Set II), though with slight differences in meaning. For example:

PCP	**Rotuman**	
	Set I	**Set II**
°*kuli* 'skin'	*?uli* 'skin'	*kiria* 'leprosy'
°*vidi* 'jump, spring'	*hiti* 'start with surprise'	*fiti* 'jump'
°*toka* 'come ashore'	*fo?a* 'come ashore'	*toka* 'settle down'

9.3.2. Word Taboo in Australia

Australian languages—as well as many others in the Pacific—are characterized by a system of **word taboo**. This can take a number of forms: One very common one is that "a person's name cannot be spoken for some time after his death. What is more, any normal vocabulary item—noun, adjective, verb etc.—that is similar in form to the banned name must also be tabooed" (Dixon 1980, 28). Imagine if this were to apply in English: When someone called *Bill* dies, we could not use the word *bill* (meaning either 'account' or 'beak of a bird'), nor probably could we use phonologically similar words like *build, billet, billy*, and perhaps *pill*. We would have to find new words . . . at least for a time.

In Australia, the tabooed word is sometimes replaced by a synonym or near synonym from within the language. In our imaginary example above, *bill* could then be replaced by (1) *check* or *account* and (2) *beak*. "But more often a new word will be borrowed from the language of a neighboring tribe" (Dixon 1980, 28). Examples:

1. "In 1975 a man named Djäyila died at Yirrkala and as a result the common verb *djäl-* 'to want, to be desirous of' was proscribed and replaced by *ḍukṭuk-*, probably a verb from another Yolŋu dialect that did have this set of meanings" (Dixon 1980, 28).

2. "In 1977 a Djapu man named Djewiny died and the loanword *dhe* 'tea' was at once tabooed at Yirrkala; another loanword *gopi* 'coffee' had its meaning extended also to cover 'tea' (little coffee is in fact drunk at Yirrkala; if disambiguation is necessary it can be referred to as *gopi yuwalk* 'real coffee')" (Dixon 1980, 122).

9.3.3. Northwest New Britain

In a series of studies, Thurston (1982, 1987, 1992) has documented the effects of language contact among a number of languages spoken in the northwest of New Britain. The area Thurston discusses is currently occupied by a number of Oceanic languages (important to this discussion are the coastal languages Kabana, Amara, Kove, and Lusi), and the Papuan language Anêm. "The Anêm are now completely surrounded by speakers of Austronesian languages. . . . Evidence suggests that Anêm is the sole surviving member of a non-Austronesian language family that once extended over much of what is now West New Britain Province. West of the Willaumez Peninsula, all of these languages, except Anêm, have been replaced by Austronesian languages which retain features of a non-Austronesian substratum" (Thurston 1992, 125).

Contact in this area between speakers of different languages, related and unrelated, has been going on for a long time, with quite far-reaching effects:

> Generations of marriage and trade across linguistic boundaries, the longstanding tradition of regional multilingualism, and the spread of languages by way of language shift have all conspired to produce regional similarity in phonology, syntax, semantics, social structure, economy, cosmology and values. . . . Aside from lexical form, the

speakers of Austronesian languages in northwestern New Britain share much more with the Anêm than they do with speakers of distant Austronesian languages that are lexically more similar. (Thurston 1992, 125)

There has been a large amount of lexical copying in both directions between the Oceanic languages and Anêm, but of more interest are changes in grammar as a result of this prolonged contact. Some of the grammatical features of Lusi (and some of the other Oceanic languages in the area) that seem to have been introduced from Anêm or its extinct relatives are described below.

1. The reciprocal is marked by a suffix to the verb, rather than by a prefix, as is widespread in Oceanic languages (see 6.4.6 above).

    Lusi

    Ti-rau-nga-ri.
    they-hit-RECIPROCAL-them
    'They fought each other.'

    Anêm

    I-pəl-ak.
    they-hit-RECIPROCAL
    'They fought each other.'

2. Tense/aspect, negation, and similar categories are marked at the end of the verb phrase, rather than by prefixes or preverbal particles, as is common in Oceanic languages (see 6.4.2 above).

    Lusi

I-rau	*ɣaea*	*mao.*
he-hit	pig	not

    'He didn't kill a pig.'

I-la	*pa*	*Rabaul*	*ɣasili.*
he-go	to	Rabaul	COMPLETIVE

    'He has (already) gone to Rabaul.'

    Anêm

U-b-i	*aba*	*mantu.*
he-kill-it	pig	not

    'He didn't kill a pig.'

U-k	*axi*	*Rabaul*	*bizang.*
he-go	to	Rabaul	COMPLETIVE

    'He has (already) gone to Rabaul.'

3. Lusi has two postpositions, *aea* purposive and *iai* locative, as well as a handful of prepositions. Oceanic languages with postpositions tend to be restricted to the New Guinea mainland. Although Anêm does not have postpositions, Thurston suggests that Lusi probably acquired its postpositions as a result of contact with one of the now extinct Papuan languages of the area.

The contact has not been one way, however. An inclusive/exclusive distinction in the first person is almost universal in Oceanic languages, but is exceedingly rare among Papuan languages (see 7.1 above). Anêm shows this distinction in possessive suffixes (though not in other pronominal forms), and it also has the inalienable/edible/neutral contrast in possessive constructions, typical of western Oceanic languages, but nonexistent in Papuan languages (Thurston 1987, 91). The long-term intimate contact between languages in this area has clearly produced major changes in the structure of these languages.

9.3.4. "Mixed" Languages?

The Anêm-Lusi situation just described gives rise to the following question: How much can Language A be influenced by Language B and still remain Language A? Or in different words, can a language be truly "mixed," not deriving from just one ancestor, but in a sense from two? There are numerous theoretical and philosophical questions involved here, and they have generated considerable debate—not to mention heat and acrimony—in the discussion of certain languages in the Pacific, especially in Melanesia.[4]

I do not wish to go into these philosophical and theoretical questions here. There are, however, a number of cases where the influence of one or more languages on another has led different reputable linguists to classify languages differently. To take some extreme examples, the following have been classified as Papuan by some linguists and as Austronesian by others: Maisin in the Oro Province of Papua New Guinea; Magori and its neighboring moribund relatives on the south coast of Papua; the languages of Santa Cruz and the Reef Islands in Solomon Islands; and the languages of Aneityum, New Caledonia, and the Loyalty Islands.

In all except the Reefs–Santa Cruz situation, the general view today is that the languages involved are originally Austronesian. Maisin and Magori have been very heavily influenced by Papuan languages, whereas Aneityum and the New Caledonian languages are probably so aberrant in their phonological and grammatical histories that they happen not to look very Austronesian. The Reefs–Santa Cruz languages, however, were probably originally Papuan languages that have been very heavily influenced by Austronesian languages.

These decisions have been reached by ignoring vocabulary for the most part and looking instead at the core of the languages' grammatical systems.

Even languages like these are not truly mixed, in the sense of having two co-equal ancestors. They are, however, cases where the influence of another language has been so strong as to make genetic affiliation very difficult to determine.

9.4. Historical Implications

In chapter 1, I discussed the way in which historical inferences can be drawn from an examination of the relationships between languages. Borrowing of vocabulary, phonology, and grammar does not constitute genetic relationship: The fact that the Fijian words *sitoa* and *sitaba* have been copied from English "store" and "stamp" does not mean that Fijian is related to English.

But although the relationship between Fijian and English is not a genetic one, there is still a historical connection between them. An examination of English words copied into Fijian, for example, provides us with information of a cultural-historical nature. They indicate what kinds of things were introduced to Fijian society and culture by English colonials, missionaries, and settlers, and what kinds of changes took place in Fijian society and culture as a result of external influence.

Let us go back to the example of Kwamera loans from West Futuna to illustrate this in a bit more detail. (Recall that this copying took place long before Europeans came to the area.) The following words relating to kava and kava-drinking were borrowed by Kwamera:

Kwamera

nɨkava	'kava'
tapuga	'chief's kava'
tamafa	'ritual spitting of kava'
nafunu	'food eaten after drinking kava'
akona	'drunk'
taporoka	'kind of canoe-shaped kava bowl'
nafáu	'kava strainer'

Clearly, this indicates a significant change in Kwamera culture. This list of words represents not just the random borrowing of a few items, but the taking over of a whole cultural complex—the preparation and drinking of kava, with its attendant rituals and behaviors (Lynch 1996).

Nor is this the end of the story of cultural contact between the Polynesian and non-Polynesian societies of southern Vanuatu. The non-Polynesian languages have also borrowed heavily from Futuna maritime vocabulary, especially where long-distance voyaging or deep-sea fishing is concerned (Lynch 1994). Futuna, on the other hand, has borrowed a number of words for varieties of yam, taro, and breadfruit from their more horticulturally inclined non-Polynesian neighbors. And perhaps most interesting of all, Futuna speakers appear to have been responsible for introducing a moiety system to neighboring Tanna. This system fell into desuetude on Futuna, but was reintroduced . . . by the Tannese (Lynch and Fakamuria 1994)! An examination of borrowed items in a language can give us significant information about the nature of contact-induced cultural change. The influence of non-Pacific languages on those of the Pacific has been considerable over the past couple of centuries or so, but Pacific Islanders have been moving around the region for thousands of years, and contact between languages has been part of the linguistic scene in the Pacific for the whole period.

Pidgins, Creoles, and Koines

Contact may have quite drastic effects on a language. But it may also lead to the creation of totally new languages, which in some senses at least qualify as "mixed" languages. Three of these new languages are, in terms of number of speakers, among the largest languages spoken in the Pacific today (although not all speakers of any of these languages speak them as their mother tongue). I use the term **Melanesian Pidgin** as a cover term for the three languages/dialects known as Tok Pisin in Papua New Guinea, Pijin in Solomon Islands, and Bislama in Vanuatu, spoken in all by perhaps three million people.[1] Hiri Motu is spoken in Papua New Guinea by about a quarter of a million people. And Fiji Hindi, one of the two major languages of Fiji, has more than 300,000 speakers. This chapter looks at these three languages and at similar languages in various parts of the Pacific.

10.1. Pidginization, Creolization, and Koineization

How do languages like Melanesian Pidgin develop? What is it about certain kinds of contact situations that gives rise to new languages?

The term **pidgin** or **pidgin language** refers to a language that develops in a multilingual contact situation, where the contact between the different groups is prolonged but relatively restricted. Trade relationships, plantations, and ships' companies are typical breeding grounds for such languages, and in situations like these the process of **pidginization** begins to take place. All speakers of a pidgin language use it as a second language, to communicate with speakers of other languages when there is no other common language. In comparison with the first languages of its speakers, a pidgin is usually simplified in pronunciation, grammar, and vocabulary. In many cases, especially in colonial situations, the vocabulary of the pidgin is drawn mainly from the politically dominant (i.e., colonial) language, whereas the grammar is often based on the language(s) of the colonized people.

Urbanization and marriage between people from different linguistic backgrounds can turn a pidgin into people's first language, especially when those people are the children of such mixed marriages growing up in towns. In these cases, the pronunciation, grammar, and vocabulary of the original pidgin language tends to expand rapidly and considerably. The language becomes more complex because it is being used for all the communicative purposes of a "normal" language. This process of expansion is referred to as **creolization**. A **creole**, or a **creole language**, is a language that has developed from a pidgin, but which is now the first language of many of its speakers.

A different kind of mixing—what is known as **dialect mixing**—produces a different kind of language. When people speaking different geographical dialects of a language are relocated and thrown together in a new community, what is known as a **koine** often develops, through a process known as **koineization**. Each dialect contributes some elements, and the resultant koine is a blend of the original dialects. While Melanesian Pidgin and Hiri Motu are the result of the processes of pidginization and creolization, Fiji Hindi is a koine.[2]

10.2. Melanesian Pidgin

Melanesian Pidgin and various Australian creoles are referred to as "English-based" or "English-lexifier" creoles. This means simply that the bulk of their vocabulary is derived from English, though some vocabulary, and much of the grammar, may have different origins. (This does *not* mean that these languages are "broken English" or "baby-talk" languages; after all, although a very significant proportion of the vocabulary of English comes from Romance languages like Latin and French, we don't consider English to be "broken Romance"!)

10.2.1. Historical Background

The late eighteenth and early nineteenth centuries saw the first prolonged and continuous contact between people living in the Pacific and outsiders. In the Pacific Islands, European explorers and missionaries were followed by whalers, sandalwooders, pearlers, bêche-de-mer[3] fishermen, and traders, all of whom had regular, if sporadic, contact with at least some people in some Pacific islands. In Australia and New Zealand, of course, contact was more intense in many areas as a result of European settlement. This contact intensified during the nineteenth century as labor recruiters began recruiting Pacific Islanders to work on plantations in various parts of the region, especially Samoa, Fiji, and Queensland. In Queensland there was also some contact between Pacific Islanders and aboriginal Australians, who themselves were often moved from their tribal homelands into situations where they lived and worked with speakers of other languages.

In all of these situations, numerous fairly unstable pidgins developed. In Melanesia and parts of Australia, these unstable pidgins developed into relatively stable languages as people who had learned different varieties in different parts of the Pacific came into contact. The contact between Europeans, mainly English speakers, Pacific Islanders (almost exclusively speakers of Oceanic languages), and aboriginal Australians was responsible for the very significant English input into the vocabulary of these creoles. But it was not just this contact that was significant in the development of Melanesian Pidgin. The contact *between* Pacific Islanders from different linguistic backgrounds was important from the beginning, became even more so later on, and was probably responsible for the Austronesian contribution to the grammar of Melanesian Pidgin.

By the latter part of the nineteenth century, English-based pidgins were spoken, in various forms and with various levels of sophistication, in almost the whole of the Pacific Basin: from New Guinea to Pitcairn Island, and from the Marshalls and Hawai'i to New Caledonia and New Zealand. In most of these places, however, the pidgins died out.[4] In some places, like New Caledonia and the British colony of Papua (the southern half of what is now Papua New Guinea), this was as a result of government policy. The governments were strongly opposed to a "bastard" form of English being used, though possibly for different reasons (the British in Papua because they saw it as a "bastard" language, the French probably because they saw it as a form of English!). In other places, like most of the countries of Polynesia, the pidgin simply became unnecessary as people from other parts of the Pacific stopped being recruited to work on plantations in these countries, and as educational levels improved. In Samoa, for example, the cessation of labor recruiting and the establishment of schools meant that pidgin English was no longer needed. Samoan was the language of communication between Samoans, while first German and then English were used for communicating with foreigners.

The situation in Melanesia and Australia was very different. First, the countries are geographically larger and linguistically more diverse than those of Polynesia and Micronesia, and it was more difficult for governments to exercise strong control over language use. Second, although recruitment of Melanesian laborers to overseas plantations stopped soon after 1900, this simply meant that laborers began moving around their own country working on newly established plantations, frequently outside their own language communities. Any plantation might have a labor force drawn from a large number of different language groups. Third, as a result of this internal mobility, men often married women who spoke a different language, and the pidgin would have been the only language used in the home. Finally, the establishment of urban centers attracted people speaking a multiplicity of languages from far and wide.

Social conditions in Melanesia and in parts of Australia, therefore, were ripe not just for the preservation and retention of the pidgin but also for its development into a creole. Children grew up speaking it as their first language; adults who had not returned to their traditional homes for many years found that they were using the pidgin/creole more and more, and their own language less and less. As the twentieth century progressed, Melanesian Pidgin became *the* language of the people in what were to become the independent states of Papua New Guinea, Solomon Islands, and Vanuatu. Australian creoles and varieties of English spoken by Aboriginal people acquired similar importance.

10.2.2. Different Histories

The Melanesian Pidgin spoken by Papua New Guineans, Solomon Islanders, and ni-Vanuatu is recognizably the same language—with recognizable differences between how it is spoken in each of these three countries. The following examples show both the similarities and the differences between these three varieties:

Tok Pisin
  Dispela pikinini i sindaun i stap na kaikai kiau wantaim kek.

Pijin
  Desfala pikinini i sidaon an kaekae eg weitim kek.

Bislama
  Pikinini ya i stap staon mo kakae eg wetem gato.
  'This child is sitting down and eating eggs and cake.'

Where do these kinds of differences come from? To answer this question, we need to look more closely at the historical development of this language.

Men from Vanuatu were first recruited to work on plantations in Queensland and Fiji in the 1860s, and a little later men from the Solomon

Islands were recruited for the same work, so there was considerable contact between ni-Vanuatu and Solomon Islanders at this time. Only a few people from this part of the Pacific, however, were recruited to work in Samoa, and then only for a short time.

Men from the German colony of New Guinea, however, did not go to Queensland or to Fiji, which were British colonies. Rather, starting in the 1880s, they went to work on the plantations in Samoa, then a German colony. For a few years they were in contact with ni-Vanuatu and Solomon Islanders, from whom they would have learned the basics of Melanesian Pidgin, but for the next few decades, the New Guinea version of Melanesian Pidgin, known today as Tok Pisin, developed in isolation both from other varieties of the language and from English. The German and Samoan languages contributed some words to early Tok Pisin, although many of these have disappeared. The major contributing languages (other than English) have been Tolai (cf. *kiau* 'egg' in the example above) and other Austronesian languages of New Britain and New Ireland, since Rabaul (where Tolai is spoken) was the headquarters of German New Guinea, and the place where most of the laborers were recruited from or returned to.

Pijin and Bislama did not undergo any of these influences. However, because the French jointly ruled the New Hebrides (now Vanuatu) with the British for most of the twentieth century, Bislama has incorporated a number of words of French origin (like *gato* 'cake' in the example above). It has also taken in quite a few words from local languages. Neither French (for obvious reasons) nor local languages (for less obvious reasons) have made any significant contribution to Pijin in Solomon Islands, however. The different colonial histories of each country, along with different labor-recruitment patterns, meant that there were significant differences in the contact situations while each version of the language was developing.

10.2.3. The Structure of Melanesian Pidgin

In recent years, the influence of English on Melanesian Pidgin has become even more dominant than in the past, not only in terms of vocabulary, but to some extent also in pronunciation and grammar as well. At the same time, there is considerably more contact today between Melanesians from different countries, and interdialectal influence is also beginning to be seen. One of the features of a language undergoing creolization is that different people speak it with different degrees of fluency. For some people, it is their first language. For others, it is very much a second language, and the way they speak it is often influenced by their first language. Those who have been educated in English often incorporate words and other linguistic features from English into their Pidgin, while less educated speakers do this much less frequently. And although all languages are changing, languages like Melanesian Pidgin are changing much faster than others.

Hence, it is often difficult to say exactly what is or is not "in" a language like Melanesian Pidgin. I try to describe the variety spoken by fluent but not highly educated speakers, but comment from time to time on common variations from these patterns.

Sound System

Melanesian Pidgin has the same five-vowel system as is found in the majority of the languages of the Pacific:

i		u
e		o
	a	

Educated speakers, however, sometimes incorporate English vowels into their speech. An educated Papua New Guinean might say /bæŋ/ or /bæŋk/ for 'bank,' whereas someone less educated will say /beŋ/.

The basic consonant system is also similar to that found in many of the Oceanic languages of Melanesia:

p	t	k	
b	d	g	
f	s		h
v	ʤ		
m	n	ŋ	
	l		
	r		
w	y		

Notable omissions, as a result of the pidginization process, are the common Melanesian fricatives /x/ and /ɣ/, which don't occur in English, and the English fricatives /θ ð z ʃ ʒ/, which are rare in Melanesian languages. Both open and closed syllables may occur, and consonant clusters are common.

Variation in the pronunciation of consonants is of two kinds. Pidgin speakers who also speak English often introduce phonemic distinctions from that language that are not made by less educated speakers. So an educated speaker might say /ʃu/ 'shoe' and /tʃetʃ/ or /tʃətʃ/ 'church' whereas an uneducated speaker would be more likely to say /su/ and /sios/.

The other kind of variation is probably related to first-language interference. Many speakers "confuse" similar sounds, probably because these sounds are not phonemically distinct in their own languages. Among the pairs of sounds commonly confused by some speakers of Melanesian Pidgin are /p/ and /b/; /t/ and /d/; /k/ and /g/; /p/ and /f/; /t/ and /s/; /h/ and absence of a consonant; /b/ and /v/; /s/ and /ʤ/; /f/ and /v/; /l/ and /r/; /v/ and /w/; and /n/ and /ŋ/. For example, some speakers of Tok Pisin say /pis/ 'fish,' and others /fis/; /tasol/ 'only' is often heard as /tatol/; and while some speakers say /haumas/ 'how much?' others would say /aumas/ or /aumat/.

The orthography is fairly straightforward, with *ng* being used to represent /ŋ/ (and *j* for /ʤ/ in Pijin and Bislama). For most speakers, voiced stops do not occur word-finally, but etymological spellings are used in Pijin and Bislama: /pik/ 'pig' and /gut/ 'good' are written *pig* and *gud* in Pijin and Bislama, but *pik* and *gut* in Tok Pisin. The diphthongs /ai/, /oi/, and /au/ are written *ai, oi,* and *au* in Tok Pisin, but *ae, oe,* and *ao* in Pijin and Bislama, so the words for 'right,' 'boy,' and 'house' are *rait, boi, haus* in Tok Pisin, but *raet, boe, haos* in Bislama.

Sentence Structure

Melanesian Pidgin is a subject-predicate language and has both verbal and verbless sentences. In verbal sentences, the phrase order is SV in intransitive sentences and SVO in transitive sentences.

Tok Pisin

Subject		Verb	Object
Wanpela	*man i*	*kam.*	0
one	man PREDICATE	come	0
'A man came/is coming.'			

	Verb	Object	
Maria i	*kilim*	*pik bilong mi.*	
Maria PREDICATE	kill TRANS	pig POSS me	
'Maria killed/is killing my pig.'			

Although there is no passive, attention can be focused on the object of a transitive clause by moving it to the front of the sentence, where it can be followed by the particle *ia* and a pause. This often translates a passive English sentence. Here is the object-focused version of the second sentence above:

Tok Pisin

Object			Subject	Verb
Pik	*bilong*	*mi ia,*	*Maria*	*i kilim.*
pig	POSS	me FOCUS,	Maria	PREDICATE
				kill:TRANS

'As for my pig, Maria killed/is killing it.'
'My pig was killed/is being killed by Maria.'

Verbless sentences follow a pattern similar to verbal sentences, with subject preceding predicate.

Pijin

Subject	**Predicate**			
Hem	*i*	*man*	*blong*	*mi.*
he	PREDICATE	man	POSS	me

'He is my husband.'

Pronouns

Pronouns in Melanesian Pidgin follow the Austronesian pattern: They distinguish at least three numbers and also show the inclusive/exclusive distinction in the first person non-singular. While the dual is common, the trial is considerably rarer. Here are the pronouns of Bislama:

Bislama

Singular

I	*mi*
you	*yu*
he/she/it	*hem*

Dual

we two INC	*yumitu*
we two EXC	*mitufala*
you two	*yutufala*
they two	*tufala*

Trial

we three INC	*yumitrifala*
we three EXC	*mitrifala*
you three	*yutrifala*
they three	*trifala*

Plural

we INC	*yumi*
we EXC	*mifala*
you	*yufala*
they	*olgeta*

There is virtually no morphophonemic variation in the pronouns.[5] The same form is used as an independent pronoun, as subject or object, or after a preposition:

Bislama

_Mi_	hang-em	ol	klos	blong	_mi_	long	laen.
I	hang-TRANS	PL	clothes	POSS	me	on	line

"I hung my clothes on the line."

Hem	i	givim	gato	ya	long	_yufala_	from
he	PREDICATE	give:TRANS	cake	this	to	you:PL	because

hem	i	laekem	_yufala_	tumas.
he	PREDICATE	like:TRANS	you:PL	very

'He/she gave the cake to you (pl.) because he/she likes you a lot.'

Nouns, Noun Phrases, and Prepositions

Nouns are almost universally invariable in form. There are no articles and only a small number of demonstratives. Tok Pisin has _dispela_ and Pijin _desfala_ 'this' (sometimes 'that'), both of which precede the noun. Bislama _ya_ 'this, that' follows the noun. The following sentences all mean much the same thing.

Tok Pisin

Dispela	man	i	laik-im	_dispela_	meri.
this	man	PREDICATE	like-TRANS	this	woman

Pijin

Desfala	man	i	laek-em	_desfala_	woman.
this	man	PREDICATE	like-TRANS	this	woman

Bislama

Man	_ya_	i	laekem	woman	_ya._
Man	this	PREDICATE	like:TRANS	woman	this

'This man likes this/that woman.'

Adjectives, numerals, and other quantifiers normally precede the noun in a noun phrase,[6] although there are some modifiers that follow the head. In Tok Pisin, all monosyllabic adjectives and numerals, as well as some that have two or more syllables, must occur with the suffix -_pela_ in this context. In Pijin and Bislama, the corresponding suffix -_fala_ is less frequently used, often occurring only when the adjective is emphasized. Here are some examples of noun phrases. The head noun is underlined.

Tok Pisin

tupela	liklik	_meri_
two	small	girl

'two little girls'

ol   gutpela   *pikinini*
PL   good   child
'the good children'

dispela   tripela   bikpela   *popo*   tasol
this   three   big   pawpaw only
'just these three big pawpaws'

Pijin

tufala   *boe*   nomoa
two   boy   only
'only two boys'

wanfala   pua   *woman*
one   poor   woman
'a poor woman'

Bislama

tu   big   *haos*   ya
two   big   house   this
'these two big houses'

tu   big-fala   *haos*   ya
two   big-EMPHATIC house this
'these two particularly big houses'

wan   smol   blu   *trak*   nomo
one   small blue car   only
'just a small blue car'

There is only a small number of prepositions (but not so small a number as some writers would have us believe). The following are the commonest prepositions in Bislama:

Bislama

long   location, direction, source, instrument, time
blong   possession, purpose, beneficiary
olsem   'like, as'
wetem accompaniment, instrument
from   cause

Examples:

Bislama

Mi kam *long* Vila *from*   wan kos.
I   come to   Vila because:of one course
'I came to Vila for a course.'

Papa	blong	yu	i		stap		wok	_wetem_	_huia?_
father	POSS	you	PREDICATE	CONTINUOUS	work	with	who

'Who is your father working with?'

Fis	_olsem_	hemia,	yu	mas	kat-em	hem	_long_
fish	like	this:one,	you	must	cut-TRANS	it	with

sap-fala	naef.
sharp-EMPHATIC	knife

'For a fish like this one, you have to cut it with a sharp knife.'

The other two dialects are slightly different. *From* does not occur in Tok Pisin, which uses the compound form *bilong wanem* 'for what?' to mark cause instead. Pijin has the same prepositions as Bislama plus *fo*, which is used to indicate purpose or tendency:

Pijin

Mifala	laek	_fo_	go.
we:EXC	want	for	go

'We want to go.'

Hem	i		man	_fo_	dring.
he	PREDICATE	man	for	drink

'He is a drunkard.'

There are no special possessive pronouns in Melanesian Pidgin. The possessive preposition (Tok Pisin *bilong*, Pijin and Bislama *blong*) may be followed by either a noun or a pronoun possessor:

Pijin

nem	blong	yu		belo	blong	sios
name	POSS	you		bell	POSS	church

| 'your name' | | | | 'the church bell' |

Verbs and the Verb Complex

Verbs are morphologically quite simple in Melanesian Pidgin. The only common affix is the transitive suffix.

Tok Pisin

Em	i		rit	i		stap.
he	PREDICATE	read	PREDICATE	be

'He/she is reading.'

Em	i		rit-_im_	dispela	buk	i		stap.
he	PREDICATE	read-TRANS	this	book	PREDICATE	be

'He/she is reading this book.'

With certain verbs, while the transitive form takes the suffix, the intransitive form is often reduplicated.

Tok Pisin

Mama	*i*	*was-im*	*ol*	*pikinini.*
mother	PREDICATE	wash-TRANS	PL	child

'Mom washed the children.'

Ol	*pikinini*	*i*	*was-was.*
PL	child	PREDICATE	INTRANSITIVE-wash

'The children washed/swam.'

The verb complex does, however, contain a number of particles marking tense-aspect and other functions. Verbs (and nonverbal predicates) take a preverbal particle *i*, which marks what follows as a predicate. This use of *i* can be seen in almost every example above.[7] In recent years, however, the use of this predicate marker has become more and more optional, especially in Tok Pisin and Pijin. Thus the two Tok Pisin sentences above are just as often heard as *Mama wasim ol pikinini* and *Ol pikinini waswas*.

The verb is very often unmarked for tense, and lack of marking can indicate either present or past. Other tenses and aspects are marked by particles, some preverbal, others postverbal.

Tok Pisin

PREVERBAL		POSTVERBAL	
bai	future	*pinis*	completed
bin	incomplete past	*i stap*	continuous
ken	optative, potential		
inap	ability		
laik	intention		
save	habitual		

Three of these particles are, or derive from, verbs: *laik*, from *laikim*, 'like, want,' *save*, which as a verb means 'know, know how to,' and *i stap*, which as a verb means 'to be (in a place).' Some examples of these tense-aspect particles (plus the negative preverbal particle *no*) follow.

Tok Pisin

Em	*i*	*no*	*save*	*kaikai*	*mit.*
he	PREDICATE	not	HABITUAL	eat	meat

'He/she doesn't eat meat.'

Yu	*bai*	*wok-im*	*pinis.*
you	FUTURE	do-TRANS	COMPLETIVE

'You will have done it.'

Pita	i	inap	karim	ol	kago	bilong	yu.
Peter	PREDICATE	able	carry:TRANS	PL	cargo	POSS	you

'Peter can carry your things.'

Mamok	i	no	bin	kam.
Mamok	PREDICATE	not	PAST	come

'Mamok didn't come.'

Reduplication of the verb for other purposes than to indicate intransitivity is relatively common, especially in Bislama. There reduplication can have the following functions: reciprocal action, random action, repeated action, plurality, intensity, and the distributive.

Bislama

Leg	blong	hem	i	solap.
leg	POSS	he	PREDICATE	swell

'His/her leg is swollen.'

Leg	blong	hem	i	sol-solap.
leg	POSS	he	PREDICATE	INTENSITY-swell

'His/her leg is really swollen.'

Ol	lif	oli	foldaon.
PL	leaf	PL:PREDICATE	fall

'The leaves fell down.'

Ol	lif	oli	fol-foldaon	long	hariken.
PL	leaf	PL: PREDICATE	RANDOM-fall	in	cyclone

'The leaves fell all over the place in the cyclone.'

10.3. The Pidgins of the Motu Traders

The Motu people, who live around Port Moresby, speak an Oceanic language. The western Motu particularly, "at the time of European contact (and for an unknown number of years before) . . . were involved in a complex network of trading relationships with linguistically related and unrelated groups east, west and inland of their present position. The most spectacular and important part of this trade . . . was the *hiri*, or annual trading voyage to the Gulf of Papua some 300 kilometres away to the west" (Dutton 1985, 20).

In the course of the *hiri* expedition, two separate (and apparently unnamed) pidgins developed. One was based mainly on the Koriki language of the western Gulf of Papua, the other on the Eleman languages of the eastern part of the Gulf. Dutton (1985) calls these the Hiri Trading

Language (Koriki variety) and the Hiri Trading Language (Eleman variety), respectively.

That, however, is by no means the end of the story. The Motu also used a pidginized version of their own language (Dutton calls this Simplified Motu) with other foreigners—originally probably in trade with their Oceanic-speaking neighbors, and later with newcomers to the area. After European contact in the late nineteenth century, they also used a variety of Melanesian Pidgin with early colonial officials and other outsiders.

The two Hiri Trading Languages were restricted to use on the *hiri*, and when that trading expedition finally ceased toward the middle of the twentieth century, the languages also died a natural death. The English-based pidgin died a less natural death: it was proscribed by the British government, which adopted instead the pidginized version of Motu as the language of contact.

The first British police force in Papua consisted of Fijians, Solomon Islanders, and Kiwais from the Daru area of western Papua. By the time the police force was being established, there were a number of other foreigners of various origins settling in the Port Moresby area. Simplified Motu soon became the lingua franca of this motley collection of people. It was spread outside Port Moresby mainly by the police on their patrols along the coast and into the interior, but also by released prisoners who were given positions of authority as village constables. The language acquired the name Police Motu, but in the 1970s, as the connotations of the word "police" were deemed pejorative, the name Hiri Motu was chosen—in the mistaken belief that Police Motu was a continuation of the language(s) spoken on the *hiri*.

The differences between the Hiri Trading Languages and Hiri (or Police) Motu can be seen in the following sentences (from Dutton 1985, 33–34).

Hiri Trading Language (Koriki Variety)

Enane	*pu*	*miai*	*anea!*		*Na*	*okuai!*
go	sago	get	come		me	give
'Go and bring some sago!'					'Give it to me!'	

Hiri Trading Language (Eleman Variety)

Abuari	*pai*	*avaia*	*abusi!*		*Ara*	*porohalaia!*
go	sago	get	come		me	give
'Go and bring some sago!'					'Give it to me!'	

Hiri (Police) Motu

Oi	*lao*	*rabia*	*oi*	*mailaia!*		*Lau*	*oi*	*henia!*
you	go	sago	you	bring		me	you	give
'Go and bring some sago!'						'Give it to me!'		

Two features give an idea of the simplified nature of Hiri Motu in comparison with Motu itself. First, Motu has the normal Oceanic contrast between direct and indirect possessive constructions and, in indirect possession, contrasts food (marked with *a-*) and other possessions (marked with *e-*):

Motu

> *(lau)*   *tama-gu*
> (I)   father-my
> 'my father'

> *(lau)*   *a-gu*   *aniani*
> (I)   POSS:FOOD-my   food
> 'my food'

> *(lau)*   *e-gu*   *ruma*
> (I)   POSS:GENERAL-my   house
> 'my house'

Hiri Motu simply uses the general possessive form for all nouns: *lauegu tamana*[8] 'my father,' *lauegu aniani* 'my food,' *lauegu ruma* 'my house.'

Second, Motu has independent pronouns, as well as subject prefixes and object suffixes to verbs. Hiri Motu uses free pronouns in all of these environments:

	Motu			**Hiri Motu**
	Independent	**Subject**	**Object**	**All environments**
Singular				
I	*lau*	*na-*	*-gu*	*lau*
you	*oi*	*o-*	*-mu*	*oi*
he/she/it	*ia*	*e-*	*-(i)a*	*ia*
Plural				
we INC	*ita*	*ta-*	*-da*	*ita*
we EXC	*ai*	*a-*	*-mai*	*ai*
you	*umui*	*o-*	*-mui*	*umui*
they	*idia*	*e-*	*-dia*	*idia*

Hiri Motu was once widely spoken in Papua (although virtually not at all in New Guinea, the northern half of Papua New Guinea), and it is one of the three official languages of Papua New Guinea (alongside English and Tok Pisin). In recent years, however, the number of its speakers, and consequently its status, have tended to decline, partly as a result of inroads into Papua by Tok Pisin, and partly because people who have been educated tend to use English in preference to Hiri Motu.

10.4. Fiji Hindi

Beginning in the late nineteenth century, more than sixty thousand indentured laborers were recruited from India to work on plantations in Fiji. Initially, these recruits came mainly from northern India, where languages of the Indo-European family are spoken. Many laborers spoke various dialects of Hindi, but many also spoke what was probably a pidgin, known as Bazaar Hindustani. By the early part of the twentieth century, however, almost half the laborers were being recruited from South India. These workers spoke the quite unrelated languages of the Dravidian family. The plantation environment brought into contact Hindi speakers from different dialects (numerically the largest group of Indians), speakers of Hindi and other Indian languages (related and unrelated), speakers of Indian languages, Fijian, and English, and finally, Indians and some of the twenty-seven thousand Pacific Islanders who were also recruited to work on Fijian plantations.

A number of languages developed or were used on the Fiji plantations, an early variety of Melanesian Pidgin, a pidginized variety of Fijian, and a pidginized variety of Hindi among them. The first of these has died out in Fiji, but the other two are still used to some extent between people of different ethnic groups who have no other common language.

In addition, however, another language also developed among Indians in Fiji. Through koineization, Fiji Hindi, or Fiji *Bāt* (= 'language') evolved, especially among ethnic Indians born in Fiji. Fiji Hindi incorporates elements from a number of Hindi dialects. Some examples of the mixture of dialects involved in the development of Fiji Hindi can be seen in the pronoun system.

	Fiji Hindi	**Hindi dialect source**
I	*ham*	Bhojpuri *ham*
you (intimate)	*tum*	Awadhi, Braj *tum*
you (formal)	*āp*	Awadhi *āp(u)*
he/she/it (near)	*ī*	Bhojpuri, Awadhi *ī*
he/she/it (remote)	*ū*	Awadhi, Bhojpuri *ū*

The formation of plural pronouns by the addition of *log* 'people' to the singular, as in *ham log* 'we,' is characteristic of Magahi.

There were other contributors to Fiji Hindi as well: Bazaar Hindustani, the Pidgin Hindi spoken on the plantations, English (as one might expect), and also Fijian. Some examples from Fijian follow.

Fiji Hindi		**Fijian source**
dakāu	'reef'	*cakau*
kūmāla	'sweet potato'	*kumala*
nangonā	'kava'	*na yaqona*

| *tabāle* | 'wife's brother' | *tavale* | 'brother-in-law' |
| *tāmabūā* | 'whale's tooth' | *tabua* | |

The result of this koineization process is a new form of Hindi different from any spoken in India.

A final complicating factor in the Hindi situation in Fiji has been the fact that, although Fiji Hindi is the first language of virtually all Fiji Indians, who speak it in informal contexts, it is not the language of formal situations. Standard (Indian) Hindi is used in schools, on radio, in print, and in other formal contexts. A situation of **diglossia** has developed in which people use one variety (Standard Hindi) in public meetings, for religious occasions, and in other formal situations, and the other variety (Fiji Hindi) in informal situations.

Language, Society, and Culture in the Pacific Context

11.1. The Vocabulary of Pacific Languages

Westerners often evaluate people and their societies on the basis of their technology. People without advanced technology are considered primitive not just technologically, but intellectually as well.

Linguists studying Australian and Pacific languages are often asked how many words there are in those languages. Underlying such a question is the assumption that such "primitive" people must speak simple languages: "By and large, the white population of present-day Australia has little knowledge of the structure or nature of Aboriginal Australian languages. Moreover, they have serious misconceptions about them. If you strike up a conversation with even well-educated white Australians you may hear that . . . '[Aboriginal languages] have only a few score words—names for common objects' " (Dixon 1980, 4).

Nothing could, as we have seen, be further from the truth. The grammars of Pacific languages are by no means simple or primitive. How do Pacific languages stand in terms of lexicon?

11.1.1. How Many Words?

When linguists are asked how many words there are in a particular language, the idea seems to be that the more words a language has, the more sophisticated it is. By implication, Pacific languages probably have many fewer words than English does, and so are less sophisticated or more primitive.

Even trying to compare dictionaries of two languages for this purpose is fraught with difficulties:

> How do we measure the number of words in a language? First, what is a word? For instance, should the compound 'firehose' be treated as a single word different from 'fire' and 'hose'? Languages differ widely as to what is considered a word. Second, are we talking about all words ever used by any speakers of that language? Or about all words used currently? Or about all the words used by an individual speaker and, presumably, stored somehow in that speaker's mind? Or about all the words ever recorded of the language? These questions show how hard it is to compare languages with respect to the number of words in them. (Simpson 1993, 123)

The other aspect of this problem relates to what forms the basis of our comparison. The simplest way to compare languages in this way is to count the entries in a dictionary (ignoring for the moment all the other problems Simpson has pointed out). But some languages (like English) have a much longer and more intensive history of dictionary compilation than do others (like those of the Pacific). So even if this were a valid way of making comparisons, it would not be a particularly productive one.

Let us pursue this a little further. Crystal (1987, 108) notes that the 1987 edition of the *Random House Dictionary of the English Language,* for example, contains some 260,000 headwords ("the bold-face items that occur at the beginning of each entry"). No dictionary of a Pacific language comes anywhere near that figure: The monolingual Fijian dictionary currently in preparation has considerably fewer than twenty thousand entries (Paul Geraghty, personal communication), and this will probably be one of the largest Pacific dictionaries when it is published. Does this mean that Pacific language vocabularies are considerably more limited than those of European languages?

In a sheer numerical sense, of course, it does. But we need to look a little more deeply into this question. Let us do a quick experiment. Below are thirty consecutive words beginning with the letter *q,* as listed on pages 1415–1416 of the 1981 edition of the *Macquarie Dictionary.* How many of these do you think are in common use? How many could you give the meaning of?[1]

quincuncial	*quinoline*	*quinquepartite*
quincunx	*quinone*	*quinquereme*
quindecagon	*quinonoid*	*quinquevalent*
quindecennial	*quinoxaline*	*quinsy*
quinella	*quinquagenerian*	*quint*
quinic acid	*Quinquagesima*	*quintain*
quinidine	*quinque-*	*quintal*
quinine	*quinquefoliate*	*quintan*

| quinoid | quinquennial | quinte |
| quinol | quinquennium | quintessence |

Dictionaries of languages like English include a vast number of highly technical, obsolete, or obscure words (like many of those listed above), nearly all of which are not known to the ordinary speaker of the language.

The average speaker of any language probably knows *and uses* somewhere between five and ten thousand words in everyday life, and may vaguely recognize a few thousand more.[2] People in a particular profession, or people who have a particular hobby or interest, will have another set of vocabulary related to that profession or interest, but other speakers of the language may probably not know those words—or at least not know how to use them accurately. Most of the 260,000 words in the Random House dictionary, for example, are probably unknown to almost all speakers of English.

When we take all of this into account, Pacific languages are not so different from English as might at first be assumed. The average speaker of a Pacific language also probably knows and uses between five and ten thousand words. People who specialize in fishing, weaving, or other professions and crafts will, of course, know additional technical terms not familiar to other people. The difference with European languages lies in the fact that most Australian and Pacific societies are relatively small-scale ones. The range of specialization of professions, crafts, and hobbies is much smaller, and hence the size of the technical or specialized vocabulary in those languages tends to be much smaller as well.

11.1.2. Specialization, Classification, and Abstraction

A second common misconception about Australian and Pacific languages concerns the degrees of abstraction they are capable of. I quote Dixon (1980, 5) again: "Some missionaries and amateur linguists who attempted to study an Australian language have contributed to the misconceptions [about them]. They have put it about that although there may be a superfluity of terms for particular objects, the languages are totally lacking in generic terms such as 'fish' or 'fowl'; this is, of course, taken as a lack of mental sophistication. The fact is that Australian languages do have quite as many generic terms as European languages."

Specific Terms

Things of cultural importance are usually obvious from a language's lexicon. The motor vehicle, for example, is of vital importance to western society, and in English we have a large number of words referring to kinds of motor vehicles (*car, truck, lorry, van, bus*), to brands of vehicles (*Toyota, Cadillac,*

Mercedes-Benz, Rolls-Royce), to models (*Toyota Corolla, Toyota Cressida, Toyota Camry*), as well as many hundreds of words referring to components of motor vehicles. In many Pacific languages, in contrast, there is often just one word, meaning 'motor vehicle (of any kind).'

But in English we have just the one word *yam* to describe a particular root-crop,[3] and we have had to borrow the word *taro* to describe another root-crop. Because these are not important food crops in English-speaking society, one word for each is probably adequate. In the Anejom̃ language of Vanuatu, where these *are* important sources of food, there are, according to my count so far, names for forty different varieties of yam, and words for over sixty named varieties of taro.

A language's vocabulary reflects what is important to its speakers. Where fine degrees of specialization are necessary or desirable, they will show up in the lexicon. Stages of growth are one common area of specialization in these languages. The coconut, of course, is perhaps the prototypical Pacific plant, and one should not be surprised to find lexical specialization in this area. In Kwamera, for example, the generic term for coconut is *napuei*; the fruit itself goes through the following named stages of development:

Kwamera

iapwas	small coconut, coconut fruit bud
kwanapuirahákw	larger coconut fruit bud
kwatigɨs	small coconut (about four inches in diameter)
kapkapeki	(intermediate stage between *kwatigɨs* and *tafa*)
tafa	young coconut before meat has begun to form
nafweruk	nut with soft meat and effervescent water
kahimaregi	nut with hard, well-developed meat
napuei mhia	ripe nut with developed flesh, which falls from the tree
kwarumahákw	fallen nut which has begun to sprout
nuvera	sprouted nut

In addition to these terms, there are terms for different parts of the nut, of the tree, and of the fronds, as well as for different varieties of coconuts and different coconut products.

The existence of areas of lexical specialization like this is not surprising. We would expect coastal people to have numerous words for different kinds of fish and fishing equipment, horticulturalists to have specialist terms for plants and their parts and growth stages, warriors to have detailed vocabulary relating to weapons, and so on. But there are also a few less expected areas of lexical specialization, like the following set of names for different kinds of noises in Yidiny:

Yidiny

dalmba	sound of cutting
mida	the noise of a person clicking his tongue against the roof of his mouth, or the noise of an eel hitting the water
maral	the noise of hands being clapped together
nyurrugu	the noise of talking heard a long way off when the words cannot quite be made out
yuyurunggul	the noise of a snake sliding through the grass
gangga	the noise of some person approaching, for example, the sound of his feet on leaves or through the grass—or even the sound of a walking stick being dragged across the ground

Generic Terms

Why have even the more charitably disposed observers held the view that Pacific languages have no generic terms? There are a few possible explanations. One is that "when objects are being named one is generally expected to be as specific as possible. If, say, a snake is seen it should be described by its species name; the generic term 'snake' would only be employed if just the tail were noticed and the species could not be identified, or in similar circumstances" (Dixon 1980, 5). A second factor is that certain abstract concepts grounded in western philosophy and culture are foreign to Pacific cultures. In a society without money, for example, terms like *money, poverty, interest, devaluation,* and so on are rare or nonexistent.

A third point is that, while abstractions do occur in Pacific languages, their nature, or the concepts they represent, may be quite different from similar concepts in European languages, because the way people look at and classify the world is different. Kinship terms are a good example of this (see 11.3).

Pacific languages also classify the natural world taxonomically (although, as we should by now expect, this classification might not necessarily exactly match a classification of the same items in a European language). A **taxonomy** is a way of classifying things or concepts in a hierarchical organization. At the "top" is a general term; the further down the hierarchy one goes, the more specific the terms become; and each lower term is included in the meaning of a higher term. If we take the generic term *fish,* then *tuna, mackerel, snapper, mullet,* and so on are all kinds of fish; *skipjack, bluefin, yellowfin,* and so on are all kinds of tuna (which is a kind of fish); and so on.

Figure 8 shows a very partial classification of terms for marine life in Anejoม̃ . The generic term *numu* refers to all fish, crustaceans, sea-urchins, sea snakes, shellfish, etc. (though in common speech *numu* often means sim-

numu marine life	numu-sgan (sea) fish	nepcev shark	nepcev-apeñ nepcev-awaraji nepcev-legeñhap nepcev-umudej nowodouyac
		inhar stingray	farfaroa inher-edej inher-mejcap̄ inmatin-namted nerenara nerenhau
		nedum̃ triggerfish	nedm̃-alis nedm̃-asin-nomñac nedum̃-hocou nedum̃-huoc
		inmokom parrotfish	inmokm-arakei inmokm-ilcai inmokm-odid inmokom-ma
	numu-ñwai freshwater fish	(numerous)	(numerous)
	numu-taregit crustaceans	nijvañ crayfish, lobster	inhaklin-najis nah najis-alp̄as nalawoñ nap-mehe nijvañ-dec
		num̃an hermit crab	num̃an-amidae num̃an-hol
		ledcei coconut crab	
	nesgaamu shellfish	(numerous)	(numerous)
	(numerous)		

Figure 8. Partial Classification of Anejom̃ Terms for Marine Life

ply 'fish'). There are a number of first-order specific terms, among them *numu-sgan* 'fish in the sea, including sharks, whales, stingrays, etc.,' *numu-ñwai* 'freshwater fish,' *numu-taregit* 'crustaceans,' *nesgaamu* 'shellfish,' *nahau* 'turtles,' and so on. Each of these has a number of subvarieties. In addition to the words given in the third column as subvarieties of sea fish (*nepcev* 'shark,' *inhar* 'stingray,' etc.), there are hundreds more: *inhet* 'needlefish,' *inhos* 'silverside,' *necna* 'sea mullet,' *najaj* 'flatfish,' *nilcam* 'wrasse,' and so on. Many of these third-order terms are further divided into more specific terms still, as partially illustrated in figure 8. Similar taxonomies could be presented in all Pacific languages for flora and fauna, especially those of economic or ritual importance to the people who speak that language.

These taxonomies reflect people's perceptions of nature, and they do not always correspond with the perceptions held by speakers of other languages. In parts of the highlands of New Guinea, for example, the cassowary is classified as an animal, not as a bird, because it does not fly. In many cultures, bats and flying foxes are classified as birds, because they do fly. Indeed, "the criteria for defining a generic term will [often] vary between neighbouring languages; in Dyirbal *yugu* 'tree' does not include within its scope stinging trees . . . or trees like pandanus which are less than a certain height, whereas the [cognate] Yidiny noun *jugi* . . . does include pandanus and stinging trees and in fact appears to be roughly coextensive with the English lexeme *tree*" (Dixon 1980, 113).

Let us look briefly at the noun classes of an Australian language, Murrinh-Patha (M. Walsh 1993). Murrinh-Patha has ten noun classes, each marked with a particle preceding the noun. These are:

Murrinh-Patha

kardu-	Aboriginal people and spirits
ku-	Non-Aboriginal people, animals, birds, fish, insects, and their products (like nests, meat, eggs, and honey)
kura-	fresh water
mi-	food and food plants, including their products (like feces!)
thamul-	spears
thu-	things used for striking: offensive weapons (other than spears), along with thunder, lightning, and playing cards (which are thrown into the center of a group)
thungku-	fire, firewood, matches, etc.
da-	times and places
murrinh-	speech and language
nanthi-	everything else

There are a number of features of interest in this system. Let us look at the first two classes first: "As in English, the category of 'higher animates' is culturally conceived. In Murrinh-Patha the category of 'higher animates' is often thought of as just involving Aboriginal people while non-Aboriginal people are classified along with other animates like snakes, birds and fish" (M. Walsh 1993, 114). The *ku*-class of other animates includes the word *ku*: this means 'meat' (the product of animals), but it also has come to mean 'money' (the product of non-Aboriginal people).

Each of the next five Murrinh-Patha classes—those marked by *kura, mi, thamul, thu,* and *thungku*—includes things with a prominent place in Murrinh-Patha culture: fresh water and its sources, fire and fire-making, spears, boomerangs and clubs, and so on. The *da*-class groups together places and times (seasons and the like), while the *murrinh*-class also suggests that speech and language are important to the culture. The final class, marked by *nanthi*, is a residual class, and includes nouns that do not fit into any of the other classes.

11.2. Counting Systems

Some Oceanic languages have an elaborate system of numeral classifiers (see chapter 6). Other aspects of counting systems in Pacific languages provide an example of the variety of semantic systems within this region. As Laycock (1975a, 219) says, "Number systems can be studied as philosophical systems in their own right, or as guides to ethnic thinking on number concepts."

11.2.1. Decimal Systems

I will begin with the system with which English speakers are most familiar, the true **decimal** system, in which there are separate individual words for the numbers one to ten, each composed of only a single morpheme,[4] and which may also have separate individual words for hundred and thousand (and perhaps higher multiples of ten as well).

The majority of the Oceanic languages have this system, although no Australian language does (at least natively),[5] and "decimal systems do not appear to exist at all in the non-Austronesian languages of the New Guinea area" (Laycock 1975a, 224). True decimal systems are found throughout Polynesia and Micronesia, in the majority of southeastern Solomons and northern Vanuatu languages, and in a minority of mainland New Guinea Oceanic languages. Some examples of decimal systems are given below (the Kiribati numerals one through nine incorporating the general classifier *ua*):

	Tongan	Fijian	Kiribati	Arosi	Nakanai
1	taha	dua	te-ua-na	ta ʻai	isasa
2	ua	rua	uo-ua	rua	ilua
3	tolu	tolu	teni-ua	oru	itolu
4	fā	vā	a-ua	hai	ivaa
5	nima	lima	nima-ua	rima	ilima
6	ono	ono	ono-ua	ono	iuolo
7	fitu	vitu	iti-ua	biu	ivitu
8	valu	walu	wani-ua	waru	iualu
9	hiva	ciwa	ruai-ua	siwa	ualasiu
10	hongofulu	tini	tabuina	tangahuru	savulu-sa
100	teau	drau	tebubua	tangarau	salatu-sasa
1000	afe	udolu	tengaa	meru	salatu-savulu

Micronesian languages are unusual in the world context in having distinct numerals for ten-power bases, in some cases as high as 10^9 (Harrison and Jackson 1984). For example:

	Kiribati	Ponapean	Woleaian
100	tebubua	epwiki	sebiugiuw
1000	tengaa	kid	sangeras
10,000	terebu	nen	sen
100,000	tekuri	lopw	selob
1,000,000	teea	rar	sepiy
10,000,000	tetano	dep	sengit
100,000,000	tetoki	sapw	sangerai
1,000,000,000		lik	

In many languages with decimal systems, there are special ways of counting certain things, especially food produce and other things of value. For example:

Fijian

bola	'ten fish,' 'a hundred canoes'
bewa	'ten bunches of bananas'
vulo	'ten *tabua* (whale's teeth)'
uduudu	'ten canoes'
koro	'a hundred coconuts'
selavo	'a thousand coconuts'

Rotuman

asoa	'two coconuts'
sava ʻa	'ten pigs, cows, fowls, eggs, cuttlefish'

sɔiga	'ten fish'	
poa	'twenty ɔlili (kind of shellfish)'	
kato'a	'a hundred fish'	

Motu and its close relatives show a system that might be referred to as an imperfect decimal system, in which some numerals represent multiplications. Here are the numerals from one through ten in Motu:

Motu

1	*ta*	6	*taura-toi*
2	*rua*	7	*hitu*
3	*toi*	8	*taura-hani*
4	*hani*	9	*taura-hani-ta*
5	*ima*	10	*gwauta*

Although there are separate words for seven and ten, six and eight appear to be '(one) two-threes' and '(one) two-fours,' and nine is '(one) two-fours-one.'

There are also imperfect decimal systems that involve subtraction. Here are the numerals one through ten in Titan (Oceanic) and Buin (Papuan). (The Buin numerals are those used with the noun class referring to things.)

	Titan	**Buin**
1	*si*	*nonumoi*
2	*luo*	*kiitako*
3	*talo*	*paigami*
4	*ea*	*korigami*
5	*lima*	*upugami*
6	*wono*	*tugigami*
7	*ada-talo*	*paigami tuo*
8	*ada-lua*	*kiitako tuo*
9	*ada-si*	*kampuro*
10	*akou*	*kiipuro*

In Titan and Buin, there are normal numerals from one through six and ten. In Titan, seven is *ada*-3, 8 is *ada*-2, and 9 is *ada*-1. Clearly subtraction is involved, although *ada* is not the word for ten. In Buin, seven is 'three less' and eight is 'two less'; nine, however, means something like 'completed.'

11.2.2. Quinary Systems

The other common numeral system in Pacific languages is a **quinary** system—one based on five. These systems have individual morphemes for the first five numerals (five may be the same word as hand). The numerals six to nine, however, are compounds whose underlying meaning is five-plus-one, five-plus-two, and so on. The numerals ten and twenty may be compounds as well, or may be separate morphemes. Such systems are found in much of New Guinea (among both Oceanic and Papuan languages), as well as in parts of Solomon Islands, Vanuatu, and New Caledonia. The examples below are from Oceanic languages, with the exception of Daga, which is Papuan.

	Lenakel	**Tigak**	**Jawe**	**Daga**
1	*karena*	*sakai*	*siic*	*daiton*
2	*kiu*	*pauak*	*seluk*	*dere*
3	*kɨsil*	*potul*	*seen*	*yampo*
4	*kuvɨr*	*poiat*	*phoec*	*bayabayapa*
5	*katilum*	*palmit*	*nim*	*nani yamunaet*
6	*katilum-karena*	*palmit sakai*	*ni-siic*	*nani yamu daiton*
7	*katilum-kiu*	*palmit pauak*	*ni-seluk*	*nani yamu dere*
8	*katilum-kɨsil*	*palmit potul*	*ni-seen*	*nani yamu yampo*
9	*katilum-kuvɨr*	*palmit poiat*	*ni-phoec*	*nani yamu*
10	*katilum-katilum*	*sangaulung*	*paidu*	*aonagaet*

Lenakel and Tigak form numerals above five by compounding on the actual numeral five, while Jawe and Daga use a modified version of the form for five. Tigak, Jawe, and Daga have independent morphemes for ten, but the Lenakel form involves addition.

Expansions of these systems are interesting. Lenakel simply continues building on the base *katilum* until nineteen (which is *katilum-katilum-katilum-kuvɨr* = 5-5-5-4 = 19).[6] Twenty is expressed as:

Lenakel
> *ieramím*   *karena*   *r-ɨka*
> person   one   he-is:not
> 'twenty'

which is similar to the system in Jawe, where the word for twenty is *siic kac* 'one man.' Both of these derive from counting all fingers and toes—"completing" a single person.

Daga is different: Here the form given above for five is *nani yamu-naet* 'hand other-nothing'; so seven is *nani yamu dere* 'two on the other hand.' Ten is *ao-na-gaet* 'up-my-INTENSIFIER'—i.e., 'only my upper appendages,' or, in other words, 'my two hands.' Counting from one to ten proceeds on the fingers, counting from eleven to nineteen on the toes, and twenty represents a complete person.

Daga
> *aonagaet*   *pusinawan*   *daiton*
> ten   my:foot   one
> 'eleven'

aonagaet	*pusin*	*yamunaet*			
ten	my:foot	five			
'fifteen'					

aonagaet	*pusin*	*yamunaet*	*pusin*	*yamu*	*daiton*
ten	my:foot	five	my:foot	other	one
'sixteen'					

apane	*daiton*
man	one
'twenty'	

Drehu shows an interesting variation on the standard quinary systems. The Drehu numerals one through twenty are given below:

Drehu

1	*caa*	6	*caa-ngömen*	11	*caa-ko*	16	*caa-hwaihano*
2	*lue*	7	*lue-ngömen*	12	*lue-ko*	17	*lue-hwaihano*
3	*köni*	8	*köni-ngömen*	13	*köni-ko*	18	*köni-hwaihano*
4	*eke*	9	*eke-ngömen*	14	*eke-ko*	19	*eke-hwaihano*
5	*trii-pi*	10	*lue-pi*	15	*köni-pi*	20	*caatr*

In Drehu, the numerals five, ten, and fifteen are *trii-pi, lue-pi,* and *köni-pi.* There seems to be a unit of five, based on a form *pi,* and these numerals are effectively *1-pi, 2-pi,* and *3-pi.* Between these units, the numerals one to four take suffixes: *-ngömen* is used between six and nine, *-ko* between eleven and fifteen, and *-hwaihano* between sixteen and nineteen. The Drehu word for twenty, *caatr,* is actually *caa atr* 'one man.'

11.2.3. Other Systems

Huli (Cheetham 1978), spoken in the Southern Highlands Province of Papua New Guinea, is quite unusual in having a base of 15, although "the last three numerals of the series, 13, 14 and 15, are also the words for body parts, even though these body parts are not referred to when counting, and the words now appear to be true numerals" (Smith 1988, 13). The Kapauku (Ekagi) of Irian Jaya (Price and Pospisil 1966) have an even more complex system—a decimal system as far as the base of 60, with higher units of 600 and 3,600, similar to the system of the ancient Babylonians (Smith 1988, 12). But most other systems that are neither decimal nor quinary have bases smaller than five.

Oceanic languages are almost exclusively decimal or quinary. The major exceptions to this generalization are some of the Oceanic languages of the Morobe Province of Papua New Guinea, which have presumably been influenced by their Papuan-speaking neighbors (Smith 1988). Adzera, for example, has only two numerals. Counting above two proceeds by addition to the base 'two.' Mapos has numerals for only one, two, and three, with four being a compound (2 + 2) and five involving the word *orund* 'hand.' Examples:

	Adzera	**Mapos**
1	*bits*	*ti*
2	*iruc*	*lu*
3	*iruc da bits*	*lal*
4	*iruc da iruc*	*lu-mba-lu*
5	*iruc da iruc da bits*	*orund vandu*
6	*iruc da iruc da iruc, etc.*	*orund vandu mb-ti, etc.*

Australian languages tend to have quite simple numeral systems. "The one obvious gap in Australian vocabularies is the lack of any system of numbers. It is usually said that there are only numbers 'one', 'two', 'several' and 'many'; some languages appear also to have 'three' although this is frequently a compound form. . . . No special significance attaches to the absence of numeral systems in Australian languages; it is simply a reflection of the absence of any need for them in traditional culture" (Dixon 1980, 107–108). Here are some examples from three widely separated Australian languages:

	Margany	**Wajarri**	**Wargamay**
1	*wakanyu*	*kurriya*	*yunggul*
2	*ura*	*kujarra*	*yaga*
3	—	*marnkurr*	*garbu*
many	*dhiwala*	*yalypa*	*dyaginy*

As in so many other ways, the Tiwi language is an exception to generalizations about Australian languages, having a quinary system.[7]

Tiwi

1	*yati*	6	*kiringarra (yati)*
2	*yirrara*	7	*kiringarra yirrara*
3	*yirrajirrima*	8	*kiringarra yirrajirrima*
4	*yatapinti*	9	*kiringarra yatapinti*
5	*punginingita*	10	*wamutirrara*

Papuan languages exhibit a great variety of numeral systems. There are quite a few languages with a **binary** system, with numerals greater than two formed by compounding. Wantoat exemplifies the classical type, while Numanggang uses the word for hand to express five; Salt-Yui allows both ways of representing five—*ana holulu* meaning roughly 'one fist,' while *sui sui tai dire* = 'two two one together.'

	Wantoat	**Numanggang**	**Salt-Yui**
1	tapatu	kutnung	taniga
2	tapaya	lufom	sutani
3	tapaya tapatu	lufom kutnung	sui tai dire
4	tapaya tapaya	lufom lufom	sui sui dire
5	tapaya tapaya tapatu	kafong ko	ana holulu, sui sui tai dire
6	tapaya tapaya tapaya	kafong ko kutnung	sui sui sui dire

Other Papuan languages have a **ternary** system, with three basic numerals. In Som the system simply involves addition (so seven is 3-3-1, etc.), while in Guhu-Samane the word for *boto* 'hand' occurs in the numeral five.

	Som	**Guhu-Samane**
1	koweran	tena
2	yarə	eseri
3	kabmə	tapari
4	oyarə oyarə	eseri sa eseri
5	oyarə oyarə kowe	boto tena
6	okabmə okabmə	boto tena ma tena

Kewa is one of the few Papuan languages with a base-four system:

Kewa

1	pameda	
2	laapo	
3	repo	
4	ki	(= 'hand')
5	(kina) kode	(= '[hand's] thumb')
6	kode laapo	(= 'thumb + two')
7	kode repo	(= 'thumb + three')
8	ki laapo	(= 'two hands')
9	ki laapona kode (pameda)	(= 'two hands, one thumb')
10	ki laapona kode laapo, etc.	(= 'two hands, two thumbs')

Laycock (1975a, 224) reports that there are also a few languages with a base-six system.

11.2.4. Tally Systems

One other type of counting system needs mentioning here. This is a **tally system**. Based on body parts, it counts the fingers of one hand, up the arm, across the face or the chest, and down to the fingers of the other hand; these are often used for counting valuables—pigs, shell-money, or other things given—and also calendrical events, such as the preparations needed for a festival. Tally systems "are used only for direct counting, or 'mapping' of a set of objects against some other measuring code. There are no 'numerals' in a tally system, so that one may not receive a reply to the question 'how many?' or find the points of the tally-system qualifying nouns, as do true numerals" (Laycock 1975a, 219).

As well as having a base-four numeral system, Kewa also has a tally system, involving a counting cycle called a *paapu*. Counting begins with the little finger on the left hand, goes through the other fingers (1–5), from the heel of the thumb up to the upper arm (6–14), the shoulder and neck (15–18), the jaw (19), the left ear (20), cheek (21), eye (22), the inside of the left eye (23) until the mid point is reached: *rikaa* 'between the eyes' = 24. Counting then proceeds in the reverse order, ending with the little finger on the right hand, which is 47.

11.3. Kinship

Kinship systems are intricately bound up with the system of social relations of a particular society. They show very clearly how language is tied in with social life and social behavior.

11.3.1. Njamal Kinship Terms

In Njamal society of northwestern Australia (Burling 1970, 21–27), as in most Australian societies, every person belongs to a **moiety**, one of two units into which a society is divided on the basis of descent. In Njamal, moieties are patrilineal: A person belongs to the same moiety as his or her father. In addition, they are exogamous—a person must marry someone from the opposite moiety. Figure 9 shows the implications in relation to a man (labeled "Ego," from the Latin word meaning 'I'), his grandparents, his parents and their siblings, his siblings and their spouses, his wife, and his children and their spouses. In this figure and the next, triangles represent males, circles represent females, and the equals sign indicates marriage. Members of Ego's moiety are shaded black, while members of the other moiety are unshaded.

Now let us see how a system of social organization like a moiety system, which is quite different from the system English speakers are used to, relates to the kinship terminology of a society. Figure 10 is the same set of relatives as in figure 9, but with a few additions. It shows the terms a male Njamal speaker uses to refer to each of those relatives.

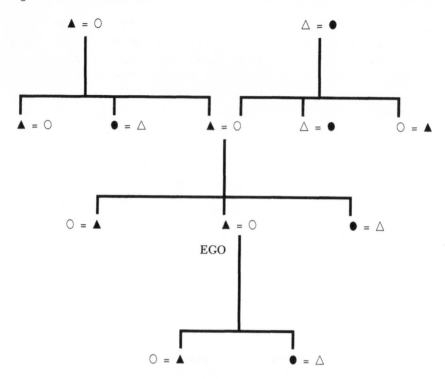

Figure 9. A Moiety System

There are a number of very significant differences between the Njamal system and that of English. Some examples follow.

1. In Ego's parents' generation, four terms are used:

   mama   all males in this generation of the same moiety—Ego's father, father's brother, and mother's sister's husband

   karna   all males in this generation of the other moiety—Ego's mother's brother and father's sister's husband

   midari   all females in this generation of the same moiety—Ego's father's sister and mother's brother's wife

   ngardi   all females in this generation of the opposite moiety—Ego's mother and her sister, and his father's brother's wife

2. The moiety system is reflected again in kinship terms for Ego's grandparents' generation. The paternal grandfather (*maili*), for example, is called by a different term from the maternal grandfather (*mabidi*), since they belong to different moieties.

3. For Ego's grandchildren's generation, the terms *maili* and *mabidi* are used again. *Maili* refers to any grandchild or any grandchild's spouse,

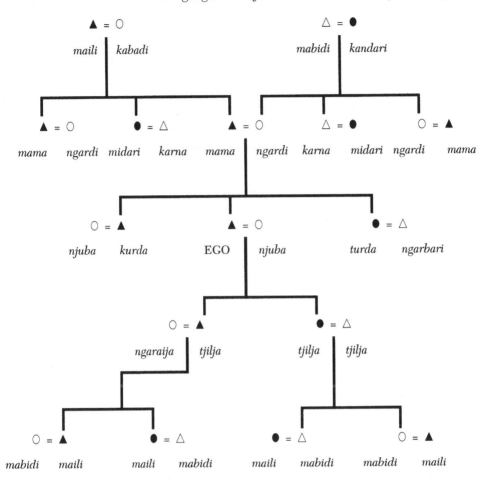

Figure 10. Njamal Kinship Terms

irrespective of sex, who is of the same moiety as Ego. *Mabidi* applies to any grandchild or grandchild's spouse, again irrespective of sex, who is of the other moiety.

Moiety membership is one of the major criteria in classifying kin. "A Njamal can apply one of these kinship terms to any Njamal however distantly he may be related. They recognize no boundary beyond which people are no longer counted as kinsmen" (Burling 1970, 23). The term *maili*, for example, not only applies in the grandparental generation to one's father's father, but also to one's father's father's brother, mother's mother's brother, mother's father's wife's brother, father's mother's husband, father's mother's sister's husband, father's mother's wife's brother, that is, to any male of this generation belonging to the same moiety.

One other feature of Njamal kinship terms is widespread in the Pacific: the reciprocal use of terms between kin two generations apart. In Njamal, for example, a man and his father's father call each other *maili*. There is often both a close bond and a fairly relaxed relationship between grandparents and grandchildren in Pacific societies, whereas the relationship between one's own generation and one's parents' (or children's) is often characterized by greater social tension. Hence the use of nonreciprocal terms, which imply more of a relationship of domination and subordination. Njamal also presents additional complications.

1. Figure 10 shows the terms for 'brother' and 'sister' as *kurda* and *turda*, respectively. These terms are used to refer only to brothers or sisters who are older than the speaker. Younger brothers and sisters are both referred to by the term *maraga*. Relative age is a factor in determining which term should be used within Ego's generation.

2. Differences in the referent of some terms may depend on the sex of the speaker.[8]

	Male speaker	**Female speaker**
njuba	wife, brother's wife	husband, sister's husband
ngarbari	wife's brother, sister's husband	[not used]
julburu	[not used]	husband's sister, brother's wife
ngaraija	sister's daughter	brother's daughter
tjilja	brother's daughter	sister's daughter

The social facts of moiety membership, relative age, and the sex of the speaker are all important in Njamal society, as the system of kinship terminology indicates.

11.3.2. Kinship and Marriage in Anejom̃

The regulation of marriage often has a great effect on the system of kinship terminology. This short case study deals with Aneityum society and the Anejom̃ language (Tepahae and Lynch 1998).

Figure 11 shows some kinship terms in Anejom̃.[9] A man calls his wife *egak*, and this term also applies to his mother's brother's daughter and his mother's sister's daughter. The reason for this is that, in traditional Anejom̃ society, a man was supposed to marry one of these cross-cousins. The term *egak* is probably better translated as 'marriageable female relative of the same generation.' The father of *egak* is called *matak*, meaning not only 'maternal uncle' but also 'father-in-law,' since one of one's maternal uncles would also be one's father-in-law. The kinship terminology of Anejom̃ is very intricately involved with the regulation of marriage in traditional Aneityumese society.

There is a further interesting twist to this system. No system works the way it should a hundred percent of the time. A young man becomes smitten with a young woman who is not one of his prescribed marriage partners, and the elders reluctantly agree for them to marry. Suppose, for example, that one of the boys in my grandchildren's generation marries my daughter. Because he is of that generation, I should call him *m̃ap̃ok* 'my grandchild.' But because he is now my son-in-law, I should also call him *nohowanig uñak* 'my son-in-law.' Neither of these sits well with me, the grandfather and father-in-law. How can the dilemma be resolved?

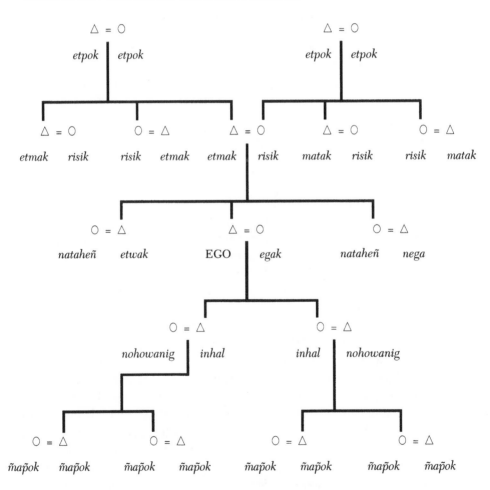

Figure 11. Anejom̃ Kinship Terms

The Aneityumese have resolved it by developing a new term, *numulai*. This term comes from *numu* 'a living person' + *lai* 'to grow or develop in an unexpected way.'[10] By referring to my grandson and son-in-law as *numulai*, I am very specifically recognizing the fact that our relationship has changed due to an "irregular" marriage.

Kinship systems have fascinated anthropologists and linguists for over a century. There is a finite number of possible kinship systems. Each system, however, has developed the way it has in order to express a complex network of social relations and a complex system of social organization. Although I have looked at just two systems here, these demonstrate how wholly language is bound up with other aspects of the life of a society.

11.4. Languages in Use

Since most Pacific languages are spoken by a few thousand people at most, one might expect them to be used in a fairly simple and uncomplicated manner—no frills, no special styles, just straightforward, down-to-earth, face-to-face communication. This view, however, is a gross oversimplification.

11.4.1. Language and Gender

In the discussion of Njamal kinship terms in 11.3.1 above, we saw that some terms are used differently depending on whether a man or a woman is speaking. The same is true of Anejoñ (see 11.3.2). For example, the term *etwak* means 'my same-sex sibling'—my brother if I am a man, but my sister if I am a woman. There are two other Anejoñ terms for siblings, and each is restricted to one sex: *Nataheñ erak* 'my sister' can be used only by men, while *natañañ erak* 'my brother' can be used only by women. Most Pacific languages probably express some distinctions in kin terms based on the sex of the speaker.

Men and women in all societies use language differently. Some differences are based on sex differences like those of the glottis and vocal folds, which result in men's generally having a lower-pitched voice than women. I am not interested in these differences here. Of much greater interest are differences based on *gender*, or the social roles of men and women.

The traditional division of labor between men and women leads, in most societies, to a difference in the vocabulary with which a speaker is familiar. In a maritime Pacific society, for example, men probably know and use more words related to house building, deep-sea fishing, hunting, warfare, and kava preparation; women tend to have a wider (active or passive) vocabulary than men in areas like basket-making and mat-weaving, shellfish, and food preparation.

Often, however, differences go deeper than this. On the island of Ngatik (near Pohnpei in Micronesia) there is reported to be a special "men's language" that incorporates quite a number of words from an early variety of Pacific Pidgin English (Clark 1979–1980, 35).[11] Among the Big Nambas in Vanuatu, on the other hand, there is a special "women's language." Women could not traditionally say the name of the chief or any senior male relative, and had to substitute other words for these names or for any word that sounded like them. If a chief or other senior male had a name that sounded like *tau* or *nauei*, then the verb *tau* 'put' would be replaced by *uln* 'let go of,' and the word *nauei* 'water' by the special replacement term *tarah* (H. Fox 1997).

Many Australian societies have special secret languages taught by older men to boys during their initiation and used only by men in certain ceremonies. Because of their ritual importance, such secret registers are not supposed to be used in front of women or uninitiated boys. "Of these registers it can in general be said that they are brilliant creations in which a very small stock of special words is made to do all the work of framing any proposition that a speaker wants to express" (Alpher 1993, 102). These secret male registers use either totally different words, or else operate on a kind of "pig Latin" basis, turning a normal word into something quite different. In some cases, the secret register involves sounds that do not occur in the standard language (Dixon 1980, 66–67).

11.4.2. The Language of Respect

In all Pacific languages, there is a right way to speak, depending on the particular context in which one is speaking. There are obscene words, which can usually only be used in the most informal—or insulting—contexts. There are euphemisms, which are used in more public circumstances or in mixed company. And there are oratorical styles, in which the underlying meanings of what is said are often obscured (at least to the uninitiated) by a series of metaphors.

In the chiefly societies of western Polynesia, there are rather more dramatically distinct speech styles, depending on whom one is talking to or about. Tongan, for example, has three styles—one for commoners, another for nobles, and the third for the king—distinguished by different vocabulary items for the same thing (Philips 1991). For example:

Tongan

Commoners	Nobles	King	
kai	*ʻilo*	*taumafa*	'eat'
mate	*pekia*	*hala*	'die'
faʻitoka	*malaʻe*	*moʻunga*	'cemetery'
kaukau	*tākele*	*fakamālū*	'bathe'
ʻalu	*meʻa*	*hāʻele*	'go'

These words are supposed to be used to and about a member of the social category concerned: "Thus [Tongan] people will say that when using Tongan words for 'go', *'alu* is used to and about Commoners, *me'a* is used to and about Nobles, and *hā'ele* is used to and about the King" (Philips 1991, 374).

This is what Tongans say *should* happen. In practice, however, things are a little different. Philips notes, for example, that kingly terms are also used when addressing God in prayers. Noble terms are used not only to and about nobles, but also to and about people in nontraditional positions of authority. She documents one case, for example, where a magistrate and the public prosecutor use noble terms to each other, but commoner terms to witnesses. Noble terms are, however, used "to raise the level of formality and politeness in public discourse generally" (378), and also in poetry "to enhance the beauty and persuasiveness of what is said" (379). The system is not rigid: It can be manipulated.

Samoan is similar to Tongan in that there are different registers, though only two, used depending on whether one is talking to or about a *matai* (a chief, an orator, or some other titled person) or a commoner. It is also similar in the way in which one can manipulate these registers: "When we test the accuracy of status/rank features to account for the actual use of RWs [respectful words] in everyday interaction, we realize that such features of the context are good predictors of performance **only in some contexts**" (Duranti 1992, 83; emphasis in the original). Formality and politeness can be signaled by the use of the respect register even when those involved do not merit this by virtue of their status. On the other hand, intimacy or common purpose can be conveyed by using the ordinary register even if one or more of the participants is *matai*.

In addition to this lexical marking, all Samoan words that contain *t* or *n* have two quite different pronunciations, depending on whether one is talking in a formal or an informal context. Formal Samoan *t* and *n* become *k* and *g* (=/ŋ/) in informal or colloquial speech. The word meaning 'bury' is *tanu* in more formal contexts, but *kagu* in informal contexts.

The fairly widespread Australian and Pacific practice of word taboo, or replacement by some other term of a word that is or sounds like the name of a recently dead person or of a chief, is one example of an **avoidance style**. There are other kinds of avoidance styles in the Pacific as well. Two such styles relate to the way one behaves linguistically (1) in the presence of certain relatives, usually in-laws, and (2) during certain kinds of food gathering and preparation. For example, "In every Australian community there are certain kin relations that demand special behaviour; typically, two people in mother-in-law/son-in-law relationship should avoid close contact and sometimes may not address one another directly. Most (perhaps all)

Australian tribes have or had a special 'avoidance' speech style which must be used in the presence of a taboo relative" (Dixon 1980, 58–59). In Dyirbal, perhaps the most extreme case of this kind in Australia, there are two words for almost every concept, one in the Guwal (everyday) style and another in the Jalnguy (avoidance) style (Dixon 1980, 61). Thus, for example, *buynyjul* means 'red-bellied lizard,' but in the presence of a taboo relative one has to use the term *jijan* instead; for *midin* 'ring-tail possum' one must substitute *jiburray*; and so on.

The Maisin of Papua New Guinea have a similar avoidance style. There, it is not just the *presence* of the in-law that is important. In Maisin, one is not allowed to use the name of an in-law in *any* circumstances, nor can one use any word that sounds like that in-law's name. One must substitute another word instead. This necessitates the generation of many pairs of words referring to the same thing. Speakers choose the one that is *not* like the name of an in-law. For example,

Maisin

isu	*gungguti*	'nose'
ikosi	*dobong*	'coconut'
mimisi	*jenje*	'sandfly'
wo	*iriri*	'fire'
gaiti	*sisari*	'dirty'
borung	*ombi*	'rain'
kimi	*damana*	'star'

If one has an in-law whose name is, or is like, *kimi*, one cannot use this word, but must use *damana* to mean 'star' instead.

The Kalam of Papua New Guinea have a similar in-law avoidance style. In addition, however, they have what has come to be called "Pandanus Language" in the literature.

> Pandanus Language is used in two ritually restricted contexts, both connected with the forest and with the preparation and consumption there of a special category of food. When people go to the forest to collect and cook *alxaw* [pandanus] nuts it is essential that they avoid Ordinary Language—otherwise, the Kalam say, the nuts will turn out to be rotten, watery or empty or the skins too hard to eat. Pandanus Language must be used throughout such expeditions, which, at least until very recently, often lasted for about three weeks. Ordinary Language must also be avoided when cassowaries, which were once fairly common in the forest, are being cut up, cooked and eaten. (Pawley 1992, 315–316)

Some examples of the differences between Ordinary Language and Pandanus Language are given below.[12]

Kalam

Ordinary Language			**Pandanus Language**		
Yakt	*magi*	*ki-p.*	*Wjblp*	*mdup*	*yok-p.*
bird	egg	excrete-it	bird	egg	put-it

'The bird has laid eggs.'

Kañm	*ñb-sp-un.*	*Sml*	*ñab*	*g-sp-un.*
banana	consume- PRESENT-we	banana	consuming	do-PRESENT- we

'We are eating bananas.'

The Kalam are not unusual in this. Many Pacific languages have special varieties that must be used in collecting forest produce, in hunting or fishing, in initiations and other rituals, and so on. In many of these cases, people believe that if they use ordinary language, the spirits guarding their prey will be alerted, and the hunting or fishing expedition will be unsuccessful. They disguise their intentions from these protective spirits by speaking in a special language in order to ensure the success of their expeditions.

11.4.3. Language and Socialization

Children learn their first language from the people around them—parents, siblings, and other members of the extended family. As Edith Bavin points out in her discussion of language and socialization among the Warlpiri of central Australia, however:

> Not all cultures have the same expectations of children. For example, in white middle-class society, preverbal children are generally considered to be potential conversation partners and a care-giver carries on 'conversations' with a child. When the child starts producing words, the care-giver often points to things and asks the child to name the object or picture. Or the care-giver helps the child to develop communicative skills by telling the child what to say to a third person. However, in other cultures, children are not necessarily encouraged to speak until they have some knowledge to give, and question-answer routines are not part of the adult-child interaction. (Bavin 1993, 86–87)

The Taiap-speakers of Gapun village in the East Sepik Province of Papua New Guinea evidence similar behavior and attitudes. In discussing Taiap views of social behavior, Kulick (1992) says that they distinguish between *hed* and *save. Hed* (Tok Pisin for 'head') refers to personal will and autonomy, but often has the negative connotations of unacceptable individualism or selfishness; *save* (Tok Pisin 'know, knowledge'), on the other hand, refers to the ability to behave appropriately and to fulfill one's roles in society. Children are born with *hed. Save*, so the people of Gapun say, "breaks open" in a child somewhere in the second or third year. "Teaching and learning are two distinct processes and . . . one can occur independently without the other. Parents consider that they can tell their children to 'call the names of things,' but that the children will only 'start to learn' once their *save* breaks open inside of them" (Kulick 1992, 120). Much of the talk Taiap villagers direct toward young children is what Kulick calls a "distraction routine." Parents do not have conversations with children; they seem simply to want to stop them from crying.

Like adults in most societies, Taiap adults have a set of baby-talk words they use to children, because the proper words are "too hard." Among them are the following (Kulick 1992, 197):

Taiap

Adult form	Baby-talk form	
mambrag	*mamak*	'spirit'
kakamatɨk	*kakam*	'millipede'
min	*mimi*	'breast'
yewɨr	*pipi*	'excrement'
nok	*soso*	'urine'
min atukun	*mimi naka*	'drink the breast!'
atɨtiŋgarana	*puparəŋgarana*	'you'd better not fall!'

This concept of proper words being too hard, however, is taken much further in Gapun village. Adults believe that the Taiap language is hard. Because children have no *save*, they will not be able to learn it well. They therefore very often use Tok Pisin in talking to children, since it is a much "easier" language. Children learn Taiap from older siblings rather than from adults.[13]

11.5. Language Use in Pacific Nations

European colonization of the Pacific brought new religions, new social and political institutions, new fashions, foods, and recreational pursuits. It also brought new languages and new ways of using language, widening the linguistic repertoires of Pacific Islanders and aboriginal Australians (and being widened by them).

11.5.1. Colonial and Other Intrusive Languages

The major colonial powers in the Pacific in recent times have been the British, Americans, Australians, New Zealanders (all of whom speak English), and the French. English and French are the two most important intrusive languages in the Pacific today. French is the official language in the French overseas territories of New Caledonia, Wallis and Futuna, and French Polynesia, and is one of the official languages (alongside Bislama and English) in Vanuatu. In almost all other Pacific countries or territories, English is the major language of external—and often internal—communication. It is also the major language of regional organizations in the Pacific (though French is sometimes used as well).

In all of these countries, some or all formal education is carried on in English or French. Educated Pacific Islanders have a reasonable knowledge of one or both of these languages, and they use them in official and often also informal situations. In many Pacific countries, a dialect of English (or French) is developing that differs from the varieties of that language spoken in metropolitan countries. These Pacific dialects often incorporate vocabulary items from vernacular languages or from languages like Melanesian Pidgin (e.g., Papua New Guinea English *bilum* 'string bag' or Vanuatu English *nakamal* 'meeting place, kava bar'), and they also show phonological differences, often as a result of the effects of the first languages of their speakers. More interesting, however, is the development of grammatical differences from neighboring first-language varieties of English, used in a highly consistent manner by virtually all well-educated and fluent speakers of English in these countries. For example:

Papua New Guinea English	**Metropolitan English**
Did he come <u>or</u>?	*Did he come?*
I read it <u>on</u> the newspaper.	*I read it <u>in</u> the newspaper.*
He can't <u>cope up with</u> it.	*He can't <u>cope with</u> it.*
Let's <u>discuss about</u> it.	*Let's <u>discuss</u> it.*
Do it <u>sometimes</u> tomorrow.	*Do it <u>some time</u> tomorrow.*
Where's the book which you read <u>it</u>?	*Where's the book which you read?*

In the region I have been dealing with, there are now only two other intrusive or colonial languages in use at the national level: Spanish is the official language of Easter Island, which is a territory of Chile, while Bahasa Indonesia is the official language of the Indonesian province of Irian Jaya. Other colonial powers used their own languages in their Pacific colonies before they were displaced. Spanish, German, and Japanese were used in parts of Micronesia, German also in New Guinea and Samoa, and Dutch in Irian Jaya.

In addition to the languages of colonial powers, other languages have entered the area. Indian laborers coming to Fiji, for example, spoke not only varieties of Hindi, but a wide range of other Indian languages, many of which (like Gujarati, Tamil, and Telugu) are still spoken there. Various Chinese languages are spoken by the small Chinese populations of almost all Pacific countries. There are immigrant communities speaking Vietnamese in Vanuatu and New Caledonia, Javanese in New Caledonia, and Japanese, Korean, Portuguese, Lao, Vietnamese, and various Philippine languages in Hawai'i. And the large numbers of European and, more recently, Asian immigrants into Australia and New Zealand have brought numerous ethnic languages to those two countries.

There have also been substantial movements of people within the Pacific. One can hear Kiribati being spoken in Solomon Islands, Tuvaluan in Nauru, East Uvea (Wallisian) and Tahitian in Vanuatu, Samoan and Tongan in Hawai'i, and most Polynesian languages in New Zealand. In a sense, these Pacific languages are also intrusive, in that they have come from somewhere else.

From the point of view of speakers of Pacific languages, languages like Melanesian Pidgin, Australian creoles, and so on could also be classed as intrusive. These languages are often used between speakers of different Pacific languages, and they are probably the primary source of borrowings into those languages. In urban areas particularly, their intrusions have progressed so far that they have become the first (and often only) language of many people.

11.5.2. Multilingualism

The arrival of these intrusive languages, and the increased social mobility of people in recent times, has led to quite complex sociolinguistic situations in the Pacific. Most people in the Pacific are at least bilingual; they use two languages on a fairly regular basis. Many people are in fact multilingual, using three or more languages regularly.

Bilingualism and multilingualism are not new in the Pacific. Particularly in Melanesia, but also to some extent in Australia, people—especially, though not exclusively, men—have always been exposed to languages other than their own, and have often used foreign languages in certain contexts. There was often considerable kudos to be gained by being multilingual. Salisbury's (1962) classic study of the Siane of the Eastern Highlands Province in Papua New Guinea, for example, showed that the overt use of a foreign language, Chuave, on formal and even informal occasions was a way of achieving and maintaining high social status.

In modern times the use of two or more languages has become more common and is no longer a male preserve. In general terms, we can differentiate between Australia, Polynesia, and Micronesia, where people tend to be bilingual, and Melanesia, where they tend to be multilingual. On most Polynesian and Micronesian islands, only one language is spoken. People speak this as their **vernacular**; it is the language they use within their own community, but normally not outside it. These people speak some other language as their **lingua franca**, the language used when dealing with (at least certain types of) outsiders. The lingua franca throughout almost all of Polynesia and Micronesia is English, except in French Polynesia and Wallis and Futuna, where it is French. Similarly, many aboriginal Australians know one Australian vernacular and use a creole or some variety of English as a lingua franca.

By contrast, most islands in Melanesia contain more than one language, and each country or territory contains a large number. Many Melanesians, therefore, speak their own vernacular, and often one or more neighboring vernaculars as well (particularly if there is a vernacular that has acquired some prestige as the result of missionary activity). Except in Irian Jaya and New Caledonia, they can usually also speak the national variety of Melanesian Pidgin (or Hiri Motu) to communicate with people from other parts of the country. And if they have been educated, they speak Bahasa Indonesia (in Irian Jaya), English (in Papua New Guinea, Solomon Islands, and Vanuatu), or French (in Vanuatu and New Caledonia), both to other citizens of their country and to outsiders. (Some educated ni-Vanuatu, in fact, speak both English and French, as well as Bislama and one or more vernaculars.)

Fiji falls somewhere between. Most Fijians speak their own dialect of Fijian plus the standard dialect; many also speak English. Similarly, most Indians speak Fiji Hindi and Standard Hindi, and many speak English. Not many Fijians speak Hindi, and not many Indians speak Fijian. English, or in some contexts Pidgin Fijian or Pidgin Hindi, is the language of interethnic communication.

In these kinds of multilingual situations, various aspects of the context determine the appropriate language to use. In the market in Vila, for example, a ni-Vanuatu would use the vernacular if the person selling vegetables came from the same language community (or possibly a nearby one), but Bislama if she didn't. During a coffee break in a Honiara office, the staff would probably talk in Pijin if they were all Solomon Islanders, but would most likely use English if some expatriates were taking part in the conversation.

Another feature of these multilingual situations is what is known as **code-switching**. Very often, even in the same conversation, people switch from one language to another. This may be because certain topics are easier to talk about in one of the languages all the participants know rather than in another, or it may be because something just sounds better in one language than in another. Whatever the reason, code-switching is a very common feature of social interaction in the multilingual Pacific.

Conversations are often carried out in two languages when the participants understand both languages fairly well, but each speaks only one of them fluently. In a Port Moresby office, for example, a Papuan worker (for whom Hiri Motu rather than Tok Pisin would be the lingua franca) might well listen to a conversation in Tok Pisin, but make his or her contribution to it in English.

11.5.3. Language in the National Context

Very few Pacific constitutions make specific reference to which language is the national language and which is the official language. Generally, the closest one gets to such a statement are sections in the constitution defining which language is authoritative, or which one(s) may be used in parliament. Constitutional provisions like the two below (from the constitutions of Kiribati and Fiji) are common.

> 127. The provisions of this constitution shall be published in a Kiribati text as well as this English text, but in the event of any inconsistency between the two texts, this English text shall prevail. (Kiribati)

> 56. The official language of Parliament shall be English, but any member of either house may address the chair in the House of which he is a member in Fijian or Hindustani [i.e., Hindi]. (Fiji)

The only reference to language in the Constitution of Papua New Guinea is the following statement in "National Goals and Directive Principles": "2(11). All persons and governmental bodies to endeavour to achieve universal literacy in [Tok] Pisin, Hiri Motu or English, and in *tok ples* or *ita eda tano gado* [i.e., vernaculars]."

In most Pacific countries, the metropolitan language (usually English) functions as the official language, although there may be no constitutional provision for this. It is the language of government, of the law and the higher courts, of higher education, and of sections of the media. The vernacular language functions as a de facto national language. It is used by the people in daily communication, in stores and offices, on public transport and in sections of the media, and often in early education and the lower courts.

This is even more true of Australia, where aboriginal vernaculars and the languages of immigrants have *no* official constitutional status. English is the official and national language, though there have recently been some efforts to give minority languages some limited status.

In Papua New Guinea and Solomon Islands, vernaculars also have no official place in the national life of the country. English is the official language, and it is very much also a de facto national language, as it is often the language people use to talk to each other. English is the language of government, of the law and the courts, of the media, and of all levels of education. Melanesian Pidgin has some status as an additional national language, as it is commonly used in daily communication and gets some exposure in the media, but its status is not comparable with that of, say, Tongan or Samoan in Tonga and Samoa.

Vanuatu is different. It is one of the few Pacific states where the national and official languages are spelled out in the constitution:

> 3 (1) The national language of the Republic is Bislama. The official languages are Bislama, English and French. The principal languages of education are English and French.
>
> (2) The Republic shall protect the different local languages which are part of the national heritage, and may declare one of them as a national language.

Pre-independence Vanuatu (then known as the New Hebrides) was in the rather unusual position of having two colonial masters, the British and the French, who ruled jointly. Some ni-Vanuatu were educated in French, others in English, and the political lines were drawn as much on the basis of language as anything else at the time of independence. Bislama was the neutral language in this situation, and it still remains the only common language, even among educated ni-Vanuatu. Although Bislama is not used in the educational system, and although laws and official government correspondence are in English and French, Bislama is used in parliament, in churches, in the media, and in other areas of daily communication.

11.5.4. Formal Education

Melanesia differs from the rest of the Pacific in terms of the languages used in the educational system. In Melanesia, schools start from the first grade in the official language, and students begin learning a totally foreign language, French or English, as soon as they enter school.[14] One major reason for this is the multiplicity of languages in these countries. Christian missions used vernaculars to some extent in primary education in the past, but now that education is a governmental concern, this no longer happens. And although there are some vernacular preschools and primary schools in some areas of Papua New Guinea, they are still in the early stages of being set up.

One interesting consequence of these policies is that almost no speakers of the largest nonmetropolitan language in the Pacific, Melanesian Pidgin, have learned to read and write their language through any formal educational system! A few have learned it through adult literacy classes; many others have taught themselves, having first learned to read and write in some other language. But the Pacific language with the largest number of speakers continues to have no place in formal education.

The Australian situation is slightly different. Some use is made of Australian languages in some areas, often through bilingual programs, where English and an Australian language are used side-by-side. For two centuries, however, there have been only negative attitudes toward aboriginal Australians and their languages. As a result, many people of aboriginal ancestry know only a variety of English, and teaching them in an Australian language is not of much help to their education.

Much more use is made of vernaculars in Polynesia and Micronesia. In many of these countries, students begin their schooling in the vernacular, not in English. English is only one subject until the middle (in Samoa or rural Fiji) or the end (in Tonga) of the primary curriculum, and vernaculars often remain subjects after the switch to English-language instruction has been made. In these countries, since the educational system has to deal with only one, or at most just a few, vernaculars, taking such an approach is relatively easy. The status of vernaculars in different parts of the Pacific relates very much to this issue of education.

11.5.5. Literacy

Literacy is often achieved through the formal educational system. In Polynesia and Micronesia, literacy rates are generally quite high, and people have usually learned to read and write their own language, often adding English later. In Melanesia, by contrast, literacy rates tend to be much lower, and those who have learned to read and write through formal education do so in English or French.

The Christian missions and the Summer Institute of Linguistics have sponsored literacy training in vernacular languages in at least some parts of Melanesia and Australia. More recently, however, there has been a burgeoning interest in vernacular literacy. Preschool programs have been established in many parts of Papua New Guinea to teach children basic literacy in their own language before they go to school. In many cases, these have operated totally or almost totally outside government education agencies.

Adult vernacular literacy has also undergone a major expansion, especially in the last few years. There are, for example, over fifteen hundred community-based literacy programs operating in Papua New Guinea, and a number of similar programs have begun in Solomon Islands and Vanuatu (Faraclas 1994). The success of these programs has caused the government of Papua New Guinea to subject its English-only policy for formal education to a critical review.

11.5.6. The Media

Almost all Pacific countries make some use of vernaculars in the media, although metropolitan languages also get considerable exposure. The balance depends on a number of factors, including how much foreign news and other material is printed or broadcast, and whether there are enough trained translators to translate foreign material into local languages. Even in Australia, where English dominates the media, minority languages still get some exposure.

The Papua New Guinea media show an interesting mixture of languages from all levels. While television is almost exclusively in English (apart from a few commercials in Tok Pisin), radio is different. National radio stations mainly use English, but have some programs in Tok Pisin and Hiri Motu. Provincial stations use mainly Tok Pisin or Hiri Motu (depending on which part of the country the station is in), but also make some use of the larger or more prominent vernaculars in the province. The two national daily newspapers are in English, and there are two weeklies, one in English and one in Tok Pisin. In the provinces, some attempt is made to use both Tok Pisin and a vernacular in provincial newsletters.

11.6. Shift, Survival, Death, Revival

The fourteen hundred languages of Australia and the Pacific are spoken by tiny populations in world terms. In addition, they have been subjected to invasion—from without, by such languages as English and French, and from within, by such languages as Melanesian Pidgin and Kriol. Australians and Pacific Islanders have incorporated these new languages into their traditional communication systems. There are, of course, a number of indigenous Pacific people who do not speak an Oceanic, Papuan, or Australian language. But for most people in the Pacific, the vernacular language exists side by side with widespread lingua francas like English or Melanesian Pidgin. At the same time, some languages have already died out as a result of depopulation, population movements, and pressure from other languages. At the beginning of the last century, for example, there were five languages spoken on the island of Erromango in Vanuatu: Today there is only one, with a few remnants of another. The situation in Australia is even more dramatic: Most of the languages spoken there two hundred years ago will not survive the next fifty years, as people of Aboriginal descent shift to English for their main, or sole, means of communication.

Linguists and other outside observers generally view such situations with alarm. The loss of a language is seen as a bad thing, and efforts should be made to preserve these languages—to the extent of running language maintenance programs, teaching children to speak their mother's tongue (which is not their mother tongue), and so on. This attitude may be an altruistic one or a paternalistic one, depending on one's point of view. But it is very much an outsider's view. What do speakers of these threatened languages themselves think of the imminent loss of their languages?

Up until the Second World War, New Zealand Māori was a dynamic language, even though it was mainly spoken in rural areas. But the war, and the movement of rural Māori to towns after it, changed all that. English came to be seen as the language with which one could get things—education, jobs, better living conditions—and the urban Māori began to abandon their language. There is evidence that this was a fairly conscious and deliberate act: Parents *chose* to speak English rather than Māori to their children, to give them as much of a head start as possible. A fairly recent survey by the New Zealand Department of Statistics showed that there were about 270,000 New Zealanders who claimed at least 50 percent Māori ancestry, and almost 100,000 more who claimed some Māori ancestry. Of those 370,000 people, only about 70,000 said they were fluent speakers of the Māori language, although another 45,000 said they could understand but not speak it.

Although the number of Māori speakers looks large from a Melanesian point of view, there was very serious concern in the Māori community, not least because very few of those fluent speakers of Māori were children or young people. It seemed likely that the number of speakers would diminish rapidly in the next couple of generations. So a number of Māori-language kindergartens called *Kōhanga Reo* ('language nests') were established. Preschool children in these did just what other preschoolers do, but through the medium of Māori rather than English. This step, combined with a resurgence of pride and interest in the language among the Māori community more generally, has probably arrested the decline, and the language will probably survive.

Similar revival programs have taken place in other parts of the Pacific. The Hawaiian language was, and probably still is, in far greater danger than Māori of totally disappearing, but intensive efforts there are also beginning to see the decline arrested.

The interesting point about these two cases—and similar cases elsewhere in the region—is that the languages involved are spoken by people who were the traditional sole occupiers of their territory, who have been invaded and colonized, but who are now reasserting their rights and identities. Following a century or more of not particularly successful assimilation, the Māori and the Hawaiians are becoming increasingly vocal on the political stage in their own country. The emblematic function of language, to which I referred in part 1, is perhaps operative here. To be a Māori, rather than just a New Zealander, involves a number of things, and one of these is the ability to speak the Māori language.

These are cases where there are active programs to revive dying languages. Some areas of Melanesia show the opposite trend. Many of the languages concerned have very small populations. In Papua New Guinea, Solomon Islands, and Vanuatu, there are over 160 languages spoken by two hundred people or fewer, and many of these are under threat of extinction. As people from these societies intermarry, as children go to school outside their home areas, and as young men and women drift to the towns looking for paid employment, the chances that they and their children will continue to speak their language are fairly remote. But the attitudes of these people toward the impending death of their languages seem to be somewhat different. Speaking of parts of the Sepik area of Papua New Guinea, for example, Foley (1986; 27–28) says: "Tok Pisin . . . is seen as an avenue by which to acquire the goods of this [Western] culture . . . with the result that in certain areas the vernacular indigenous languages are being abandoned in favour of Tok Pisin, which is being acquired as a first language. This is occurring not just in urban areas, but also in rural areas. Murik, a language of the lake country west of the mouth of the Sepik river . . . is dying, and is not spoken by younger people in the villages. It is being replaced by Tok Pisin."

I have already referred to Kulick's (1992) important study of the Taiap speakers of Gapun village in the Sepik. Tok Pisin was introduced into the village by men returning from working on plantations, and for some years it was a men's language only. Christianization and other social changes after the Second World War exposed women to Tok Pisin, with the result that all adults now know both Taiap and Tok Pisin.

But this in itself is no explanation for the fact that children in Gapun village, as in some other parts of Papua New Guinea, are learning Tok Pisin rather than (in this case) Taiap as their first language. In many parts of the Pacific, people retain their own vernacular even though they use another language on a daily basis. Why are Gapun children growing up speaking Tok Pisin rather than Taiap as their first language? "The reasons for the enthusiasm toward and the spread of Tok Pisin throughout the verbal repertoires of all villagers, eventually even those who rarely if ever left Gapun, were not so much 'pragmatic' or 'socioeconomic,' as those terms are commonly used in the sociolinguistic literature, as they were 'cosmological,' in the broadest anthropological sense of that word" (Kulick 1992, 249). That is, the arrival of Europeans, or new conditions, and of a new religion was seen as "the harbinger of a new way of life. Their presence in New Guinea came to be understood in terms of an impending metamorphosis that would transform every aspect of the villagers' lives, including their physical beings. . . . In their eagerness for the metamorphosis to occur, villagers immediately seized upon language as a 'road,' a way of making it happen" (Kulick 1992, 249).

To some extent, of course, these attitudes are similar to those of the postwar urban Māori. The new language is seen as the key to change, to advancement, to success, however measured and perceived. The difference is that the people Foley and Kulick are talking about see themselves as Papua New Guineans, as citizens of a country with the same rights as other citizens. A shift from one language to another does not really threaten this identity. In contrast, the Māori and the Hawaiians view language as a mark not only of cultural but also of ethnic identity, and they manipulate language as a political tool.

CONCLUSION

Ideas about Pacific Languages

When I first went to see the man who has become our family doctor in Port Vila, he asked what I did, and then said that he had visited the university library here and had seen rows and rows of dictionaries and grammars of languages spoken by just a few hundred speakers. "Fascinating", he said, "fascinating . . . but bloody useless!"

Attitudes like these are held by both westerners and many Pacific Islanders, though perhaps for different reasons. Many westerners see Pacific Island languages as not being really serious subjects of study: They do not have a "literature," they are not used in education, they have no real place in the national—let alone the international—domain. Linguists who study these languages are seen as dilettantes who should be doing something more "serious." Many Pacific Islanders have slightly different views. For example, they often look on a dictionary as an important archive or museum piece recording "old" words that are dropping out of the language. But they feel that their language really does not have much of a future when faced with competition from international languages.

Most Pacific languages have neither been vilified to the extent that Melanesian Pidgin or Fiji Hindi have nor subjected to the extreme pressures of survival that Māori, Hawaiian, Murik, or Taiap have felt. Virtually all of them, however, have well and truly entered the twentieth century, and are spoken side-by-side with introduced languages or other recently developed lingua francas.

Rapid social changes in the Pacific have affected Pacific languages no less rapidly. This is perhaps most evident in the area of lexical borrowing, as discussed in chapter 9. Grandparents shudder when their grandchildren interlard their vernacular with English-derived terms—and are sure that their language will not survive another generation!

To a large extent, this could be construed as just the typical conservatism of the elderly: "Things were better in our time, these modern fads and fashions are no good." But there are some cases where the grandparents may have a point. Clark (1982), in studying words of English origin borrowed into Ifira-Mele,[1] distinguishes between necessary and unnecessary borrowings. A necessary borrowing is one where the thing or concept to which the word refers is new to the culture and, even though the possibility of a compound using existing words, a monomorphemic loan is usually simpler. Some examples of necessary borrowings are:

Ifira-Mele

aeani	'iron'	*fooko*	'fork'
marseni	'medicine'	*laemu*	'lemon, lime'
nakitae	'necktie'	*peelo*	'bell'

Unnecessary borrowings are those that replace an already existing word in the language. This has happened in Ifira-Mele with most of the numerals, possibly because of the constant use of English/Bislama numerals in counting money, telling time, and in mathematics classes, and partly also because the higher numerals in Ifira-Mele are longer than their English/Bislama equivalents. But there are other cases, like the following:

Ifira-Mele

Borrowing		Original word
taemu	'time'	*malo*
staaji	'start'	*tuulake*
insaiji	'inside'	*iroto*
auji	'go out'	*tave*
puroomu	'broom'	*niisara*
wooka	'work'	*wesiwesi*

In discussing the replacement of *wesiwesi* 'work' by *wooka*, Clark (1982, 139) says that his middle-aged informants "condemned *wooka* as an abusive borrowing, when a perfectly good indigenous synonym existed." In a sense, older speakers of the language have, in many cases, come reluctantly to accept necessary change. But they often also see the unnecessary incorporation of foreign words into their language as a sure sign that the language is not going to survive. As one elderly ni-Vanuatu man said to me, "My grandchildren think they're speaking our language, but they're really speaking Bislama."

Change has, of course, been taking place for millennia. The Pacific region has had a long and complex history. When the first settlers came, and where they came from, we don't really know—but we can be fairly sure that it was at least fifty thousand years ago. By the time the Anglo-Saxons were subduing

the Celtic people of Britain, virtually all the islands of the Pacific had been settled, many by successive waves of people speaking different languages.

Many westerners—and indeed many Pacific Islanders as well—hold the
view that, once a particular island or area was settled, the inhabitants remained in place. Only with the coming of Europeans were their eyes
opened to the outside world. But of course the Pacific region was not like
this at all. Contact of various kinds—warfare, invasion, trade, intermarriage,
ceremonial exchange, and so on—took place between near neighbors or between peoples whose homes were thousands of kilometers apart, between
people who spoke similar or at least related languages and between those
whose languages were unrelated. The European intruders who entered this
region in the eighteenth and nineteenth centuries were really just the latest
of a series of "foreigners" who contacted Pacific peoples. Pacific languages
have been changing throughout this whole period as a result of external
pressures and internal processes. They have survived these changes and will
continue to survive others.

When the first Fiji Hindi dictionary ever published appeared some years
ago (Hobbs 1985), it was greeted with howls of protest and derision from
the Fiji Hindi–speaking community. "There is no such language as Fiji
Hindi!" said one writer to a newspaper. "Hindi in Fiji is a sub-standard
Bhojpuri which has been corrupted," said another.

Attitudes like these toward creoles and similar languages are common
throughout the world. Such languages are often seen by outsiders as "broken," "bastardized," or "baby-talk" versions of proper languages. Speaking of
what is now known as Tok Pisin, for example, Sir Hubert Murray (1924, 10),
an Australian colonial administrator, said, "It is a vile gibberish . . . and should
be discouraged." Major Eustace Sanders, a British colonial official who served
on Malaita in Solomon Islands, had similar views about Pijin: "The only *lingua
franca* [is] pigeon English which consists of the English word in the
Melanesian context. It is a queer sounding garbled business and not in any
way satisfactory" (quoted in Keesing 1990, 156). Even the names of these languages—Pidgin, Pijin, Broken, and so on—have negative connotations.[2]

This could all be simply dismissed as another example of western ethno-
centrism if many speakers of these languages did not share the same
views—as the case of Fiji Hindi illustrates. Speaking of Solomon Islands,
Keesing (1990, 162) says:

> It is perhaps surprising . . . that so many Solomon Islanders have ac-
> cepted uncritically an ideology depicting Pijin as a bastardized form of
> English. . . . Many well educated Solomon Islanders echo the colonial

view that Pijin has 'no grammar,' even though in speaking and under-standing Pijin, those who express this view use (unconsciously) a grammar so complex and intricate and powerful that (like the grammars of all languages) it defies formal description.

The attitude of many speakers of Melanesian Pidgin toward their language could be described as schizophrenic. On the one hand, they use it frequently, in all kinds of situations; on the other, they see it as not a "real" language.

This schizophrenia is perhaps most pronounced in Vanuatu. Bislama has higher constitutional status in Vanuatu than any nonmetropolitan language in any other Pacific country. It is the language of parliament, of churches, of government offices, and of social functions. Because half the educated population is English-educated and the other half French-educated, Bislama is the linguistic cement holding the nation of Vanuatu together. Highly educated ni-Vanuatu from different islands prefer to speak to each other in Bislama rather than in English,[3] and there is a distinct feeling of national pride in the public use of Bislama.

But Bislama is not used in the school system, either as a medium of instruction or as a subject, and attempts to introduce it have met with the kind of attitudes expressed in Keesing's description of the Solomon Islands situation: "it's not a real language," "it has no grammar," "it's only a language for casual conversation." Vanuatu may be unique among the countries of the world in allowing a child to be punished for speaking the constitutionally recognized national language on school grounds!

Yet another aspect of this complex issue concerns the replacement of vernaculars by Melanesian Pidgin in parts of Melanesia. People in some parts of Papua New Guinea are abandoning their vernacular in favor of Tok Pisin. They see Tok Pisin as the key to the future, rather than as a "rubbish" language to be used only where no other can serve.

The situation in Fiji is somewhat different. Fiji Indians grow up speaking Fiji Hindi at home. At school, they are exposed to two prestige languages, Standard Hindi and English. Unlike Melanesian Pidgin, Fiji Hindi is never written. Literacy is taught in Standard Hindi, and the association of the standard language with the sacred books of Hinduism gives Standard Hindi great prestige. English too is obviously a prestigious language in Fiji—the language of higher education, the international language, the language of business, and, increasingly, the language Fiji Indians need to know to emigrate from post-coup Fiji. The result has been that Fiji Hindi has very low status in Fiji, especially among its native speakers.

Pacific Islands languages, whether indigenous or more recently developed, are worthy subjects of study in their own right. A language represents a culture of a people. Even if that people is numerically small and does not play an important part on the world stage, its culture and, by implication, its language, are no less worthy of study than the languages of larger or more influential peoples. It is true that the *usefulness* in a global sense of even languages like Fijian or Samoan pales into insignificance beside the usefulness of English or French. But that does not mean that these languages should be discounted altogether.

Change in the languages of Pacific Islanders, as in all languages, is inevitable, natural, and not something to be universally deplored. Certain changes may be undesirable for all sorts of reasons, but it is in the nature of language to change, and resisting change is counterproductive.

What of the future? Dixon (1990, 230–231), in suggesting that every language with fewer than ten thousand speakers is at risk of extinction, rather gloomily predicts that 80 percent of the languages in the Pacific and Asia may have died out by the end of the twenty-first century. Even languages like Melanesian Pidgin are seen by some as being under threat from English: "It would seem that in the future Tok Pisin has nowhere to go but down. . . . This does not mean that Tok Pisin will die a rapid, or even an easy, death. . . . But it does mean that, in perhaps 50 years' time, Tok Pisin will most likely be being studied by scholars among a small community of old men" (Laycock 1985, 667). Although the potential for language death is a serious one for some Pacific languages, I feel that Dixon and Laycock are unnecessarily pessimistic. The vast majority of Pacific languages are not, or not yet, moribund. As long as a community is sufficiently viable to remain a community (irrespective of absolute size), and as long as such a community has pride in its language as part of its overall cultural heritage, the language will survive. It will change, as internal and external mechanisms cause it to develop different words, pronunciations, and expressions, and these changes will be rued by the older generation—as they always are. But change is endemic to language and is an element of its vitality.

There are, of course, languages that have died out or are currently under serious threat. For some threatened languages, there are programs of reinvigoration and resurgence: Hawaiian and Māori are probably the best known of these. Both involve serious attempts to teach young children the language in a structured or semistructured environment, in the hope that, unlike their parents, they will become fluent in the language of their ancestors.

Arguments rage, of course, about the worth of such programs. At one end of the spectrum are those who feel that all languages should be preserved and, if possible, used more widely than they are now, and who propose programs to encourage—and even almost to force—young people, and often adults, to learn their "own" language. At the other end are those who say that languages should be left alone. If people want to shift to another language that they think is more useful, it is their right to do so. Very often this debate is held in the rarefied circles of academe, without much input from the speakers of the languages themselves. Those speakers will, of course, have the final say (and perhaps the last laugh) by choosing the course of action that seems most sensible and practical from their perspective.

The Pacific area has probably seen more change taking place in its languages than any other part of the world—certainly than any other region with a comparable population. The multiplicity of different languages and language types, with different histories, has always been one of the intriguing features of this region for both Pacific Islanders and outsiders alike. As long as Pacific Islanders continue to recognize that their languages are both their past and their future, the unity in diversity so characteristic of the Pacific will continue to make this region unique.

Suggestions for Further Reading

Chapter 1

Crystal's *Cambridge Encyclopedia of Language* (1987, 2d ed. 1998) provides a wealth of information on many of the topics covered in this chapter in a very readable and accessible format.

There are hundreds of general introductions to **descriptive linguistics**. Aitchison (1978) provides a good, readable general introduction. Finegan and Besnier (1979) and Crowley, Lynch, Siegel, and Piau (1995) go into rather more technical detail; these are useful because many of their examples are from Pacific languages.

Aitchison (1981) is a very readable discussion of **language change**, while Crowley (1992, 3d ed. 1997) not only provides perhaps the clearest introduction to **historical and comparative linguistics** currently available but also uses Pacific examples to illustrate many technical concepts.

Chapter 2

Sebeok (1971) and Wurm (1975, 1976) contain a number of articles relevant to the distribution of and history of research into Pacific languages. Schütz (1972, 1994) provides thorough and sensitive treatments on the history of research into Fijian and Hawaiian, respectively. Schütz (1994) is a particularly fine piece of scholarship. The language atlas of the Pacific region edited by Wurm and Hattori (1981) is worth detailed examination.

Chapter 3

Various aspects of the establishment of the Austronesian family and its subgroups are covered by Blust (1978a, 1984a, 1984b), Clark (1979), Dempwolff

(1934–1938), Geraghty (1983), Grace (1955, 1959, 1968), Jackson (1983), Lynch, Ross, and Crowley (1998), Lynch and Tryon (1985), Pawley (1972), Pawley and Ross (1995), Ross (1988), Tryon (1976, 1995), Tryon and Hackman (1983), and Wurm (1976). (References to some of the classics of the nineteenth century and the early part of the twentieth can be found in the bibliography of Ross 1988.)

Readers interested in cultural reconstruction should consult Blust (1980), Chowning (1991), Pawley and Ross (1995), and a number of papers in Geraghty (1998), Lynch and Pat (1996), and Pawley and Ross (1994),

Chapter 4

The major general comprehensive works on the history of **Papuan** languages are Foley (1986) and Wurm (1975, 1982). McElhanon and Voorhoeve (1970) provides an illustration of the kinds of techniques used in establishing a Papuan phylum, while Pawley (1995) shows how the comparative method can be applied to these languages.

Good general works on **Australian** languages include Dixon (1980) and Yallop (1981). O'Grady and Tryon (1990) is a collection of articles in which the comparative method is applied to a number of Australian language groups.

Chapter 5

There is no single volume dealing with the sound systems of the Austronesian languages, such descriptions generally being incorporated in larger comparative or grammatical studies. Haudricourt et al. (1979) provides considerable information on New Caledonian phonologies, as does Krupa (1982) for Polynesian. Tryon (1994) and Lynch, Ross, and Crowley (1998) give briefer outlines of the phonologies of a wide range of Austronesian languages.

Foley (1986, chap. 3) and Dixon (1980, chaps. 6 and 7) provide general overviews of the phonology of Papuan and Australian languages, respectively. A fairly representative sample of Australian phonologies can be found in the handbooks edited by Dixon and Blake (1979, 1981, 1983).

Chapter 6

Lynch, Ross, and Crowley (1998) provides a general coverage of Oceanic grammar, as well as sketch grammars of almost four dozen Oceanic languages. Ross (1988) contains general information on the grammars of Western Oceanic languages, while Blust (1978b), Tryon (1973), and Haudricourt (1971) contain general grammatical information on the languages of the Admiralties, Vanuatu, and New Caledonia, respectively. Bender (1971, 1984) provide general information on Micronesian languages, as does Krupa (1982) for Polynesian languages. For further details on any specific Oceanic language, consult appendix 1, below.

Chapter 7

The best general introduction to the structure of Papuan languages is Foley (1986). Wurm (1975, 1982) also provide useful general information on a range of Papuan languages. Collections of articles on a number of languages include Dutton (1975) and Franklin (1973, 1981). More detailed information on individual languages can be found in the bibliographies to these works or in appendix 1, below.

Chapter 8

Dixon (1980) is a very good general survey of Australian languages, and it contains as well quite a detailed description of grammatical structure. Sketch grammars of particular languages, or treatments of particular grammatical categories across a range of Australian languages, may be found in Dixon (1976) and in Dixon and Blake (1979, 1981, 1983). Appendix 1, below, gives sources for a number of individual languages.

Chapter 9

Apart from the studies by Biggs on Rotuman and Thurston in northwest New Britain, mentioned in this chapter, there are a number of other useful works about this topic. Collections of articles include Dutton (1992), Dutton and Tryon (1994), and Pawley and Ross (1994). Implications for prehistoric contact on the classification of modern languages are discussed by Lynch (1981a, 1981b) and Pawley (1981). Among case studies of individual languages or language communities, those by Siegel (1987) on Fiji and J. Lee (1987) on the Tiwi of Australia are of considerable interest.

Chapter 10

Verhaar (1990) is a collection of articles on **Melanesian Pidgin**. For specific varieties of Melanesian Pidgin, the following should be consulted:

1. **Tok Pisin**: Dutton with Thomas (1985), Mihalic (1971), Mühlhäusler (1979), Verhaar (1995), and Wurm and Mühlhäusler (1985).
2. **Pijin**: Simons and Young (1978).
3. **Bislama**: Crowley (1990a, 1990b), Tryon (1987).

On **Hiri Motu** and the **Hiri Trading Languages**, Dutton (1985) is the best historical source. Grammatical treatments may be found in Wurm and Harris (1963) and Dutton and Voorhoeve (1974).

For **Fiji Hindi** and other contact languages in Fiji, Siegel (1987) is the authoritative source. Siegel (1977) is a brief introduction to the grammar of Fiji Hindi, and Hobbs (1985) is a dictionary of the language.

Among discussions of Australian creoles, the following are of interest: for **Broken** (Torres Strait Creole), see Schnukal (1988); for **Kriol** (Northern Territory Creole), see Harris (1986) and Sandefur (1986).

Chapter 11

General coverages of the relationship between **language, culture, and so-cial organization**, and the nature of the lexicons of Pacific languages, can be found in Dixon (1980), Foley (1986), Walsh and Yallop (1993), and Wurm (1975, 1976, 1977). Smith (1988) provides a good discussion of the range of **numeral and counting systems** found in parts of the region.

There is a growing literature on **languages in use** in both traditional and modern societies. Important studies on socialization include Kulick (1992) and Schieffelin (1990) on New Guinea societies and Ochs (1988) on Samoa. There are a number of Pacific-oriented studies in Duranti and Goodwin (1992) dealing with various aspects of the **context** of language use.

As far as **language and education** are concerned, Baldauf and Luke (1990), Benton (1981), Brumby and Vászolyi (1977), and Mugler and Lynch (1996) provide a fairly wide coverage.

Conclusion

Most of the general surveys I have referred to above contain some reference to attitudes toward and ideas about Pacific languages. There are a number of articles specifically on this topic in the *Handbook of Tok Pisin* (Wurm and Mühlhäusler 1985).

Appendices

APPENDIX 1

Data Sources

Below is a list of all languages from which data have been quoted in the book, arranged on a broad genetic basis, together with their general locations (see the maps in chapter 2) and the sources from which the data were taken. JL indicates that some or all of the data are from my own knowledge or unpublished research; PNG = Papua New Guinea.

	Location	**Sources**
Austronesian Languages		
Non-Oceanic		
Chamorro	Micronesia	Topping (1973)
Palauan	Micronesia	Josephs (1975)
Oceanic		
Adzera	PNG	Holzknecht (1989), Smith (1988)
A'jië	New Caledonia	Fontinelle (1976), Lichtenberk (1978)
Anejom̃	Vanuatu	Lynch (1982a, 1998), JL
Aroma	PNG	Crowley (1992), JL
Arosi	Solomon Is.	Capell (1971), Lynch and Horoi (1998)
Banoni	PNG	Lincoln (1976)
Big Nambas	Vanuatu	G. Fox (1979)
Carolinian	Micronesia	Jackson and Marck (1991)
Cèmuhî	New Caledonia	Rivierre (1980)

Drehu	New Caledonia	Moyse-Faurie (1983), Tryon (1968a)
Fijian	Fiji	Geraghty (1983), Milner (1972), Schütz (1985), Schütz and Komaitai (1971), JL
Hawaiian	Polynesia	Elbert and Pukui (1979)
Hula	PNG	Crowley (1992)
Iaai	New Caledonia	Ozanne-Rivierre (1976), Tryon (1968b)
Ifira-Mele	Vanuatu	Clark (1982)
Jawe	New Caledonia	Haudricourt and Ozanne-Rivierre (1982)
Kilivila	PNG	Senft (1986)
Kiribati	Micronesia	Groves, Groves, and Jacobs (1985)
Kosraean	Micronesia	K. Lee (1975)
Kwamera	Vanuatu	Lindstrom (1986), Lindstrom and Lynch (1994)
Labu	PNG	Siegel (1984)
Lagoon Trukese	Micronesia	Dyen (1965), Goodenough and Sugita (1980)
Lenakel	Vanuatu	Lynch (1978), JL
Lewo	Vanuatu	Early (1994)
Lusi	PNG	Thurston (1982, 1987, 1992)
Maisin	PNG	Ross (1984), JL
Manam	PNG	Lichtenberk (1983)
Māori	Polynesia	Bauer (1993), Biggs (1969), Hohepa (1967)
Mapos	PNG	Smith (1988)
Mari	PNG	Holzknecht (1989)
Maringe	Solomon Is.	Ross (1988), White (1988)
Marshallese	Micronesia	Bender (1969)
Mekeo	PNG	Jones (1992)
Mokilese	Micronesia	Harrison (1976)
Mono-Alu	Solomon Is.	Fagan (1986), Ross (1988)
Motu	PNG	Lister-Turner and Clark (n.d.), Crowley (1992), JL
Nadrau Fijian	Fiji	Geraghty (1983)
Nakanai	PNG	Johnston (1980)
Nakanamanga	Vanuatu	Schütz (1969)

Nauruan	Micronesia	Kayser (1936), Rensch (1993)
Nehan	PNG	Ross (1988), Todd (1978)
Niuean	Polynesia	McEwen (1970)
Nukuoro	Micronesia	Carroll (1965)
Paamese	Vanuatu	Crowley (1982)
Pije	New Caledonia	Haudricourt and Ozanne-Rivierre (1982)
Ponapean	Micronesia	Rehg (1981)
Port Sandwich	Vanuatu	Charpentier (1979)
Puluwat	Micronesia	Elbert (1974)
Raga	Vanuatu	D. Walsh (1966)
Rapanui	Polynesia	Krupa (1982), Langdon and Tryon (1983)
Rarotongan	Polynesia	Savage (1980)
Ririo	Solomon Is.	Laycock (1982b)
Rotuman	Fiji	Churchward (1940), Biggs (1965)
Roviana	Solomon Is.	Ross (1988), Corston (1998)
Samoan	Polynesia	Duranti (1992), Marsack (1962), Milner (1966), Pawley (1966b)
Sinagoro	PNG	Crowley (1992), Kolia (1975)
Sissano	PNG	Laycock (1973)
Southwest Tanna	Vanuatu	Lynch (1982b)
Sye	Vanuatu	Crowley (1995), Lynch (1983)
Tahitian	Polynesia	Tryon (1970)
Tigak	PNG	Beaumont (1979)
Titan	PNG	Ross (1988)
To'aba'ita	Solomon Is.	Lichtenberk (1984)
Tolai	PNG	Mosel (1980, 1984), Ross (1988)
Tongan	Polynesia	Churchward (1953), Philips (1991)
Trukese (*see* Lagoon Trukese)		
Ulithian	Micronesia	Sohn and Bender (1973)
Vinmavis	Vanuatu	Crowley (1998)
Wayan Fijian	Fiji	Pawley and Sayaba (1990)
West Futuna	Vanuatu	Dougherty (1983)
Woleaian	Micronesia	Harrison and Jackson (1984)
Xârâcùù	New Caledonia	Haudricourt et al. (1979)

| Yabêm | PNG | Bradshaw (1979), Ross (1993) |
| Yapese | Micronesia | Jensen (1977) |

Papuan Languages

Abelam	PNG	Laycock (1965)
Abu'	PNG	Nekitel (1986)
Alamblak	PNG	Bruce (1984), Foley (1986)
Anêm	PNG	Thurston (1982, 1987, 1992)
Anggor	PNG	Litteral (1981)
Awa	PNG	Loving and Loving (1975)
Baniata	Solomon Is.	Todd (1975)
Barai	PNG	Olson (1975)
Bilua	Solomon Is.	Todd (1975)
Buin	PNG	Laycock (1975b, 1982a)
Daga	PNG	Murane (1974)
Enga	PNG	Lang (1973)
Fore	PNG	Scott (1978)
Grand Valley Dani	Irian Jaya	Foley (1986)
Guhu-Samane	PNG	Smith (1988)
Huli	PNG	Cheetham (1978)
Iatmul	PNG	Foley (1986)
Kalam	PNG	Pawley (1966a, 1992), Foley (1986)
Kamasau	PNG	Sanders and Sanders (1980)
Kapauku (Ekagi)	Irian Jaya	Price and Pospisil (1966), Smith (1988)
Kâte	PNG	Foley (1986)
Kewa	PNG	Franklin (1971), Franklin and Franklin (1978)
Kobon	PNG	Davies (1980)
Koita	PNG	Dutton (1975)
Korafe	PNG	Farr and Farr (1975)
Kuman	PNG	Piau (1981, 1985), JL
Magi	PNG	Thomson (1975)
Manem	Irian Jaya	Foley (1986)
Melpa	PNG	Cochran (1977)
Mountain Koiari	PNG	Garland and Garland (1975)
Nimboran	Irian Jaya	Foley (1986)
Numanggang	PNG	Smith (1988)
Pawaian	PNG	Trefry (1969)
Rotokas	PNG	Firchow and Firchow (1969)

Salt-Yui	PNG	Irwin (1974)
Selepet	PNG	Kulick (1992)
Som	PNG	Smith (1988)
Taiap	PNG	Kulick (1992)
Toaripi	PNG	Franklin (1973)
Vanimo	PNG	Ross (1980)
Wahgi	PNG	Phillips (1976)
Wantoat	PNG	Smith (1988)
Waskia	PNG	Ross and Paol (1978)
Wiru	PNG	Foley (1986)
Yeletnye	PNG	Henderson (1975)
Yimas	PNG	Foley (1986)

Australian Languages

Alawa	Sharpe (1972)
Anguthimri	Crowley (1981)
Bandjalang	Crowley (1978, 1992)
Diyari	Dixon (1980)
Djapu	Morphy (1983)
Dyirbal	Dixon (1980)
Gooniyandi	McGregor (1994)
Gumbaynggir	Eades (1979)
Guugu Yimidhirr	Haviland (1979)
Kaitij	Dixon (1980)
Kalkatungu	Dixon (1980)
Kunjen	Sommer (1969)
Lardil	Dixon (1980)
Margany	Breen (1981)
Murrinh-Patha	M. Walsh (1993)
Njamal	Burling (1970)
Pitta-Pitta	Blake (1979)
Tiwi	J. Lee (1987)
Uradhi	Crowley (1983)
Wajarri	Douglas (1981)
Walmajarri	Dixon (1980)
Wargamay	Dixon (1981)
Warlpiri	Bavin (1993)
Western Desert	Dixon (1980)
Wunambal	Vászolyi (1976)
Yanyuwa	Bradley (1992)
Yaygir	Crowley (1979)

Yidiny		Dixon (1980)
Yukulta		Keen (1983)

Creoles, Pidgins, and Koines

Bislama	Vanuatu	Crowley (1990a, 1990b), Tryon (1987), JL
Fiji Hindi	Fiji	Siegel (1977, 1987)
Hiri Trading Languages	PNG	Dutton (1985)
Hiri Motu	PNG	Dutton (1985)
Melanesian Pidgin (*see* Bislama, Pijin, Tok Pisin)		
Pijin	Solomon Is.	Simons and Young (1978)
Police Motu (*see* Hiri Motu)		
Tok Pisin	PNG	Dutton with Thomas (1985), Mihalic (1971), JL

APPENDIX 2

Phonetic Symbols

As much as is possible in this book, I use the standard orthographies of the languages I describe. In discussing the sound systems of these languages, however, phonetic symbols representing the sounds are used. In addition, some Pacific languages do not have a standard—or any—orthography, so phonetic symbols are used in quoting data from these languages.

The symbols I use are given in the following charts, with a brief description of some of the sounds they represent. Different linguists occasionally use different symbols to represent the same sound. I have tried to be as consistent as possible with the use of phonetic symbols in this book, often changing the orthography of some of the original sources for this purpose. The system used here is based on the International Phonetic Alphabet, but deviates from it in a number of respects.

Symbols not on these charts, usually representing sounds referred to only once in this book, are explained when they are used.

Vowel Symbols

	Front		Central	Back
	Unrounded	Rounded	Unrounded	Rounded
HIGH				
Close	i	ü	ɨ	u
Open	I			U
MID				
Close	e	ö	ə	o
Open	ɛ			ɔ

LOW

Close	æ	œ		ʌ
Open			a	ɒ

Length is marked by a colon following the vowel: /a/ is a vowel of normal length, whereas /a:/ is a long vowel. Nasalization is marked by a tilde above a vowel: /ã/ is the nasalized version of /a/.

The technical terms used in describing consonants and vowels may be found in the glossary at the end of the book. A very brief guide to the pronunciation of the sounds symbolized above, especially the vowels and some of the unfamiliar consonant symbols, follows.

Vowels

Approximate pronunciations of some of these vowels are as follows. (Pronunciation is in educated Australian English unless otherwise indicated.)

Front Vowels

[i] as in *heed*
[I] as in *hit*
[e] as in French *été* 'summer'
[ɛ] as in *bet*
[æ] as in *bat*

[ü] as in French *rue* 'street'

[ö] as in French *feu* 'fire'
[æ] as in French *peur* 'fear'

Central Vowels

[ɨ] as in New Zealand English *this*

[ə] as in *ago, father*

[ʌ] as in *but*
[a] as in *bard*

Back Vowels

[u] as in *pool*
[U] as in *pull*
[o] as in *saw*
[ɔ] as in *pot*

[ɒ] as in BBC English *party*

Consonants

Symbols that look like, and are pronounced roughly like, the corresponding English letter are not discussed here. Less familiar symbols are briefly explained below.

Consonant Symbols

	velarized bilabial	bilabial	labio dental	dental	alveolar	retroflex	alveo palatal	palatal	velar	labio velar	glottal
voiceless stops: oral	pʷ	p		t̪	t	ṭ	tʸ	c	k	kʷ	ʔ
prenasalized	ᵐpʷ	ᵐp		ⁿt̪	ⁿt	ⁿṭ	ⁿtʸ	ⁿc	ᵑk	ᵑkʷ	ᵑʔ
voiced stops: oral	bʷ	b		d̪	d	ḍ	dʸ	j	g	gʷ	
prenasalized	ᵐbʷ	ᵐb		ⁿd̪	ⁿd	ⁿḍ	ⁿdʸ	ⁿj	ᵑg	ᵑgʷ	
voiceless affricates				ts̪	ts		tʃ				
voiced affricates				dz̪	dz		dʒ				
voiceless fricatives	fʷ	ɸ	f	θ	s	ṣ	ʃ		x	xʷ	h
voiced fricatives	vʷ	β	v	ð	z	ẓ	ʒ		ɣ	ɣʷ	
voiced nasals	mʷ	m		n̪	n	ṇ	ñ		ŋ	ŋʷ	
voiced laterals				l̪	l	ḷ	λ		ɬ		
voiced flap					r	ṛ					
voiced trill: oral					r̃						
prenasalized					ⁿr̃						
voiced semivowels	w					r		y			

English Sounds with Unfamiliar Symbols

The following are English sounds, though the symbols are not always familiar.

[tʃ] as in <u>ch</u>ur<u>ch</u>   [ʤ] as in <u>j</u>u<u>dge</u>
[θ] as in <u>th</u>ink   [ð] as in <u>th</u>ey
[ʃ] as in <u>sh</u>irt   [ʒ] as in rou<u>ge</u>
[ŋ] as in si<u>ng</u>i<u>ng</u>   [ɾ] as in <u>r</u>un

Non-English Sounds

Stops.   Prenasalized stops are made with a nasal sound at the same time as the stop: [ᵐb], for example, is a bit like the *mb* in *timber*, but is a single sound rather than two. Dental stops have the tongue tip touching the teeth, retroflex stops have the tongue tip curled back to the roof of the mouth, and palatal stops are made with the blade of the tongue on the roof of the mouth.

Fricatives.   The bilabial fricatives [β ɸ] are very similar to English [f v], except that both lips are used, and the teeth are not. The velar fricatives [x ɣ] parallel the stops [k g], except that a little air is allowed to escape.

Nasals.   [ñ] is pronounced as in Spanish *señor*.

Laterals.   [λ] is pronounced like *ly* run quickly together, while [ɬ] is pronounced like *gl* run together.

Flaps and trills.   [r] is a single flap, as in Spanish *pero* 'but,' while [r̃] is a trill or roll, as in Spanish *perro* 'dog.'

APPENDIX 3

Sample Phoneme Systems

Vowel Systems

Micronesia

	Kosraean				**Mokilese**	
i	ɨ	u		i		u
e	ə	o		e		o
ɛ	ʌ			ɛ		ɔ
æ	a	ɒ			a	

Melanesia: Austronesian

	Port Sandwich				**Labu**	
i	ü		u		i		u
e	ö		o		e		o
					ɛ		ɔ
		a				a	

	Iaai					**Xârâcùù**				
i	ü		u		i	ĩ	ɨ	ɨ̃	u	ũ
e	ö	ə	o		e		ə		o	
ɛ	œ		ɔ		ɛ	ɛ̃		ʌ̃	ɔ	ɔ̃
	a					a	ã			

Australia

Anguthimri

i	i:	ĩ	ü			u	u:
e	e:	ẽ	ö			o	
æ	æ:	æ̃					
				a	a:	ã	

Consonant Systems

Micronesia

Note: The symbol /R/ is used here to refer to a Nauruan consonant described as "a kind of r whose exact nature is unknown. It may be palatalized. . . . It sounds partially devoiced and appears to be quite fortis" (Nathan 1973, 482).

Nauruan

p^w	p	t	k	k^w
b^w	b	d	g	g^w
m^w	m	n	ŋ	$ŋ^w$
m^w:	m:	n:	ŋ:	$ŋ^w$:
		r̃		
		R		
w		y		

Kosraean

p^w	p	t^w	t			k^w	k
f^w	f		s	$ʃ^w$	ʃ		
m^w	m	n^w	n			$ŋ^w$	ŋ
		l^w	l				
			r				

Yapese

p	p′	t	t′	ṭ		k	k′	ʔ
b		d		ḍ		g		
f	f′	θ	θ′	ṣ				h
m	m′	n	n′			ŋ	ŋ′	
		l	l′					
		r̃						
w	w′			y	y′			

Melanesia: Austronesian

Port Sandwich

```
pʷ    p     t     c     k
bʷ    b     d           g
ᵐbʷ   ᵐb    ⁿr          ᵑg
            s           x
vʷ    v
mʷ    m     n           ŋ
            l
            r̃
```

Banoni

```
p     t     ts    k
b     d     dz    g
            s              h
v                 γ
m     n           ŋ
      r̃
```

Ririo

```
p     t     ts    k     ʔ

ᵐb    ⁿd    ⁿdz   ᵑg
      s
v     z           γ
m           n     ŋ
      l
      r
```

Adzera

```
p     t     c     k     ʔ
ᵐp    ⁿt    ⁿ̃c    ᵑk    ᵑʔ
b     d     j     g
            ñj
f     s                 h
m     n                 ŋ
r
                  w     y
```

Pije

```
pʰʷ   pʰ          tʰ          kʰ
pʷ    p           t     c     k
ᵐbʷ   ᵐb          ⁿd    ñ̃j    ᵑg
      ɸ     f      s           x
            v
mʷ    m           n     ñ     ŋ
m̥ʷ    m̥           n̥     ñ̥     ŋ̥
                  l
                  l̥
w                       y
w̥                       y̥
```

Drehu

```
p     t           ṭ     c     k
b     d           ḍ           g
f     θ     s                 x     h
      ð     z
m     n           ñ     ŋ
m̥    n̥           ñ̥     ŋ̥
      l
      l̥
w
w̥
```

Melanesia: Papuan

Awa

```
p   t   k   ʔ
b       g
    s
m   n
    r
w   y
```

Abau

```
p       k
        s   h
m   n
    r
w   y
```

Kobon

```
            p
b  d        g
f  s        x   h
            v
   ts
   dz
m  n   ñ        m
   l  ḷ  λ
   r̃
w      y   ŋ
```

Kâte

```
p   t   k   ᵏp
b   d   g   ᵍb
f   s       h
v
    ts
    dz
m   n   ŋ

r
y
```

Wahgi

```
p           t       k
ᵐb          ⁿd      ⁿg
        ⁿd̰z̰
        s̰
m   n̰       n       ŋ
    l̰       l       ɫ
w       y
```

Australia

Anguthimri

```
p   ṯ̰   t   tʳ   tʸ   k   ʔ
ᵐb  ⁿḏ̰  ⁿd  ⁿdʳ  ⁿdʸ  g
v   ð̰        ʒ   ɣ
m   ṉ̰   n        ñ   ŋ
        l
        r
w            y
```

APPENDIX 4

Glossary of Technical Terms

This glossary of technical terms used in the text is intended to assist the general reader to understand the basic meanings of those terms. For this reason, many technicalities and intricacies have been deliberately omitted.

ablative. A case marking the direction from which the action proceeds.

absolute dating. In prehistory, the assignment of an actual (approximate) date for a particular event (say, the breakup of a language family). *See also* **relative dating**.

absolutive. The case of the object and the intransitive subject in an ergative language.

accusative language. A language (like English) where the subjects of transitive and intransitive verbs are marked in the same way and the object of transitive verbs is marked differently. Also called nominative-accusative languages.

active voice. A sentence is in the active voice when the subject of the verb is also the performer of the action, as in *John hit the dog*. *See also* **passive voice**.

adjective. A class of words whose function is to describe nouns.

adjunct, adjunct construction. A construction, common in Papuan languages, in which a noun or an adjective (an **adjunct**) is bound closely with a verb, expressing an idea that is often expressed by a single verb in other languages.

affix. A morpheme attached to a root. An affix may not occur by itself. *See also* **infix, prefix, suffix**.

affricate. A consonant combining a stop with a fricative release, like the sound of ch [tʃ] in English *chin*.

agent.   (1) The performer of an action; often the semantic (but not the grammatical) subject in a passive sentence, like *Fred* in *The window was broken by Fred.* (2) The subject of a transitive verb in an ergative language.

alienable possession.   A construction in which the possessor is in control of the relationship with what is possessed. *See also* **inalienable possession**.

allative.   A case marking the direction toward which action proceeds.

alveolar.   Made by the tip of the tongue touching the ridge behind the top teeth, as for [t d].

alveopalatal.   Made with the front part of the tongue touching the front of the roof of the mouth as far forward as the alveolar ridge, as for [ʃ].

anaphoric.   Referring to something already mentioned.

antipassive.   A structure found in ergative languages to derive intransitive sentences from underlying transitive ones.

aorist.   A tense that marks an action as non-future but does not specify whether it is present or past.

apical.   Made with the tip of the tongue, like [t].

apicolabial.   A sound produced with the tip of the tongue touching the top lip.

applicative.   Marking the instrument with which the action was performed, the reason for the performance of the action, and similar roles. Often referred to as the "remote transitive."

article.   A morpheme that marks some aspect of the class or reference of a noun. The English articles *a* and *the*, for example, mark a noun as indefinite and definite, respectively.

aspect.   Expresses the duration of the event or state referred to by the verb, or the manner in which the action or state is carried out. The difference between *He went* and *He was going* in English is one of aspect (punctiliar vs. continuous). *See also* **tense**.

aspiration.   The puff of air accompanying the production of certain sounds. English *p* and *t* in words like *peach* and *tick* are aspirated; in words like *speech* and *stick* they are not aspirated.

asterisk (°).   Symbol used to mark an utterance as not (normally) occurring, either (1) because it is ungrammatical, e.g., °*They will went today* or (2) because it is a reconstruction for a particular protolanguage, and has not actually been attested, e.g., Proto Oceanic °*paka-* 'causative prefix.'

Australian.   A language family consisting of nearly all aboriginal languages of Australia.

Austronesian.   A large family of languages, whose members are found in a few areas on the Asian mainland, in island Southeast Asia, Madagascar, parts of the New Guinea area, most of the rest of Melanesia, and in Micronesia and Polynesia.

auxiliary. A morpheme with little semantic content that functions to carry tense and sometimes other grammatical information in the verb phrase, like *did* in *Did you see it?*

avoidance style. A variety of a language in which the speaker has to avoid certain terms (e.g., names of recently dead people or of in-laws).

back vowel. A vowel made with the highest part of the tongue in the back of the mouth, like those in English *sue* and *saw*.

benefactive. A case marking the beneficiary of an action.

binary numeral system. A system of counting based on two.

bilabial. A consonant made with both lips, like [m].

borrowing. A process whereby speakers of one language adopt some features of another language. Sometimes called **copying.**

bound morpheme. *See* **affix.**

case. An indication of the role of a noun phrase in a clause or sentence.

causative. Bringing about the action of a verb or the quality of a noun or adjective. Compare Tongan *mohe* 'to sleep' and *fakamohe* 'to put (someone) to sleep,' with the causative prefix *faka-*.

central vowel. A vowel in which the highest part of the tongue is in the center of the mouth, as in English *bird* and *bard*.

classifier. A morpheme marking a noun as belonging to a particular class.

clause. A group of phrases containing one predicate.

clitic. An affix attached to a phrase rather than a word, like the English possessive suffix *'s*, which is attached to the last word in the possessor noun phrase, as in *the President of the United States of America's hat*.

close vowel. A vowel made with more tension than its **open** equivalent; the vowel in English *seat* is close, but the vowel in *sit* is open.

closed syllable. A syllable ending in a consonant. *See* **open syllable.**

coarticulated sound. A single sound involving two simultaneous but different articulations. The labial-velar stop /^{k}p/ is an example.

code-switching. A situation in a bilingual or multilingual context where people switch from using one language to using another one.

cognate. Words in different languages whose meanings correspond and whose forms are related through regular sound correspondences. Cognates by implication all derive from a single protoform.

comitative. A marker of accompaniment, like *with* in *He came with me*.

common ancestor. The language ancestral to a group of related languages. A common ancestor may be either known through documentary records or else hypothesized or inferred (in which case it is referred to as a protolanguage).

common article.   An article used with common nouns.

common noun.   A noun that is not the name of a specific individual.

comparative linguistics.   *See* **historical-comparative linguistics**.

completive.   An aspect that marks an action as completed.

compound preposition/postposition.   A compound of a locational noun and a preposition (or postposition) introducing a prepositional (or postpositional) phrase—for example, *in back of*, compared with *behind*.

conjugation.   A set of verbal affixes. Different verbs take different affixes, which thus distinguish different conjugational classes or conjugations (as in Latin).

conjunction.   A morpheme joining two clauses, like *and, if, or*.

consonant cluster.   Two or more consonants coming together with no intervening vowel.

consonant length.   A **long consonant** takes almost twice as long to articulate as a **short consonant**. Difference in consonant length is phonemic in many languages.

construct suffix.   A suffix added to a directly possessed noun, or to a possessive marker when the possessor is a noun phrase.

continuous.   An aspect marking action as continuing over a period of time.

copying.   *See* **borrowing**.

creole.   A **pidgin** language that becomes the first language of a significant number of people and that (in comparison with the pidgin) is much less simplified. The process by which creoles develop is known as **creolization**.

dative.   A case marking the receiver of the object or the person spoken to.

daughter language.   A descendant of a protolanguage.

decimal numeral system.   A system of counting based on ten.

demonstrative.   A morpheme locating a noun in space (or time), often with reference to its position with respect to the speaker and the addressee, like English *this, that*.

dental.   Made by the tongue touching the top teeth, like the two English *th*-sounds [θ ð].

derivational affix.   An affix that turns one part of speech into another, like English *-ize*, which turns nouns into verbs.

descriptive linguistics.   The branch of linguistics that deals with the analysis and description of the grammars of languages.

diacritic.   Any mark added to a letter. Accents are the most common diacritics.

dialect.   Differences between communities' ways of speaking the same language that are not great enough to prevent normal communication between the communities concerned. Dialectal differences may be phonological, grammatical, or lexical.

dialect chain.   A series of dialects without any clear language boundary between any two neighboring dialects, although people whose dialects are not neighboring speak what seem to be different languages.

dialect mixing.   *See* **koine**.

diglossia.   A situation in which two quite different dialects of a language are used side by side, one in formal contexts and the other in informal contexts (such as Standard Hindi and Fiji Hindi in Fiji).

digraph.   Two letters representing a single phoneme. In English (and many other languages), for example, the digraph *ng* represents the single sound [ŋ].

direct possession.   A type of construction in which a possessive pronoun is directly attached to the possessed noun, e.g., Motu *tama-gu* 'my father,' where -*gu* 'my' is directly suffixed to *tama* 'father.' *See also* **indirect possession**.

directional particle.   A particle marking the direction of the action or some other spatial or contextual reference.

discontinuous morpheme.   A morpheme occurring in two separate parts, like the French negative *ne* preceding the verb and *pas* following it.

distant demonstrative.   A demonstrative referring to someone or something distant from both speaker and addressee.

dual number.   Referring to two and only two.

emblematic function of language.   The use of linguistic features—often deliberately exaggerated or created—to mark a group's identity and to accentuate its differences from other groups.

ergative (or **ergative-absolutive**) **language.**   A language in which the subject of a transitive verb is marked in one way and the subject of an intransitive verb and the object of a transitive verb are marked in a different way. The **ergative case** is the case of the transitive subject.

exclusive first person.   A pronoun referring to the speaker and some other person or persons, but not the person(s) being spoken to, for example, Bislama *mifala* 'we (he and I, they and I).' *See also* **inclusive first person**.

family tree.   A schematic representation of the subgroups of a language family and thus of the degrees of relationship between member languages.

final verb.   The last verb in the sentence. In a language with a **switch-reference** system, this is the verb fully marked for tense-aspect and features of the subject.

flap.   A consonant made by one very fast strike of the tongue on the alveolar ridge. In fast casual speech, the *dd* in English *ladder* is often pronounced as a flap [r].

free morpheme.   A morpheme that may stand on its own as a word.

fricative.   A consonant made by allowing a small amount of air to escape under considerable friction, as with English [f v s z].

front vowel.   A vowel made with the highest part of the tongue in the front of the mouth, as in English *seat* and *set*.

genetic inheritance, genetic relationship.   Descended from a common ancestor (said of languages). Deriving from phonemes or words in the ancestor language (said of phonemes, words, and so on).

glottal.   Made in the glottis, like [h].

glottal stop.   A consonant, symbolized [ʔ], in which the stream of air is completely stopped in the glottis. (Cockneys are supposed to substitute a glottal stop for *tt* in words like *butter* and *better*.)

glottalization.   Simultaneous closure of the glottis in the production of a nonglottal consonant.

glottochronology.   A technique, now shown to be unreliable, for dating the splits in a protolanguage.

goal.   The noun phrase at which the action of the verb is aimed.

habitual.   An aspect indicating that an action is performed regularly as a habit or custom.

head.   The main word in a phrase.

high vowel.   A vowel made with the tongue high in the mouth, like the vowels in English *see* and *sue*.

historical-comparative linguistics.   The branch of linguistics that seeks to discover the history of a group of languages through comparing them. Sometimes referred to as **comparative linguistics**.

imperative.   The modality of a command.

imperfective.   An aspect indicating that action is not seen as completed.

inalienable possession.   A construction in which the possessor does not control possession. Often used of body parts or relatives. *See* **alienable possession**.

inceptive.   An aspect indicating that action is seen as beginning.

inchoative.   Inceptive.

inclusive first person.   A pronoun including the speaker and the person or persons spoken to, e.g., Bislama *yumi* 'we (you and I).' *See also* **exclusive first person**.

independent pronoun.   A pronoun that may occur alone, as opposed to other types of pronouns, which occur only as prefixes or suffixes.

indirect possession.   A construction in which a possessive pronoun is not attached to the possessed noun (as in **direct possession**) but to some other morpheme, e.g., Motu *e-gu ruma* 'my house,' where *-gu* 'my' is attached to the possessive marker *e-* and not to the noun *ruma* 'house.'

infix. An **affix** inserted inside a root. Tolai, for example, changes verbs into nouns with the infix *-in-*, as in *mat* 'die,' *m-in-at* 'death.' *See also* **prefix, suffix**.

instrumental. A case marking the instrument with which the action is performed.

intentional. An aspect marking the fact that the subject intends to perform the action.

intermediate demonstrative. A demonstrative referring to someone or something near the addressee but not near the speaker.

interstage language. An intermediate protolanguage, which is both a daughter of the common ancestor of a whole family and the ancestor of one subgroup of that family.

intransitive. A verb with no object; a clause or sentence containing such a verb as the main verb: e.g., *They are sleeping. See also* **transitive**.

irrealis. An aspect or mood marking an action or state as not real, i.e., not having taken place or existing. *See also* **realis**.

isolate. A language that appears to be related to no other language.

koine. A language that develops (through a process known as **koineization**, sometimes called **dialect mixing**). out of contact between and mixing of a number of dialects.

labiodental. Consonants produced by touching the top teeth to the bottom lip, like [f v].

labiovelar. Velar consonants produced with simultaneous lip-rounding, like [kʷ].

laminal. Made with the blade of the tongue, like *sh* in English (phonetically [ʃ]).

language family. A group of related languages deriving from a common ancestor (actual or hypothesized).

Lapita. A distinctive pottery style found in the Pacific. **Lapita culture** refers to the culture associated with this pottery style, assumed to be the culture of speakers of Proto Oceanic and its immediate descendants.

lateral. A sound made when air passes around the sides of the tongue; [l] is a typical lateral.

lexicostatistics. A statistical technique for measuring the degree of relationship between languages by comparing similarities in basic or noncultural vocabulary.

lingua franca. A language used as a common language between people who speak different **vernaculars**.

linguistics. The systematic study of language.

locative. A case marking the place where an action takes place.

long consonant.   *See* **consonant length**.

long vowel.   *See* **vowel length**.

low vowel.   A vowel made with the tongue low in the mouth, like the vowels in English *back* and *bark*.

macron.   A bar over a vowel, used in many Pacific (and other) languages to indicate vowel length: e.g., *ā* = [a:].

medial verb.   In a language with a switch-reference system, any but the last verb in a sentence. Medial verbs usually do not mark tense or subject but do indicate whether the next subject is the same or different.

Melanesian Pidgin.   Cover term for the different English-lexifier pidgins/creoles spoken in Melanesia, specifically Tok Pisin (Papua New Guinea), Pijin (Solomon Islands), and Bislama (Vanuatu).

metathesis.   A morphophonemic process by which phonemes change places. Adding the Lenakel trial suffix *-hel* to the pronoun *kami-* 'you' produces *kamhiel* 'you three' (not °*kamihel*), with metathesis of *i* and *h*.

mid vowel.   A vowel made with the tongue between the high and low positions, like the vowels in English *bed* and *bird*.

"mixed" language.   A language that has been so heavily influenced by one or more unrelated languages that its family membership is not obvious.

modality.   *See* **mood**.

moiety.   One of two units into which is a society is divided, all members of the society belonging to one or the other moiety.

mood.   Marker of whether the event or state described by the verb is seen as being actual/realized or non-actual/unrealized.

morpheme.   The smallest meaningful unit in a language. The English word *ungodly* contains three morphemes, the prefix *un-*, the root *god*, and the suffix *-ly*.

morphology.   (1) The study of morphemes; (2) the way in which morphemes combine to form words in a language.

morphophonemics.   The study of sound changes that take place when morphemes combine to form words.

nasal.   A sound produced through the nose. Consonants like [m n] are nasals, and vowels like those in French *vin blanc* are nasal vowels.

nominal sentence.   A sentence in which the predicate is not a verb phrase. *See also* **verbal sentence**.

nominalizer.   A morpheme that converts a verb into a noun; the process is called **nominalization**.

non-Austronesian.   *See* **Papuan**.

non-Pama-Nyungan.   Languages in the north-west of Australia, distinguished from Pama-Nyungan languages by having prefixes as well as suffixes.

noun class.   Nouns that take a different set of affixes for the same functions belong to different noun classes (like the Latin declensions).

noun phrase.   A phrase in which the head is a noun.

number.   The marking in a noun, verb, or some other word of linguistically recognized categories relating to the number of participants—like singular, dual, plural.

numeral.   An exact number (*two, three, seventeen,* etc.). *See* **quantifier**.

numeral classifier.   A classifier used with a numeral in a noun phrase to mark the class of the head of the phrase.

object.   The goal of the action of an active verb. In the sentence *The boy hit the dog,* the object is *the dog.*

object marker.   A form of a pronoun that occurs within a verb complex to mark the person and number of the object.

Oceanic.   A subgroup of the Austronesian family. It includes all the languages of Polynesia and almost all the Austronesian languages of Melanesia and Micronesia.

open syllable.   A syllable ending in a vowel. *See* **closed syllable**.

open vowel.   *See* **close vowel**.

orthography.   The letters used to represent the sounds or phonemes of a language; spelling.

palatal.   Produced by touching the blade of the tongue to the palate. The *y* sound of many languages is a palatal consonant.

Pama-Nyungan.   Cover term for a large group of Australian languages distinguished mainly by a suffixing morphology.

Papuan.   Cover term for a number of language families in Melanesia not belonging to the Austronesian family.

particle.   Words whose principal function is grammatical. Particles are pronounced and/or written as separate words rather than as **affixes**.

passive voice.   A sentence is in the passive voice when the subject of the verb is the goal of the action: e.g., *The dog was hit by John. See* **active voice**.

paucal.   Referring to a small number, though more than two.

penultimate stress.   Stress applied to the next-to-last syllable of words.

phoneme.   A significant unit of sound in a particular language.

phonemics.   *See* **phonology**.

phonetics.   The study of the sounds used in languages.

phonology.   (1) The study of the significant sounds and the sound patterns of a particular language; (2) the sound system of a language.

phrase.   A group of words functioning as a unit in a clause.

phylum.   A group of related **stocks**.

pidgin.   A simplified language, usually no one's first language, which develops (through the process of **pidginization**) in a multilingual contact situation to allow for intergroup communication.

Polynesian Outliers.   Genetic members of the Polynesian linguistic subgroup that are spoken outside geographical Polynesia.

possessive affix.   A pronominal form marking the person and number of the possessor.

possessive classifier.   A classifier used in a possessive construction to mark the class of the possessed noun.

possessive marker.   A marker used in an indirect possessive construction, to which pronoun affixes are attached.

postpositions.   Grammatical markers that follow noun phrases, marking them as postpositional phrases, and that either indicate the relationship between them and other noun phrases or mark their function in the sentence. *See* **preposition**.

predicate.   That part of a clause that comments on the topic or subject. In a verbal sentence, the predicate is a verb phrase, but in a nominal sentence it may be a noun phrase, an adjective phrase, etc.

prefix.   An **affix** that precedes the root, like *re-* in *rewrite*. *See also* **infix, suffix**.

prehistory.   That part of the past before the period covered by written records.

prenasalization.   The production of a nasal immediately before, and as part of, the production of a following sound. For example, both the *d* and *b* in Fijian *dabe* 'sit'—phonetically [ⁿdaᵐbe]—are prenasalized.

prepositions.   Grammatical markers that precede a noun phrase and indicate the relationship between it and other noun phrases or mark its function in the sentence. Prepositions in English include *in, to, for, from, by, with, at*, and so on. *See also* **postpositions**.

prepositional phrase.   A noun phrase introduced by a preposition; e.g., *In the morning they walked to the store.*

proper article.   An article used with proper nouns.

proper noun.   The name of a specific individual.

prosodic features.   *See* **suprasegmental phonology**.

Proto Australian.   The protolanguage from which all Australian languages are presumed to have derived.

Proto Austronesian.   The protolanguage from which all members of the Austronesian family are presumed to have derived.

protolanguage.   The hypothesized common ancestor of a group of languages that, on the basis of comparative evidence, appear to be genetically related.

Proto Oceanic.   The protolanguage from which all members of the Oceanic subgroup of Austronesian are presumed to have derived.

proximate demonstrative.   A demonstrative referring to someone or something near the speaker.

quantifier.   A morpheme marking approximate number (like *some, few, many*).

quinary numeral system.   A system of counting based on five.

realis.   An aspect or mood marking the fact that the action or state actually happened or existed. *See also* **irrealis**.

reciprocal.   Performing an action on each other, as in *They kissed each other*.

reconstruction.   A procedure by which, through comparison of cognate forms, an educated guess is made about the phonemes, words, or grammatical structures of a protolanguage.

reduplication.   A process whereby all (**complete reduplication**) or part (**partial reduplication**) of a word or root is repeated, usually involving a different grammatical function or a slight change in meaning: e.g., Hawaiian *ʻaki* 'to take a nip and let go,' *ʻaki-ʻaki* 'to nibble (as a fish),' *ʻa-ʻaki* 'to nip repeatedly.'

regular sound correspondence.   In cognate words in two or more languages, the systematic and predictable correspondence of a particular sound in one language to a particular sound in the other language(s).

related languages.   Languages descended from a common ancestor.

relative dating.   In prehistory, a statement that one event took place before (or after) another, without the assignment of an actual date to either event. *See* **absolute dating**.

relative pronoun.   The pronoun that takes the place of a noun when one sentence is embedded in another, like *who* in *The man who came yesterday will come again today*.

retroflex.   Produced with the tip of the tongue turned back to the roof of the mouth.

rhotic.   Any *r-* like sound.

root.   A morpheme to which affixes can be attached.

rounded vowel.   A vowel made with the lips rounded, like [u] in *do* and [o] in *short*.

segmental phonology.   That area of phonology dealing with the segments of speech—consonants and vowels. *See also* **suprasegmental phonology**.

semivowel.   A consonant with vowel-like qualities, like [w] and [y], which are similar in some ways to [u] and [i].

sentence.   A group of one or more clauses that can stand alone without requiring the addition of any more phrases.

sequential.   An aspect indicating that an action follows the action of the previous verb.

serial construction.   A construction involving the stringing together of two or more verbs in a single clause.

shared innovation.   A change from the protolanguage shared only by certain members of the family. Shared innovations are one of the criteria for delimiting a **subgroup**.

short consonant.   *See* **consonant length**.

short vowel.   *See* **vowel length**.

sound correspondence.   *See* **regular sound correspondence**.

split-ergative language.   One in which certain nouns function ergatively and others (including pronouns) function accusatively.

stative.   Expressing a state rather than an event or an action.

stock.   A group of related families. *See also* **phylum**.

stop.   A sound whose production involves the complete blockage of the air flow, like English [p t k].

stress.   Emphasis placed on one of the syllables of a word, making it more prominent than the others, as in the third syllable of *university*.

subgroup.   A group of languages within a family, more closely related to each other than any is to any other language.

subject.   The topic in a nominal sentence, or the doer of the action or experiencer of the state in a verbal sentence.

subject marker.   A form of a pronoun occurring within a verb complex to mark the person and the number of the subject.

suffix.   An **affix** following the root, like *-ing* in *raining*. *See also* **infix, prefix**.

suprasegmental phonology.   The area of phonology that deals with aspects of speech that cannot be segmented, like stress, tone, and intonation. *See also* **segmental phonology**.

switch-reference.   A grammatical category marked on verbs that indicates whether the subject of a verb is the same as, or different from, the subject of some other verb.

taxonomy.   A classification of words in which there is a generic, overarching term and a number of levels of specific terms. The lower-level terms are members of the higher-level terms' families.

tense.   The time of the action or state referred to by the verb in relation to the time of speaking or writing (or, occasionally, in relation to some other time): The difference between *I went, I am going*, and *I will go*, is one of tense—past, present, and future. In many cases, a marker of tense also marks **aspect**; such markers are referred to as **tense-aspect** markers.

ternary numeral system. A system of counting based on three.

thematic consonant (vowel). A consonant (or vowel) not present when the root occurs alone, but which surfaces when an affix is added: e.g., in Palauan *char* 'price,' one must add the thematic vowel *a* before any possessive suffix. Historically, thematic vowels or consonants may have been part of the root that were lost except in such environments.

tone. For our purposes, changes in pitch that causes changes in meanings of a word. Such tone is **phonemic tone**.

transitive. Having an object (of a verb); containing such a verb as the main verb (of a clause or a sentence). Example: *They are eating ice cream. See* **intransitive**.

trial number. Referring to three and only three.

trigraph. Three letters representing a single phoneme.

trill. A series of very fast flaps giving a rolling sound (phonetically [r]) found, for example, in Scots English.

unrounded vowel. A vowel made with the lips not rounded, like the vowels of *seed* and *sad*.

velar. Made in the back of the mouth, like [k].

velarized bilabial. A bilabial sound produced by simultaneously raising the tongue at the back of the mouth, giving an accompanying *w*-sound: e.g., [mʷ].

verb. A class of words expressing actions and states.

verb complex. A phrase in which the head is a verb.

verb root. The form of the verb with no affixes.

verb serialization. *See* **serial construction**.

verbal sentence. A sentence whose predicate is a verb complex. *See also* **nominal sentence**.

vernacular. The language of a community, which is little used outside that community.

voice. *See* **active voice; passive voice**.

voiced and voiceless sounds. A sound is voiced if the vocal folds vibrate during its production, and voiceless if they do not: The voiced sounds [b v z] have voiceless equivalents [p f s].

vowel copying. Occurs in an affix whose vowel is a complete copy of some other vowel in the root. In Bislama, when the verbs *kuk* 'cook', *kil* 'hit,' and *sem* 'shame' take the transitive suffix vowel +*m*, the vowel is a copy of the vowel of the root: *kuk-um, kil-im, sem-em*.

vowel length.   A **long vowel** takes almost twice as long to articulate as a **short vowel**. Difference in vowel length is phonemic in many languages.

word.   The smallest freely pronounceable unit in a language.

word taboo.   A practice whereby the name of a relative of a particular category, or of a recently dead person, or any word that sounds like that name, may not be uttered. A synonym or a borrowed word must be used in its place.

Notes

CHAPTER 1

1. Some linguists use the term "**verb phrase**" to represent this type of unit, but others use it to refer to the verb complex together with the object. I do not use the term in this book.

2. The first and third sentences could stand on their own with the assistance of context, that is, they would both be acceptable answers to the question "Who were killing the cats?" They could not, however, stand in isolation, or as, say, the first sentence in a conversation.

3. See section 2.1 in the next chapter for a discussion of the concept of dialect.

CHAPTER 2

1. In the absence of other evidence, the number of speakers in the region would lead us to predict the existence of about six languages, not fourteen hundred, assuming that all the world's languages had an equal number of speakers.

2. The points of the Polynesian Triangle are Hawai'i to the north, New Zealand to the southwest, and Easter Island to the southeast.

3. Crowley (1994) estimates that Paamese currently has about 4,750 speakers, although Tryon and Charpentier (1989) put the number of speakers at around 2,400. Even with changes of this order in the figures for some other languages, however, no Vanuatu language has anywhere near 10,000 speakers.

4. The Western Desert language has a variety of local dialect names, but no indigenous name for the whole language.

5. The name Nakanamanga, both widely and commonly used by speakers of the language, may have been avoided by missionaries who had some experience with Fijian, since this term is obscene in that language.

CHAPTER 3

1. The family was for a long time called "Malayo-Polynesian," but because this term appeared to exclude the languages of Melanesia and Micronesia, most scholars have adopted the term "Austronesian" (lit., southern islands).

2. Most of the groups mentioned here correspond to those listed in Pawley and Ross 1995, an admirable summary of the current state of research. (Exactly how a small group of Oceanic languages in northeast Irian Jaya is related to the rest of the languages of the subgroup is still not clear.) In a few cases, I have incorporated more recent research. In such cases I have specified the source. Lynch, Ross, and Crowley (1998) suggest that groups five through eight may belong to a single Central-Eastern Oceanic group.

3. For a brief discussion of lexicostatistics, see 1.3.3, above.

4. I do not list the actual terms here. For both a list and more detailed discussion, see Chowning (1991) and Pawley and Ross (1995).

CHAPTER 5

1. Recall from the discussion in chapter 1 that the sounds of languages are organized into a number of sound units, or phonemes. In discussing individual pronunciations of words, linguists use square brackets [ ], while phonemes are written between slant lines / /. I use italics for single letters. Appendix 2 provides a chart of the phonetic symbols used in this book, and appendix 3 gives some examples of the vowel and consonant systems of a number of Pacific languages.

2. I make occasional reference in this section to the two non-Oceanic languages spoken in Micronesia, Palauan and Chamorro.

3. The contexts need not concern us here. But see 6.2.1 below and Churchward (1940, 14).

4. The phonetic explanation for this seems to be that the production of voiceless obstruents involves greater muscle tension and a higher larynx than does the production of voiced obstruents, and greater muscle tension and a higher larynx are associated with higher pitch (Clark and Yallop 1990, 282–283).

5. The Rotokas voiced phonemes /v r g/ are pronounced as nasals [m n ŋ] in some phonetic environments.

6. Tone marking has been omitted from these examples so as not to obscure the placement of stress.

7. "On the whole these [tonal systems] seem better analyzed as pitch-accent systems rather than as genuine tonal systems. The vast majority of such Papuan languages have a single contrast between high and low tone, and this suggests a pitch-accent system with a contrast between accented syllables and unaccented ones" (Foley 1986, 63).

8. Unfortunately, the sources do not show full contrast, as there appears to be no word /nǎ/ that would contrast with the other three words listed here.

9. The Rapanui (Easter Island) *rongorongo* may be an exception to this, although it was apparently a system of mnemonics rather than a writing system per se.

10. Many nonlinguists do not conceive of the glottal stop as a proper consonant, but more as a "break" between two vowels. In his grammar of Tongan, Churchward is at pains to correct this misconception and to stress the consonantal nature of the glottal stop: "To call it the break, as is sometimes done, is convenient but is rather misleading" (Churchward 1953, 1).

11. The Catholic forms have eventually been adopted, partly because they correspond most closely to the English system, and partly due to the influence of *Wantok* newspaper, the first Tok Pisin newspaper, which was originally produced by the Catholic Church.

12. This principle was taken to its ridiculous extreme in Erromango (Vanuatu), where early missionaries wrote /au/ as *x* and /oi/ as *c*.

13. The only violation of this principle has been the use of the digraph *dr* to represent /$^n\bar{r}$/. The controversy, which surfaces every so often, usually takes the form of pressure to revise Fijian orthography more in the direction of English, and to write *mb*, *th*, and so on for what are currently written as *b* and *c*.

14. This convention is based on German orthography.

CHAPTER 6

1. Note that the Fijian pronouns given here (and elsewhere) have a preposed personal article (see 6.2.2 below), which is *i* in the Nadrau dialect given here and *o* in Standard Fijian and some other dialects. I sometimes refer to Standard (Bauan) Fijian simply as "Fijian," but specify other varieties by name (e.g., "Nadrau Fijian").

2. The Nehan forms are those used in past tense. Non-past forms are slightly different, involving the loss of initial *k* in most persons and the replacement of *k* with *m* in the first person exclusive and the second person plural.

3. The variation in the third person plural in Kiribati is between animate (*-iia*) and inanimate (*-i*) objects.

The forms given for the subject markers in table 5 are what appear to be the underlying forms. There is considerable variation in current usage as a result of changes in progress in this system (see Lynch 1995).

4. In citing Rotuman data, I use standard orthographic symbols for consonants, but phonetic symbols for vowels, since the system of vowel diacritics in Rotuman orthography is somewhat unwieldy.

5. Many of these languages probably once did have at least one article, deriving from the Proto Oceanic common article °*na*. In Vanuatu especially, however, this article has become attached to the noun and now forms part of the noun root, though it may be removed in certain contexts (cf. the discussion on pluralization in Anejoṁ in the previous section).

6. In Fijian, *ko* tends to be used quite often in writing where *o* is used in speech, while *a* is sometimes used instead of *na*. This variation is not important for our purposes here. I will continue to gloss articles as "a" or "the," adding additional information (personal, plural, etc.) where relevant.

7. *Ke* is most often used before words beginning with *a*, *e*, *o*, and *k*, while *ka* tends to precede words beginning with *i*, *u*, and any consonant except *k*.

8. The numeral for one does not usually follow the same pattern in these languages.

9. The vowels of some of the possessive markers in both languages undergo morphophonemic changes in various environments. Note that, in both Paamese and Fijian, the markers for food and for passivity are formally identical. As some languages mark these two categories differently, there is good reason for believing that these were distinct in Proto Oceanic.

10. Generally, however, the form, function, and semantics of possessive classifiers are different from those of numeral classifiers. Some languages, like Kiribati and Kilivila, for example, have elaborate numeral classifier systems but no correspondingly elaborate possessive classifier systems.

11. I say "for the most part" because there are vestiges of the direct construction in some of these languages (cf. Wilson 1982, 35–40).

12. The Nukuoro orthography used here differs slightly from that in the original source (Carroll 1965): I write the simple stops *p t k* and the long stops *pp tt kk*; Carroll writes the simple stops *b d g* and the long stops *p t k*.

13. I use the term "verb complex" in place of "verb phrase," which has different meanings in different theoretical approaches to linguistics. The term "particle" refers to words that have a *grammatical* function (marking tense or negation, for example) rather than a *lexical* one (denoting some thing, action, or quality in the real world), but which are pronounced and written as separate words and not as prefixes or suffixes.

14. Thus *I had drunk* (completive), *I used to drink* (habitual), *I was drinking* (continuous), and *I drank* (punctiliar) illustrate different aspects of the English verb in the past tense.

15. Rotuman is somewhat unusual in having no preverbal subject markers and in marking the person and number of the subject of a stative verb by a suffix:

Iris	*la*	*joni-eris.*
they	FUTURE	run:away-they:STATIVE

"They will run away."

16. To some extent, this consonant reflects an earlier morpheme-final consonant that has been lost in word-final position. Take, for example, Fijian *kini* 'pinch,' whose transitive form is *kini-ti*. This verb derives from Proto Oceanic °*giñit*, and the intransitive form *kini* has lost the final °*-t* quite regularly. The transitive form *kini-ti* derives from °*giñit-i*, from which °*-t-* was not lost because it was no longer word-final. By no means all thematic consonants, however, can be explained in this way. On the basis of comparative evidence, one would expect the transitive form of the Fijian verb *gunu* 'drink' to be *gunu-mi*, but it is in fact *gunu-vi*.

17. The fact that the pronoun object is not part of the verb complex but a separate phrase can be seen from sentences that emphasize the object by placing it first:

Iik	*ka,*	*r- im-eiua-in*	*mun.*
you	that,	he-PAST-lie-TRANS	again

'He lied to **you** again.'

18. In some of these languages both transitive and object marking occur together only when the object is human or animate.

19. Passive and transitive are closely linked concepts, and this suffix is presumably the same historically as the *-Ci* transitive suffix. There has been considerable debate in the literature over whether the *-Ci* suffix marks passive or transitive in other Polynesian languages, a matter I do not take up here. See, for example, Biggs (1974), Chung (1977, 1978), Clark (1973, 1981), Hohepa (1969), Lynch (1972), Milner (1973), and Tchekhoff (1973).

20. The Kiribati numerals given here include the general classifier *-ua*.

21. "Accusative" here is short for "nominative-accusative" (subject in the nominative case, object in the accusative case). "Ergative" is short for "ergative-absolutive," defined later.

22. This is probably a result of influence from one or more neighboring non-Austronesian languages (most of which have SOV preferred order) on a language ancestral to the Oceanic languages of southern mainland Papua New Guinea. See chapter 9 for further discussion.

23. Verb-initial languages do allow some flexibility when the subject or object is emphasized. Some Oceanic languages have flexible phrase order, but certain grammatical contexts may require one order and others another.

CHAPTER 7

1. The marking on nouns and other noun phrase constituents varies for number (*aleman n-ahe* 'the man went,' *alemam m-ahe* 'the men went'), and in some classes the markers are not phonologically identical in all environments (*numataʻ kw-aheʻ* 'the woman went').

2. The Anggor verbs in the examples below are more complex morphologically than illustrated here, but I have simplified the analysis for purposes of illustration.

3. The numerous morphophonemic changes in Enga verb roots and suffixes need not concern us here, but note that the root meaning "go" appears as both *p-* and as *pá-* in the examples.

CHAPTER 8

1. Given my lack of first-hand experience with Australian languages, I have relied very heavily in this chapter on Dixon's *The Languages of Australia* (1980), which is an excellent introduction to the topic; and I am grateful to Terry Crowley and Nick Thieberger for their assistance.

2. Pronouns may take case suffixes, and in many cases the combination pronoun + case suffix has fused to produce a pronoun form impervious to analysis. In such cases I give the intransitive subject form of the pronoun.

3. This discussion of case marking relies heavily on the discussion in Dixon (1980), especially his treatment of case in Yidiny (294–301).

4. The Tiwi language of Bathurst and Melville Islands is an exception. Dixon (1980, 488) says that Tiwi "is probably unique in Australia in having no case inflections of any type; local relations are shown by prepositions."

5. The last example is the version used by female speakers. Male speakers dispense with the prefix *nya-* with nouns of this class, saying simply *yabi arrkula* "one good man/boy."

6. When the consonant-initial prefixes are followed by a consonant, a vowel intervenes.

7. In some split-ergative languages, proper nouns—or even all nouns referring to humans—behave like pronouns, while other nouns behave ergatively.

CHAPTER 9

1. Note also that these words have adapted to another phonological feature of Motu—the fact that every syllable must be open. (Examples are from Crowley 1992, 85.)

2. Not all consonants are included in these tables. In order not to clutter the picture, I have concentrated only on those pertinent to the point I am making.

3. A third of his correspondences are classed as indeterminate. There are no diagnostic differences between the two sets (since, for example, phonemes like °*m* and °*n* are reflected as *m* and *n* in both set I and set II).

4. Readers interested in this debate might wish to consult, in the first instance, the summaries in Lynch (1981b) or Thurston (1987, 89–93), and the more detailed discussions in Capell (1976) for mixed languages and Biggs (1972) against them.

CHAPTER 10

1. Recall the discussion in chapter 2 relating to the indeterminacy of the terms "language" and "dialect." This is another case in point. Tok Pisin, Pijin, and Bislama are mutually intelligible, and under this criterion should be classified as dialects of a single language. Each, however, functions as the national language of the country in which it is spoken, and under this sociopolitical criterion each could be viewed as a separate language.

2. As to the origin of these terms, the term "pidgin" may derive from the China Coast Pidgin English word *pijin*, meaning 'business': thus *Pidgin English* meant 'business (trading) English.' The term "creole" comes originally from Portuguese *crioulo*, meaning a person of European descent brought up in the colonies. *Koine* is the Greek word meaning 'common,' and was used to refer to the standard Attic Greek that replaced other Greek dialects.

3. Bêche-de-mer is sometimes translated 'sea-cucumber.' The name Bislama—the Vanuatu variety of Melanesian Pidgin—ultimately derives from the word "bêche-de-mer." "Bêche-de-mer English" was one name given to this early trade language.

4. One exception to this statement is Hawai'i. Because of the recruitment of Asian laborers, the need for a pidgin remained.

5. There are one or two very minor exceptions to this statement, most notably the widespread pronunciation of the third person singular pronoun *em* as *en* after a preposition in Tok Pisin, as in, *Em i givim long en* 'He gave it to him.'

6. A notable exception is the adjective meaning 'bad,' which follows the noun, as in Pijin *Mi kaekae fis nogud* 'I ate a/some bad fish.'

7. If the subject is *mi* 'I,' *yu* 'you,' or *yumi* 'we (inclusive),' *i* is not used. In Bislama, *i* is replaced by *oli* if the subject is third person plural.

Ol	pikinini	oli	spolem	garen	blong	yu.
PL	child	PL:PREDICATE	damage:TRANS	garden	POSS	you

'The kids have messed up your garden.'

8. The Hiri Motu word *tamana* 'father' derives from the Motu form *tama-na* 'his/her father.' The Motu third person suffix *-na* has become part of the Hiri Motu root. Hiri Motu has also fused the (optional) Motu free pronoun and the possessive pronoun as a single form: *(lau) e-gu > lauegu* 'my,' *(oi) e-mu > oiemu* 'your,' etc.

CHAPTER 11

1. Even the spellcheck on my computer doesn't recognize four of these words: *quinic (acid)*, *quinquagenerian*, *quinque-*, and *quinquefoliate*.

2. In a study of German children aged between eighteen months and eleven years, Wagner (1985, quoted in Crystal 1987, 244) found that they used *on average* three thousand different words in a single day, with the eleven-year-old using five thousand words in a day!

3. In fact, in some dialects of English, *yam* refers to the sweet potato, an entirely different root-crop.

4. In some languages with a decimal system the word for "ten" includes the word for "one": "one-ten" = "ten," parallelling "two-ten" = "twenty," "three-ten" = "thirty," and so on.

5. Many languages have borrowed numerals from other languages either because they do not have higher ones, because their own higher numerals are inconveniently long compounds, or simply because such numerals are used mainly in "modern" contexts (money, time, airline flight numbers, and so on).

6. The length of such compounds is one reason for borrowing numerals. Most Lenakel speakers today do not express the numeral nineteen by the long-winded compound *katilum-katilum-katilum-kuvir*, but instead use the much more concise Bislama borrowing *naintin*.

7. Forms for numerals vary depending on what is counted. Where there is variation, I have cited the forms for (male) humans.

8. Even though all kinship terms can be extended almost without limit, my translations include only the more immediate relatives.

9. The suffix *-k* on some of these kin terms means 'my.' Note that some kinship terms are directly possessed (grandparents, all relatives in the parents' generation, same-sex siblings, wife, and grandchildren), but others are indirectly possessed (opposite-sex siblings and children are the most notable of these).

10. The verb *lai* is generally used of plants and trees that are much shorter or taller than the norm, or that have developed flowers of the "wrong" color or leaves of the "wrong" shape.

11. Clark cites Fischer's (1957, 27) report that all the male inhabitants of Ngatik are said to have been massacred by some European sailors (who presumably spoke some variety of Pidgin English). These sailors then married the local women and remained on the island.

12. Kalam words like *wjblp* 'bird' look unpronounceable because Kalam orthography does not mark the neutral vowel /ə/, which occurs predictably between any two consonants. *Wjblp* is phonemically something like /wəjəbələp/.

13. This behavior has obvious implications for a shift in language-use patterns. See 11.6 below.

14. In Vanuatu, some schools are English medium, others French medium.

CONCLUSION

1. I say "words of English origin" because in many cases, in Ifira-Mele as in most parts of Melanesia, the *immediate* source is much more likely to be the local variety of Melanesian Pidgin (in this case, Bislama).

2. There ought perhaps to be an attempt to find some less negatively loaded name for languages like Melanesian Pidgin. Gillian Sankoff, for example, has referred to the varieties of Melanesian Pidgin as "the Bislamic languages," and certainly the name Bislama does not have the negative connotations to an English speaker that names like Pijin or Broken might have.

3. Interestingly, French-educated ni-Vanuatu tend to use French with each other much more than English-educated ni-Vanuatu use English in these situations. This may, however, have more to do with attitudes emanating from metropolitan France than from any local view of Bislama.

References

Aitchison, Jean
  1978   *Teach yourself linguistics.* 2d ed. Sevenoaks, U.K.: Hodder and
          Stoughton.
  1981   *Language change: Progress or decay?* Bungay, U.K.: Fontana
          Paperbacks.

Alpher, Barry
  1993   "Out-of-the-ordinary ways of using a language." In *Language and cul-
          ture in Aboriginal Australia*, edited by Michael Walsh and Colin
          Yallop, 97–106. Canberra: Aboriginal Studies Press.

Baldauf, Richard, and Allan Luke, eds.
  1990   *Language planning and education in Australasia and the South
          Pacific.* Clevedon, U.K.: Multilingual Matters.

Bauer, Winifred
  1993   *Maori.* London: Routledge.

Bavin, Edith
  1993   "Language and culture: Socialisation in a Warlpiri community." In
          Language and culture in Aboriginal Australia, edited by Michael
          Walsh and Colin Yallop, 85–96. Canberra: Aboriginal Studies Press.

Beaumont, Clive H.
  1979   *The Tigak language of New Ireland.* Canberra: Pacific Linguistics,
          B-58.

Bellwood, Peter
  1978   *Man's conquest of the Pacific: The prehistory of Southeast Asia and
          Oceania.* Auckland: Collins.

1995   "Austronesian prehistory in Southeast Asia: Homeland, expansion and transformation." In *The Austronesians: Historical and comparative perspectives*, edited by Peter Bellwood, James J. Fox, and Darrell Tryon, 96–111. Canberra: Dept. of Anthropology, Research School of Pacific Studies, Australian National University.

Bender, Byron W.
1969   *Spoken Marshallese*. Honolulu: University of Hawai'i Press.
1971   "Micronesian languages." In *Current trends in Linguistics*. Vol. 8, *Linguistics in Oceania*, edited by Thomas A. Sebeok, 426–465. The Hague: Mouton.

————, ed.
1984   *Studies in Micronesian Linguistics*. Canberra: Pacific Linguistics, C-80.

Bender, Byron W., and Judith W. Wang
1985   "The status of Proto-Micronesian." In *Austronesian linguistics at the 15th Pacific Science Congress*, edited by Andrew Pawley and Lois Carrington, 53–92. Canberra: Pacific Linguistics, C-88.

Benton, Richard A.
1981   *The flight of the amokura: Oceanic languages and formal education in the South Pacific*. Wellington: New Zealand Council for Educational Research.

Biggs, Bruce
1965   "Direct and indirect inheritance in Rotuman." *Lingua* 14: 383–415.
1969   *Let's learn Maori*. Wellington: A. H. and A. W. Reed.
1972   "Implications of linguistic subgrouping with special reference to Polynesia." In *Studies in Oceanic culture history*, edited by Roger C. Green and Marion Kelly, 3: 143–152. Pacific Anthropological Records no. 13. Honolulu: Bernice Pauahi Bishop Museum.
1974   "Some problems of Polynesian grammar." *Journal of the Polynesian Society* 83: 401–426.

Blake, Barry J.
1979   "Pitta-Pitta." In *Handbook of Australian languages*, edited by R. M. W. Dixon and Barry J. Blake, 183–242. Canberra: Australian National University Press.

Blust, Robert A.
1978a   "Eastern Malayo-Polynesian: A subgrouping argument." In *Second International Conference on Austronesian Linguistics: Proceedings*, edited by S. A. Wurm and Lois Carrington, 181–234. Canberra: Pacific Linguistics, C-61.
1978b   *The Proto-Oceanic palatals*. Wellington: Polynesian Society.

1980   "Early Austronesian social organization: The evidence of language." *Current Anthropology* 21: 205–247, 415–419.

1984a   "Malaita-Micronesian: An Eastern Oceanic subgroup?" *Journal of the Polynesian Society* 93 2: 99–140.

1984b   "More on the position of the languages of Eastern Indonesia." *Oceanic Linguistics* 22–23: 1–28.

Bradley, John (with Jean Kirton and the Yanyuwa Community)
1992   "*Yanyuwa wuka*: Language from Yanyuwa country." Unpublished computer file.

Bradshaw, Joel
1979   "Obstruent harmony and tonogenesis in Jabêm." *Lingua* 49: 189–205.

Breen, J. G.
1981   "Margany and Gunya". In *Handbook of Australian languages*, edited by R. M. W. Dixon and Barry J. Blake, 2: 275–393. Canberra: Australian National University Press.

Bruce, Les
1984   *The Alamblak language of Papua New Guinea (East Sepik)*. Canberra: Pacific Linguistics, C-81.

Brumby, Ed, and Eric Vászolyi, eds.
1977   *Language problems and Aboriginal education*. Mount Lawley, Western Australia: Mount Lawley College of Advanced Education.

Burling, Robbins
1970   *Man's many voices: Language in its cultural context*. New York: Holt, Rinehart and Winston.

Capell, A.
1971   *Arosi grammar*. Canberra: Pacific Linguistics, B-20.

1976   "Austronesian and Papuan 'mixed' languages: General remarks." In *New Guinea area languages and language study*. Vol. 2, *Austronesian languages*, edited by S. A. Wurm, 527–579. Canberra: Pacific Linguistics, C-39.

Carroll, Vern
1965   *An outline of the structure of the language of Nukuoro*. Polynesian Society Reprints, Series No. 10. Wellington: Polynesian Society.

Charpentier, Jean-Michel
1979   *La langue de Port-Sandwich (Nouvelles-Hébrides): Introduction phonologique et grammaire*. Langues et Civilisations à Tradition Orale 34. Paris: Société d'Etudes Linguistiques et Anthropologiques de France.

Cheetham, Brian
    1978   "Counting and number in Huli." *Papua New Guinea Journal of Education* 14: 16–27.

Chowning, Ann
    1991   "Proto Oceanic culture: The evidence from Melanesia." In *Currents in Pacific linguistics: Papers on Austronesian languages and ethnolinguistics in honour of George W. Grace*, edited by Robert Blust, 43–75. Canberra: Pacific Linguistics, C-117.

Chung, Sandra L.
    1977   "Maori as an accusative language." *Journal of the Polynesian Society* 86: 355–370.
    1978   *Case marking and grammatical relations in Polynesian*. Austin: University of Texas Press.

Churchward, C. Maxwell
    1940   *Rotuman grammar and dictionary*. Sydney: Australasian Medical Publishing.
    1953   *Tongan grammar*. Nukuʻalofa, Tonga: Vavaʻu Press.

Clark, John, and Colin Yallop
    1990   *An introduction to phonetics and phonology*. Oxford: Blackwell.

Clark, Ross
    1973   "Transitivity and case in Eastern Oceanic." *Oceanic Linguistics* 12: 559–605.
    1979   "Language." In *The prehistory of Polynesia*, edited by Jesse D. Jennings, 249–270. Canberra: Australian National University Press.
    1979–   "In search of Beach-la-mar: Towards a history of Pacific Pidgin
    1980   English." *Te Reo* 22–23: 3–64.
    1981   Review of *Case marking and grammatical relations in Polynesian*, by Sandra L. Chung. *Language* 57: 198–205.
    1982   "'Necessary' and 'unnecessary' borrowing". In *Papers from the Third International Conference on Austronesian Linguistics*. Vol. 3, *Accent on variety*, edited by Amran Halim, Lois Carrington, and S. A. Wurm, 137–143. Canberra: Pacific Linguistics, C-76.

Cochran, Anne M.
    1977   "Alphabet design for Papua New Guinea languages." Unpublished master's thesis, University of Papua New Guinea.

Codrington, R. H.
    1885   *The Melanesian languages*. Oxford: Clarendon Press.

Corston, Simon
    1998   "Roviana". In *The Oceanic languages*, edited by John Lynch, Malcolm Ross, and Terry Crowley. London: Curzon Press.

Crowley, Terry
1978   *The Middle Clarence dialects of Bandjalang*. Canberra: Australian Institute of Aboriginal Studies.
1979   "Yaygir." In *Handbook of Australian languages*, edited by R. M. W. Dixon and Barry J. Blake, 363–384. Canberra: Australian National University Press.
1981   "The Mpakwithi dialect of Anguthimri." In *Handbook of Australian languages*, edited by R. M. W. Dixon and Barry J. Blake, 2: 147–194. Canberra: Australian National University Press.
1982   *The Paamese language of Vanuatu*. Canberra: Pacific Linguistics, B-87.
1983   "Uradhi." In *Handbook of Australian languages*, edited by R. M. W.Dixon and Barry J. Blake, 3: 307–428. Canberra: Australian National University Press.
1990a   *Beach-la-Mar to Bislama: The emergence of a national language in Vanuatu*. Oxford: Clarendon Press.
1990b   *An illustrated Bislama-English and English-Bislama dictionary*. Vila, Vanuatu: Pacific Languages Unit and Vanuatu Extension Centre, University of the South Pacific.
1992   *An introduction to historical linguistics*. 2d ed. Auckland: Oxford University Press.
1993   "Tasmanian Aboriginal language: Old and new identities." In *Language and culture in Aboriginal Australia*, edited by Michael Walsh and Colin Yallop, 51–71. Canberra: Aboriginal Studies Press.
1994   "Linguistic demography in Vanuatu: Interpreting the 1989 census results." *Journal of Multilingual and Multicultural Development* 15/1: 1–16.
1995   "The Erromangan (Sye) language of Vanuatu." Unpublished typescript.
1998   "Vinmavis." In *The Oceanic languages*, edited by John Lynch, Malcolm Ross, and Terry Crowley. London: Curzon Press.

Crowley, Terry, John Lynch, Jeff Siegel, and Julie Piau
1995   *The design of language: An introduction to descriptive linguistics*. Auckland: Longman.

Crystal, David
1987   *The Cambridge encyclopedia of language*. Cambridge: Cambridge University Press.

Davies, H. J.
1980   *Kobon phonology*. Canberra: Pacific Linguistics, B-68.

Dempwolff, Otto
1934–   Vergleichende Lautlehre des austronesischen Wortschatzes.
1938   *Zeitschrift für Eingeborenen-Sprachen* 15, 17, 19 (full issues).

Dixon, R. M. W.
1980   *The languages of Australia*. Cambridge: Cambridge University Press.
1981   "Wargamay." In *Handbook of Australian languages*, edited by R. M. W. Dixon and Barry J. Blake, 2: 1–144. Canberra: Australian National University Press.
1991   "The endangered languages of Australia, Indonesia and Oceania." In *Endangered languages*, edited by R. H. Robins and E. M. Uhlenbeck, 229–255. Oxford: BERG.

———, ed.
1976   *Grammatical categories in Australian languages*. Linguistic Series, no. 22. Canberra: Australian Institute of Aboriginal Studies.

Dixon, R. M. W., and Barry J. Blake, eds.
1979   *Handbook of Australian languages*. Canberra: Australian National University Press.
1981   *Handbook of Australian languages*. Vol. 2. Canberra: Australian National University Press.
1983   *Handbook of Australian languages*. Vol. 3. Canberra: Australian National University Press.

Dougherty, Janet W. D.
1983   *West Futuna–Aniwa: An introduction to a Polynesian Outlier language*. University of California Publications in Linguistics, vol. 102. Berkeley: University of California Press.

Douglas, Wilfred H.
1981   "Watjarri." In *Handbook of Australian languages*, edited by R. M. W. Dixon and Barry J. Blake, 2: 197–272. Canberra: Australian National University Press.

Duranti, Alessandro
1992   "Language in context and language as context: The Samoan respect vocabulary." In *Rethinking context: Language as an interactive phenomenon*, edited by Alessandro Duranti and Charles Goodwin, 77–99. Studies in the Social and Cultural Foundations of Language 11. Cambridge: Cambridge University Press.

Duranti, Alessandro, and Charles Goodwin, eds.
1992   *Rethinking context: Language as an interactive phenomenon*. Studies in the Social and Cultural Foundations of Language 11. Cambridge: Cambridge University Press

Dutton, T[om] E.
1975   "A Koita grammar sketch and vocabulary." In *Studies in languages of central and south-east Papua*, edited by T. E.Dutton, 281–412. Canberra: Pacific Linguistics, C-29.

1985   *Police Motu: Iena sivarai.* [Port Moresby]: University of Papua New Guinea Press.

————, ed.
1975   *Studies in languages of central and south-east Papua.* Canberra: Pacific Linguistics, C-29.
1992   *Culture change, language change: Case studies from Melanesia.* Canberra: Pacific Linguistics, C-120.

Dutton, T[om] E., with Dicks Thomas
1985   *A new course in Tok Pisin (New Guinea Pidgin).* Canberra: Pacific Linguistics, D-67.

Dutton, Tom [E.], and Darrell T. Tryon, eds.
1994   *Language contact and change in the Austronesian world.* Trends in Linguistics—Studies and Monographs 77. Berlin: Mouton de Gruyter.

Dutton, T[om] E., and C. L. Voorhoeve
1974   *Beginning Hiri Motu.* Canberra: Pacific Linguistics, D-24.

Dyen, Isidore
1965   *A sketch of Trukese grammar.* New Haven, Conn.: American Oriental Society.

Eades, Diana
1979   "Gumbaynggir." In *Handbook of Australian languages,* edited by R. M. W. Dixon and Barry J. Blake, 244–361. Canberra: Australian National University Press.

Early, Robert
1994   "A grammar of Lewo, Vanuatu." Unpublished Ph.D. thesis, Australian National University.

Elbert, Samuel H.
1974   *Puluwat grammar.* Canberra: Pacific Linguistics, B-29.

Elbert, Samuel H., and Mary Kawena Pukui
1979   *Hawaiian grammar.* Honolulu: University Press of Hawai'i.

Fagan, Joel L.
1986   *A grammatical analysis of Mono-Alu (Bougainville Straits, Solomon Islands).* Canberra: Pacific Linguistics, B-96.

Faraclas, Nicholas
1994   "Successful language maintenance in Papua New Guinea." Paper delivered to the Australian Language Institute Workshop on Language Shift and Maintenance in the Asia Pacific Region, Melbourne.

Farr, James, and Cynthia Farr
    1975   "Some features of Korafe morphology." In *Studies in languages of central and south-east Papua*, edited by T[om] E. Dutton, 731–769. Canberra: Pacific Linguistics, C-29.

Finegan, Edward, and Niko Besnier
    1979   *Language: Its structure and use*. San Diego: Harcourt Brace Jovanovich.

Firchow, Irwin B., and Jacqueline Firchow
    1969   "An abbreviated phoneme inventory." *Anthropological Linguistics* 11/9: 271–276.

Fischer, J. L.
    1957   *The Eastern Carolines*. New Haven, Conn.: Human Relations Area Files.

Foley, William A.
    1986   *The Papuan languages of New Guinea*. Cambridge: Cambridge University Press.

Fontinelle, Jacqueline de la
    1976   *La langue de Houaïlou (Nouvelle-Calédonie)*. Langues et Civilisations à Tradition Orale 17. Paris: Société d'Etudes Linguistiques et Anthropologiques de France.

Fox, G. J.
    1979   *Big Nambas grammar*. Canberra: Pacific Linguistics, B-60.

Fox, Helen
    1996   "An honorific sub-dialect used among Big Nambas women." In *Oceanic studies: Proceedings of the First International Conference on Oceanic Linguistics*, edited by John Lynch and Fa'afo Pat. Canberra: Pacific Linguistics, C-133.

Franklin, Karl J.
    1971   *A grammar of Kewa, New Guinea*. Canberra: Pacific Linguistics, C-16.

————, ed.
    1973   *The linguistic situation in the Gulf District and adjacent areas, Papua New Guinea*. Canberra: Pacific Linguistics, C-26.
    1981   *Syntax and semantics in Papua New Guinea languages*. Ukarumpa, Papua New Guinea: Summer Institute of Linguistics.

Franklin, Karl J., and Joice Franklin
    1978   *A Kewa dictionary, with supplementary grammatical and anthropological materials*. Canberra: Pacific Linguistics, C-53.

Gabelentz, H. C. von der
1861–   *Die melanesischen Sprachen nach ihrem grammatischen Bau und*
1873   *ihrer Verwandschaft unter sich und mit den malaiisch-polynesischen*
        Sprachen. Abhandlungen der philologisch-historischen Classe der
        königlich sächsischen Gesellschaft der Wissenschaften. 2 vols.
        Leipzig: S. Hirzel.

Garland, Roger, and Susan Garland
1975   "A grammar sketch of Mountain Koiali." In *Studies in languages of*
        central and south-east Papua, edited by T[om] E. Dutton, 413–470.
        Canberra: Pacific Linguistics, C-29.

Geraghty, Paul A.
1983   *The history of the Fijian languages.* Oceanic Linguistics Special
        Publication, no. 19. Honolulu: University of Hawai'i Press.

———, ed.
1998   *Proceedings of the Second International Conference on Oceanic*
        Linguistics. Canberra: Pacific Linguistics.

Goodenough, Ward H., and Hiroshi Sugita
1980   *Trukese-English dictionary.* Philadelphia: American Philosophical
        Society.

Grace, George W.
1955   "Subgrouping Malayo-Polynesian: A report of tentative findings."
        American Anthropologist 57: 337–339.
1959   *The position of the Polynesian languages within the Austronesian*
        (Malayo-Polynesian) language family. International Journal of
        American Linguistics Memoir 16.
1968   "Classification of the languages of the Pacific." In *Peoples and cultures*
        of the Pacific, edited by Andrew P. Vayda, 63–79. New York: Natural
        History Press.
1981   *An essay on language.* Columbia, S.C.: Hornbeam.

Greenberg, Joseph H.
1971   "The Indo-Pacific hypothesis." In *Current trends in linguistics.* Vol. 8,
        Linguistics in Oceania, edited by Thomas A. Sebeok, 807–871. The
        Hague: Mouton.

Groves, Terab'ata R., Gordon W. Groves, and Roderick Jacobs
1985   *Kiribatese: An outline description.* Canberra: Pacific Linguistics,
        D-64.

Harris, J. W.
1986   *Northern Territory pidgins and the origin of Kriol.* Canberra: Pacific
        Linguistics, C-89.

Harrison, Sheldon P.
  1976   *Mokilese reference grammar*. Honolulu: University Press of Hawai'i.

Harrison, Sheldon P., and Frederick H. Jackson
  1984   "Higher numerals in several Micronesian languages." In *Studies in Micronesian languages*, edited by Byron W. Bender, 61–79. Canberra: Pacific Linguistics, C-80.

Haudricourt, André-G.
  1971   "New Caledonia and the Loyalty Islands." In *Current trends in linguistics*. Vol. 8, *Linguistics in Oceania*, edited by Thomas A. Sebeok, 359–396. The Hague: Mouton.

Haudricourt, André-G., and Françoise Ozanne-Rivierre
  1982   *Dictionnaire thématique des langues de la région de Hienghène (Nouvelle-Calédonie)*. Langues et Civilisations à Tradition Orale, Asie-Austronésie 4. Paris: Société d'Etudes Linguistiques et Anthropologiques de France.

Haudricourt, André-G., Jean-Claude Rivierre, Françoise Rivierre,
C. Moyse-Faurie, and Jacqueline de la Fontinelle
  1979   *Les langues mélanésiennes de Nouvelle-Calédonie*. Collection *Eveil* no. 13. Noumea: D. E. C., Bureau Psychopédagogique.

Haviland, J. B.
  1979   "Guugu Yimidhirr." In *Handbook of Australian languages*, edited by R. M. W. Dixon and Barry J. Blake, 27–180. Canberra: Australian National University Press.

Hazlewood, David
  1850a   *A Feejeean and English and an English and Feejeean dictionary*. Vewa [Viwa]: Wesleyan Mission Press.
  1850b   *A compendious grammar of the Feejeean language*. Vewa [Viwa]: Wesleyan Mission Press.

Henderson, J. E.
  1975   "Yeletnye, the language of Rossell Island." In *Studies in languages of central and south-east Papua*, edited by T[om] E. Dutton, 817–834. Canberra: Pacific Linguistics, C-29.

Hobbs, Susan
  1985   *Fiji Hindi–English, English–Fiji Hindi dictionary*. Suva: Ministry of Education.

Hohepa, Patrick W.
  1967   *A profile generative grammar of Maori*. Supplement to *International Journal of American Linguistics* 33/2. International Journal of American Linguistics, Memoir 20. Indiana University Publications in Anthropology and Linguistics.

1969   "The accusative-to-ergative drift in Polynesian languages." *Journal of the Polynesian Society* 78: 295–329.

Holzknecht, Susanne
1989   *The Markham languages of Papua New Guinea*. Canberra: Pacific Linguistics, C-115.

Irwin, Barry
1974   *Salt-Yui grammar*. Canberra: Pacific Linguistics, B-35.

Jackson, Frederick H.
1983   "The internal and external relationships of the Trukic languages of Micronesia." Unpublished Ph.D. diss., University of Hawai'i.

Jackson, Frederick H., and Jeffrey C. Marck
1991   *Carolinian-English dictionary*. Honolulu: University of Hawai'i Press.

Jensen, John Thayer
1977   *Yapese reference grammar*. Honolulu: University Press of Hawai'i.

Johnston, R. L.
1980   *Nakanai of New Britain: The grammar of an Oceanic language*. Canberra: Pacific Linguistics, C-70.

Jones, Alan A.
1992   "Towards a lexicogrammar of Mekeo." Unpublished Ph.D. thesis, Australian National University.

Josephs, Lewis S.
1975   *Palauan reference grammar*. Honolulu: University Press of Hawai'i.

Kayser, Alois
1936   *Nauru grammar*. Mimeograph. Nauru: Administration of Nauru. Reprinted with introductory notes as Karl H. Rensch, ed. *Nauru grammar* (Canberra: Embassy of the Federal Republic of Germany, 1993).

Keen, Sandra
1983   "Yukulta." In *Handbook of Australian languages*, edited by R. M. W. Dixon and Barry J. Blake, 3: 191–304. Canberra: Australian National University Press.

Keesing, Roger M.
1990   "Solomons Pijin: Colonial ideologies." In *Language planning and education in Australasia and the South Pacific*, edited by Richard Baldauf, Jr., and Allan Luke, 150–165. Clevedon, U. K.: Multilingual Matters.

Kolia, J. A.
1975   "A Balawaia grammar sketch and vocabulary." In *Studies in languages of central and south-east Papua*, edited by T[om] E. Dutton, 107–226. Canberra: Pacific Linguistics, C-29.

Krupa, Viktor
1982   *The Polynesian languages: A guide*. London: Routledge and Kegan Paul.

Kulick, Don
1992   *Language shift and cultural reproduction: Socialization, self, and syncretism in a Papua New Guinean village*. Studies in the Social and Cultural Foundations of Language 14. Cambridge: Cambridge University Press.

Lang, Adrienne
1973   *Enga dictionary with English index*. Canberra: Pacific Linguistics, C-20.

Langdon, Robert, and Darrell Tryon
1983   *The language of Easter Island: Its development and Eastern Polynesian relationships*. Laie, Hawai'i: Institute for Polynesian Studies.

Laycock, D. C.
1965   *The Ndu language family (Sepik District, New Guinea)*. Canberra: Pacific Linguistics, C-1.
1973   "Sissano, Warapu, and Melanesian pidginization." *Oceanic Linguistics* 12: 245–277.
1975a   "Observations on number systems and semantics." In *New Guinea area languages and language study*. Vol. 1, *Papuan languages and the New Guinea linguistic scene*, edited by S. A. Wurm, 219–233. Canberra: Pacific Linguistics, C-38.
1975b   "The Torricelli Phylum." In *New Guinea area languages and language study*. Vol. 1, *Papuan languages and the New Guinea linguistic scene*, edited by S. A. Wurm, 767–780. Canberra: Pacific Linguistics, C-38.
1982a   "Melanesian linguistic diversity: A Melanesian choice?" In *Melanesia: Beyond diversity*, edited by R. J. May and H. N. Nelson, 33–38. Canberra: Australian National University, Research School of Pacific Studies.
1982b   "Metathesis in Austronesian: Ririo and other cases." In *Papers from the Third International Conference on Austronesian Linguistics*. Vol. 1, *Currents in Oceanic*, edited by Amran Halim, Lois Carrington, and S. A. Wurm, 269–281. Canberra: Pacific Linguistics, C-74.
1985   "The future of Tok Pisin." In *Handbook of Tok Pisin (New Guinea Pidgin)*, edited by S. A. Wurm and P. Mühlhäusler, 665–668. Canberra: Pacific Linguistics, C-70.

Lee, Jennifer
    1987   *Tiwi today: A study of language change in a contact situation.*
            Canberra: Pacific Linguistics, C-96.

Lee, Kee-dong
    1975   *Kusaiean reference grammar.* Honolulu: University Press of Hawai'i.

Leenhardt, Maurice
    1946   *Langues et dialectes de l'Austro-Mélanésie.* Travaux et Mémoires 46.
            Paris: Institut d'Ethnologie.

Lichtenberk, Frantisek
    1978   A sketch of Houailou grammar. Honolulu: University of Hawai'i
            Working Papers in Linguistics 10/2: 74–116.
    1983   *A grammar of Manam.* Oceanic Linguistics Special Publication no.
            18. Honolulu: University of Hawai'i Press.
    1984   *To'aba'ita language of Malaita, Solomon Islands.* Working Papers in
            Anthropology, Archaeology, Linguistics, Maori Studies no. 65.
            Auckland: Department of Anthropology, University of Auckland.

Lincoln, Peter C.
    1976   "Describing Banoni, an Austronesian language of southwest
            Bougainville." Unpublished Ph.D. diss., University of Hawai'i.

Lindstrom, Lamont
    1986   *Kwamera dictionary—Nikukua sai nagkiariien Nininife.* Canberra:
            Pacific Linguistics, C-95.

Lindstrom, Lamont, and John Lynch
    1994   *Kwamera.* Languages of the World/Materials 02. Munich: Lincom
            Europa.

Lister-Turner, R., and J. B. Clark
    n.d.   *A grammar of the Motu language of Papua.* 2d ed. Edited by Percy
            Chatterton. Sydney: New South Wales Government Printer.

Litteral, Shirley
    1981   "The semantic components of Anggor existential verbs." In *Syntax
            and semantics in Papua New Guinea languages,* edited by Karl J.
            Franklin, 125–149. Ukarumpa, Papua New Guinea: Summer Institute
            of Linguistics.

Loving, Richard, and Aretta Loving
    1975   *Awa dictionary.* Canberra: Pacific Linguistics, C-30.

Lynch, John
    1972   "Passives and statives in Tongan." *Journal of the Polynesian Society*
            81: 5–18.
    1978   *A grammar of Lenakel.* Canberra: Pacific Linguistics, B-55.

1981a   "Austronesian 'loanwords' (?) in Trans–New Guinea Phylum vocabulary." *Pacific Linguistics* A-61: 165–180.

1981b   "Melanesian diversity and Polynesian homogeneity: The other side of the coin." *Oceanic Linguistics* 20: 95–129.

1982a   "Anejom grammar sketch." *Pacific Linguistics* A-64: 93–154.

1982b   "South-west Tanna grammar outline and vocabulary." *Pacific Linguistics* A-64: 1–91.

1994   "Melanesian sailors on a Polynesian sea: Maritime vocabulary in southern Vanuatu." In *Austronesian terminologies: Continuity and change*, edited by A. K. Pawley and M. D. Ross, 289–300. Canberra: Pacific Linguistics, C-127.

1995   "The Anejom̃ subject marking system: Past, present and future". *Oceanic Linguistics* 34/1: 13–26.

1996   "Kava-drinking in southern Vanuatu: Melanesian drinkers, Polynesian roots." *Journal of the Polynesian Society* 105, 1: 27–40.

1998   "Anejom̃." In *The Oceanic languages*, edited by John Lynch, Malcolm Ross, and Terry Crowley. London: Curzon Press.

1998   "Linguistic subgrouping in Vanuatu and New Caledonia: Some preliminary hypotheses." In *Proceedings of the Second International Conference on Oceanic Linguistics*, edited by Paul Geraghty. Canberra: Pacific Linguistics.

————, ed.

1983   *Studies in the languages of Erromango*. Canberra: Pacific Linguistics, C-79.

Lynch, John, and Kenneth Fakamuria

1994   "Borrowed moieties, borrowed names: Sociolinguistic contact between Tanna and Futuna-Aniwa, Vanuatu." *Pacific Studies* 17/1: 79–91.

Lynch, John, and Rex Horoi

1998   "Arosi." In *The Oceanic languages*, edited by John Lynch, Malcolm Ross, and Terry Crowley. London: Curzon Press.

Lynch, John, and Faʻafo Pat, eds.

1996   *Oceanic studies: Proceedings of the First International Conference on Oceanic Linguistics*. Canberra: Pacific Linguistics, C-133.

Lynch, John, Malcolm Ross, and Terry Crowley

1998   *The Oceanic languages*. London: Curzon Press.

Lynch, John, and D. T. Tryon

1985   "Central-Eastern Oceanic: A subgrouping hypothesis." In *Austronesian Linguistics at the 15th Pacific Science Congress*, edited by Andrew Pawley and Lois Carrington, 31–52. Canberra: Pacific Linguistics, C-88.

McElhanon, Kenneth A., and C. L. Voorhoeve
   1970   *The Trans–New Guinea phylum: Explorations in deep-level genetic relationships*. Canberra: Pacific Linguistics, B-16.

McEwen, J. M.
   1970   *Niue dictionary*. Wellington: Department of Maori and Island Affairs.

McGregor, William
   1994   "Gooniyandi." In *Aboriginal words*, edited by Nick Thieberger and William McGregor, 193–213. Sydney: Macquarie Library.

Marsack, C. C.
   1962   *Teach yourself Samoan*. London: English Universities Press.

Mihalic, F.
   1971   *The Jacaranda dictionary and grammar of Melanesian Pidgin*. Milton, Queensland: Jacaranda Press.

Milner, G. B.
   1966   *Samoan dictionary (Samoan-English, English-Samoan)*. Auckland: Polynesian Press.
   1972   *Fijian grammar*. 3d ed. Suva: Government Press.
   1973   "It is aspect (not voice) which is marked in Samoan." *Oceanic Linguistics* 12: 621–639.

Morphy, Frances
   1983   "Djapu." In *Handbook of Australian languages*, edited by R. M. W. Dixon and Barry J. Blake, 3: 1–188. Canberra: Australian National University Press.

Mosel, Ulrike
   1980   *Tolai and Tok Pisin: The influence of the substratum on the development of New Guinea Pidgin*. Canberra: Pacific Linguistics, B-73.
   1984   *Tolai syntax and its historical development*. Canberra: Pacific Linguistics, B-92.

Moyse-Faurie, Claire
   1983   *Le drehu: Langue de Lifou (Iles Loyauté)*. Langues et Cultures du Pacifique 3. Paris: Société d'Etudes Linguistiques et Anthropologiques de France.

Mugler, France, and John Lynch, eds.
   1996   *Pacific languages in education*. Suva: Institute of Pacific Studies, University of the South Pacific.

Mühlhäusler, Peter
   1979   *Growth and structure of the lexicon of New Guinea Pidgin*. Canberra: Pacific Linguistics, C-52.

Murane, Elizabeth
    1974   *Daga grammar*. Norman, Oklahoma: Summer Institute of Linguistics.

Murray, J. H. P.
    1924   *Notes on Colonel Ainsworth's report on the Mandated Territory of New Guinea*. Port Moresby: Government Printer.

Nathan, Geoffrey S.
    1973   "Nauruan in the Austronesian language family." *Oceanic Linguistics* 12: 479–501.

Nekitel, Otto
    1986   "A sketch of nominal concord in Abuʿ (an Arapesh language)." *Pacific Linguistics* A-70: 177–205.

Ochs, Elinor
    1988   *Culture and language development: Language acquisition and language socialization in a Samoan village*. Studies in the Social and Cultural Foundations of Language 6. Cambridge: Cambridge University Press.

O'Grady, G. N., and D. T. Tryon, eds.
    1990   *Studies in comparative Pama-Nyungan*. Canberra: Pacific Linguistics, C-111.

Olson, Mike
    1975   "Barai grammar highlights." In *Studies in languages of central and south-east Papua*, edited by T[om] E. Dutton, 471–512. Canberra: Pacific Linguistics, C-29.

Ozanne-Rivierre, Françoise
    1976   *Le iaai: Langue mélanésienne d'Ouvéa (Nouvelle-Calédonie)*. Langues et Civilisations à Tradition Orale 20. Paris: Société d'Etudes Linguistiques et Anthropologiques de France.

Pawley, Andrew [K.]
    1966a   "The structure of Kalam: A grammar of a New Guinea Highlands language." Unpublished Ph.D. diss., University of Auckland.
    1966b   "Samoan phrase structure." *Anthropological Linguistics* 8/5: 1–63.
    1972   "On the internal relationships of the Eastern Oceanic languages." In *Studies in Oceanic culture history*, edited by Roger C. Green and Marion Kelly, 3: 1–142. Pacific Anthropological records no. 13. Honolulu: Bernice Pauahi Bishop Museum.
    1981   "Melanesian diversity and Polynesian homogeneity: A unified explanation for language." In *Studies in Pacific languages and cultures in honour of Bruce Biggs*, edited by Jim Hollyman and Andrew Pawley, 269–309. Auckland: Linguistic Society of New Zealand.

1992   "Kalam Pandanus language: An old New Guinea experiment in language engineering." In *The language game: Papers in memory of Donald C. Laycock*, edited by Tom Dutton, Malcolm Ross, and Darrell Tryon, 313–334. Canberra: Pacific Linguistics, C-110.

1995   "C. L. Voorhoeve and the Trans New Guinea hypothesis." In *Tales from a concave world: Liber amicorum Bert Voorhoeve*, edited by Connie Baak, Mary Bakker, and Dick van der Meij, 83–123. Leiden: Leiden University.

Pawley, Andrew [K.], and Malcolm Ross

1995   "The prehistory of the Oceanic languages: A current view." In *The Austronesians: Historical and comparative perspectives*, edited by Peter Bellwood, James J. Fox, and Darrell Tryon, 39–74. Canberra: Australian National University, Research School of Pacific Studies, Department of Anthropology.

———, eds.

1994   *Austronesian terminologies: Continuity and change.* Canberra: Pacific Linguistics, C-127.

Pawley, Andrew [K.], and Timoci Sayaba

1990   "Possessive-marking in Wayan, a western Fijian language: Noun class or relational system?" In *Pacific Island languages: Essays in honour of G. B. Milner*, edited by Jeremy H. C. S. Davidson, 147–171. London and Honolulu: School of Oriental and African Studies, University of London, and University of Hawai'i Press.

Philips, Susan U.

1991   "Tongan speech levels: Practice and talk about practice in the cultural construction of social hierarchy." In *Currents in Pacific linguistics: Papers on Austronesian languages and ethnolinguistics in honour of George W. Grace*, edited by Robert Blust, 369–382. Canberra: Pacific Linguistics, C-117.

Phillips, Donald J.

1976   *Wahgi phonology and grammar.* Canberra: Pacific Linguistics, B-36.

Piau, Julie Anne

1981   "Kuman classificatory verbs." *Language and Linguistics in Melanesia* 13/1–2:3–31.

1985   "The verbal syntax of Kuman." Unpublished master's thesis, Australian National University.

Price, D. J. de Solla, and Leopold Pospisil

1966   "A survival of Babylonian arithmetic in New Guinea?" *Indian Journal of the History of Science* 1: 30–33.

Ray, S. H.
1926   *A comparative study of the Melanesian island languages*. Cambridge: Cambridge University Press.

Rehg, Kenneth L.
1981   *Ponapean reference grammar*. Honolulu: University Press of Hawaiʻi.

Rensch, Karl H., ed.
1993   *Nauru grammar*. Reprint of Alois Kayser, *Nauru grammar* (1936), with introductory notes. Canberra: Embassy of the Federal Republic of Germany.

Rivierre, Jean-Claude
1980   *La langue de Touho: Phonologie et grammaire du cèmuhî (Nouvelle-Calédonie)*. Langues et Civilisations à Tradition Orale 38. Paris: Société d'Etudes Linguistiques et Anthropologiques de France.

Ross, M[alcolm] D.
1980   "Some elements of Vanimo, a New Guinea tone language." *Pacific Linguistics* A-56: 77–109.
1984   "Maisin: A preliminary sketch." *Pacific Linguistics* A-69: 1–82.
1988   *Proto Oceanic and the Austronesian languages of western Melanesia*. Canberra: Pacific Linguistics, C-98.
1993   "Tonogenesis in the North Huon Gulf chain." In *Tonality in Austronesian languages*, edited by Jerold A. Edmondson and Kenneth J. Gregorson, 133–150. Oceanic Linguistics Special Publication, no. 24. Honolulu: University of Hawaiʻi Press.
1995   "Is Yapese Oceanic?" Paper presented to the Second International Conference on Oceanic Linguistics, Suva, Fiji, July.
1996   "On the genetic affiliation of the Oceanic languages of Irian Jaya." *Oceanic Linguistics* 35/2: 259–271.

Ross, Malcolm, and John Natu Paol
1978   *A Waskia grammar sketch and vocabulary*. Canberra: Pacific Linguistics, B-56.

Salisbury, Richard
1962   "Notes on bilingualism and language change in New Guinea." *Anthropological Linguistics* 4/7: 1–13.

Sandefur, J. R.
1986   *Kriol of North Australia: A language coming of age*. Darwin: Summer Institute of Linguistics.

Sanders, Arden G., and Joy Sanders
1980   "Phonology of the Kamasau language." *Pacific Linguistics* A-56: 111–135.

Savage, Stephen
    1980   *A dictionary of the Maori language of Rarotonga.* 2d ed. Suva: Institute of Pacific Studies, University of the South Pacific, and Cook Islands Ministry of Education.

Schieffelin, Bambi B.
    1990   *The give and take of everyday life: Language socialization of Kaluli children.* Studies in the Social and Cultural Foundations of Language 9. Cambridge: Cambridge University Press.

Schnukal, Anna
    1988   *Broken: An introduction to the creole language of Torres Strait.* Canberra: Pacific Linguistics, C-107.

Schütz, Albert J.
    1969   *Nguna grammar.* Oceanic Linguistics Special Publication, no. 5. Honolulu: University of Hawai'i Press.
    1972   *The languages of Fiji.* Oxford: Clarendon Press.
    1985   *The Fijian language.* Honolulu: University of Hawai'i Press.
    1994   *Voices of Eden: A history of Hawaiian language studies.* Honolulu: University of Hawai'i Press.

Schütz, Albert J., and Rusiate T. Komaitai
    1971   *Spoken Fijian.* Honolulu: University Press of Hawai'i.

Scott, Graham K.
    1978   *The Fore language of Papua New Guinea.* Canberra: Pacific Linguistics, B-47.

Sebeok, Thomas A., ed.
    1971   *Current trends in linguistics.* Vol. 8, *Linguistics in Oceania.* The Hague: Mouton.

Senft, Gunter
    1986   *Kilivila: The language of the Trobriand Islanders.* Berlin: Mouton de Gruyter.

Sharpe, Margaret C.
    1972   *Alawa phonology and grammar.* Australian Aboriginal Studies no. 37. Linguistic Series no. 15. Canberra: Australian Institute of Aboriginal Studies.

Siegel, Jeff
    1977   *Say it in Fiji Hindi.* Sydney: Pacific Publications.
    1984   "Introduction to the Labu language." *Pacific Linguistics* A-69: 83–159.
    1987   *Language contact in a plantation environment: A sociolinguistic history of Fiji.* Cambridge: Cambridge University Press.

Simons, Linda, and Hugh Young
    1978   *Pijin blong yumi: A guide to Solomon Islands Pijin*. Honiara: Solomon Islands Christian Association.

Simpson, Jane
    1993   "Making dictionaries." In *Language and culture in Aboriginal Australia*, edited by Michael Walsh and Colin Yallop, 123–144. Canberra: Aboriginal Studies Press.

Smith, Geoffrey P.
    1988   "Morobe counting systems." *Pacific Linguistics* A-76: 1–132.

Sohn, Ho-min, and B. W. Bender
    1973   *A Ulithian grammar*. Canberra: Pacific Linguistics, C-27.

Sommer, Bruce A.
    1969   *Kunjen phonology: Synchronic and diachronic*. Canberra: Pacific Linguistics, B-11.

Spriggs, Matthew
    1995   "The Lapita culture and Austronesian prehistory in Oceania." In *The Austronesians: Historical and comparative perspectives*, edited by Peter Bellwood, James J. Fox, and Darrell Tryon, 112–133. Canberra: Australian National University, Research School of Pacific Studies, Department of Anthropology.

Tchekhoff, Claude
    1973   "Verbal aspects in an ergative construction: An example in Tongan." *Oceanic Linguistics* 12: 607–620.

Tepahae, Philip, and John Lynch
    1998   "The language of family in Aneityum." In *Violence in Paradise: Proceedings of the Conference on Violence and the Family in Vanuatu*, edited by Andonia Piau-Lynch. Canberra: Research School of Pacific and Asian Studies, Australian National University.

Thomson, N. P.
    1975   "Magi phonology and grammar—fifty years afterwards." In *Studies in languages of central and south-east Papua*, edited by T[om] E. Dutton, 599–666. Canberra: Pacific Linguistics, C-29.

Thurston, William R.
    1982   *A comparative study in Anêm and Lusi*. Canberra: Pacific Linguistics, B-83.
    1987   *Processes of change in the languages of north-western New Britain*. Canberra: Pacific Linguistics, B-99.
    1992   "Sociolinguistic typology and other factors effecting change in north-western New Britain, Papua New Guinea." In *Culture change,*

language change: Case studies from Melanesia, edited by Tom Dutton, 123–139. Canberra: Pacific Linguistics, C-120.

Todd, Evelyn M.
1975   "The Solomon language family." In *New Guinea area languages and language study*. Vol. 1, *Papuan languages and the New Guinea linguistic scene*, edited by S. A. Wurm, 805–846. Canberra: Pacific Linguistics, C-38.
1978   "A sketch of Nissan (Nehan) grammar." In *Second International Conference on Austronesian Linguistics: Proceedings*, edited by S. A. Wurm and Lois Carrington, 1181–1239. Canberra: Pacific Linguistics, C-61.

Topping, Donald M.
1973   *Chamorro reference grammar*. Honolulu: University Press of Hawai'i.

Trefry, David
1969   *A comparative study of Kuman and Pawaian*. Canberra: Pacific Linguistics, B-13.

Tryon, D[arrell] T.
1968a   *Dehu grammar*. Canberra: Pacific Linguistics, B-7.
1968b   *Iai grammar*. Canberra: Pacific Linguistics, B-8.
1970   *Conversational Tahitian*. Canberra: Australian National University Press.
1973   "Linguistic subgrouping in the New Hebrides: A preliminary approach." *Oceanic Linguistics* 12: 303–351.
1976   *New Hebrides languages: An internal classification*. Canberra: Pacific Linguistics C-50.
1987   *Bislama: An introduction to the national language of Vanuatu*. Canberra: Pacific Linguistics, D-72.
1995   "Proto-Austronesian and the major Austronesian subgroups." In *The Austronesians: Historical and comparative perspectives*, edited by Peter Bellwood, James J. Fox, and Darrell Tryon, 17–38. Canberra: Australian National University, Research School of Pacific Studies, Department of Anthropology.

————, ed.
1994   *Comparative Austronesian dictionary*. Berlin: Mouton de Gruyter.

Tryon, D[arrell] T., and J.-M. Charpentier
1989   "Linguistic problems in Vanuatu." *Ethnies* 4/8–10: 13–17.

Tryon, D[arrell] T., and B. D. Hackman
1983   *Solomon Island languages: An internal classification*. Canberra: Pacific Linguistics, C-72.

Vászolyi, E.
1976   "Wunambal." In *Grammatical categories in Australian languages*, edited by R. M. W. Dixon, 629–646. Linguistic Series, no. 22. Canberra: Australian Institute of Aboriginal Studies.

Verhaar, John W. M.
1995   *Toward a reference grammar of Tok Pisin: An experiment in corpus linguistics*. Oceanic Linguistics Special Publication, no. 26. Honolulu: University of Hawai'i Press.

———, ed.
1990   *Melanesian Pidgin and Tok Pisin*. Amsterdam: John Benjamins.

Wagner, K. R.
1985   "How much do children say in a day?" *Journal of Child Language* 12: 475–487.

Walsh, D. S.
1966   "The phonology and phrase structure of Raga." Unpublished master's thesis, University of Auckland.

Walsh, Michael
1993   "Classifying the world in an Aboriginal language." In *Language and culture in Aboriginal Australia*, edited by Michael Walsh and Colin Yallop, 107–122. Canberra: Aboriginal Studies Press.

Walsh, Michael, and Colin Yallop, eds.
1993   *Language and culture in Aboriginal Australia*. Canberra: Aboriginal Studies Press.

White, Geoffrey M.
1988   *Cheke Holo (Maringe/Hograno) dictionary*. Canberra: Pacific Linguistics, C-97.

Wilson, William H.
1982   *Proto-Polynesian possessive marking*. Canberra: Pacific Linguistics, B-85.

Wurm, S. A.
1982   *The Papuan languages of Oceania*. Tübingen: Gunther Narr Verlag.

———, ed.
1975   *New Guinea area languages and language study*. Vol. 1, *Papuan languages and the New Guinea linguistic scene*. Canberra: Pacific Linguistics, C-38.
1976   *New Guinea area languages and language study*. Vol. 2, *Austronesian languages*. Canberra: Pacific Linguistics, C-39.

1977   *New Guinea area languages and language study.* Vol. 3, *Language, culture, society, and the modern world.* Canberra: Pacific Linguistics, C-40.

1979   *New Guinea and neighbouring areas: A sociolinguistic laboratory.* The Hague: Mouton.

Wurm, S. A., and John B. Harris
1963   *Police Motu: An introduction to the trade language of Papua (New Guinea) for anthropologists and other fieldworkers.* Canberra: Pacific Linguistics, B-1.

Wurm, S. A., and Shirô Hattori, eds.
1981   *Language atlas of the Pacific area.* Part 1, *New Guinea area, Oceania, Australia.* Canberra: Pacific Linguistics, C-66.

Wurm, S. A., and P. Mühlhäusler, eds.
1985   *A handbook of Tok Pisin (New Guinea Pidgin).* Canberra: Pacific Linguistics, C-70.

Yallop, Colin
1981   *Australian Aboriginal languages.* London: André Deutsch.

Index

The following do *not* appear in this index:
1. Names of authors listed in the References.
2. Names of languages listed in Appendix 1 or located on Maps 3–11.
3. Names of Papuan language families which appear *only* in Table 4.
4. Technical terms listed alphabetically in Appendix 4.
5. English, French, etc., where these languages are used to illustrate a point of grammar.

General categories (such as *Polynesia, languages of*) are indexed only where a generalization is made about that category, and not when a specific member of the category (e.g., *Hawaiian* or *Tongan*) is referred to.

About the Author

John Lynch is professor of Pacific languages at the University of the South Pacific's Emalus Campus in Vanuatu. He is the author of *Lenakel Dictionary, A Grammar of Lenakel*, and *An Annotated Bibliography of Vanuatu Languages*. He is co-author of *The Design of Language* and *The Oceanic Languages*, and co-editor of *Pacific Languages in Education*.

CPSIA information can be obtained
at www.ICGtesting.com
Printed in the USA
FSHW010741310819
61556FS